NEW POLITICS IN
WESTERN EUROPE

NEW DIRECTIONS IN
COMPARATIVE AND INTERNATIONAL POLITICS

Series Editors
Peter Merkl and Haruhiro Fukui

NEW POLITICS IN WESTERN EUROPE

The Rise and Success of Green Parties and Alternative Lists

EDITED BY
FERDINAND MÜLLER-ROMMEL

WESTVIEW PRESS
BOULDER, SAN FRANCISCO, & LONDON

New Directions in Comparative and International Politics

This Westview softcover edition is printed on acid-free paper and bound in softcovers that carry the highest rating of the National Association of State Textbook Administrators, in consultation with the Association of American Publishers and the Book Manufacturers' Institute.

Published in 1989 in the United States of America by Westview Press, Inc., 5500 Central Avenue, Boulder, Colorado 80301, and in the United Kingdom by Westview Press, Inc., 13 Brunswick Centre, London WC1N 1AF, England

Library of Congress Cataloging-in-Publication Data
New politics in Western Europe : the rise and success of green parties
   and alternative lists / edited by Ferdinand Müller-Rommel.
      p.   cm.—(New directions in comparative and international
politics)
   Includes bibliographies.
   ISBN 0-8133-7529-0
   1. Political parties—Europe.   2. Environmental policy—Europe.
3. Grünen (Political party).   4. Europe—Politics and
government—1945–   .   I. Müller-Rommel, Ferdinand.   II. Series.
JN94.A979N49   1989
324.24—dc19   87-35198
                                                                      CIP

Printed and bound in the United States of America

∞   The paper used in this publication meets the requirements of the American National
     Standard for Permanence of Paper for Printed Library Materials Z39.48-1984.

10   9   8   7   6   5   4   3   2

Contents

Tables and Figures

Preface

This book seeks to provide an introduction to the green party phenomenon in Western Europe that will enable the student of comparative politics to acquire detailed understanding of these parties and to compare them meaningfully across countries.

Although there is a considerable knowledge on the Greens in Germany, hardly anything is known about the green parties in other European countries. This finding is rather astonishing, since green parties are currently represented in eight national parliaments (Finland, Switzerland, Luxembourg, Federal Republic of Germany, Belgium, Austria, Italy, Sweden). In some countries, the Greens already have profound effects on the process of coalition building, while in other countries they challenge traditional institutional patterns and mobilize conventional parties in changing their policy. Hence, the Greens have become a political force in several European party systems. However, in spite of this development, students and scholars who wish to know more about the Greens cross-nationally have to go back to newspaper analysis. Even setting the language problems aside, there is an inadequate media-coverage of the Greens in most European counties.

This book is primarily written for an audience that wishes to deal with recent trends in European party systems and wants to be informed about the knowledge we have gained on the Greens in various countries. The book provides a comprehensive coverage of all green parties that are organized on the national level of political systems. Excluded are green parties that only operate on the local, district and regional level. Since the reader should be able to make comparisons between green parties in various European countries, all national case-studies were organized in the same format. Authors were invited to examine the distinctive characteristics of green parties in each country under the following sub-headings:

• *Development of the green party:* highlighting particularly the party-splits and the institutional and the constitutional setting in which the green parties have developed.

• *Organizational structure:* centralized versus decentralized; administrative bodies, e.g. decision-making process, party control versus leadership-role, parliamentary party group; membership and finance; relationship to new social movements.

• *Electoral support:* percentage of votes obtained in elections; analysis of socio-demographic characteristics of green party voters, e.g., with regard to education, class, ethnicity, age, and sex.

• *Programatic profile:* emphasis upon economic, social, international issues; individualism, civil rights, ecology, disarmament, the Third World, leftism.

• *Government participation:* number and length of times in government (nationally, regionally, locally); coalition partners.

• *Outlook:* level of main strategic emphasis; what is the future of the green party?

Aside from national case-studies (chapters 2–14), this book also draws some initial comparative conclusions concerning the supporters of green parties in advanced industrial countries, and on their new style of political participation (chapters 15–16).

A book of this sort can be put together only with the assistance of individuals and institutions. I owe great debt to the University of Lüneburg and the German National Science Foundation (*Deutsche Forschungsgemeinschaft*) which both provided me with generous financial support. For the assistance in organizing and typing the manuscript I am particularly grateful to Christel Amirmontaghemi, Bettina Krüger, Tanja Sprengel, Kevin Becnel, and Jacque Petrucci. Needless to say, the contributors of this book are in a real sense the authors. They deserve credit for any success which the book might enjoy. However, any errors or inadequacies are the editor's responsibility or are due to the intractable nature of green party organizations in Europe. Finally, I am indebted to Uwe Thaysen at the University of Lüneburg whose unceasing encouragement and thoughtful advice—not only in context with this book—was always greatly appreciated. This book is dedicated to him.

Ferdinand Müller-Rommel
Lüneburg, West-Germany, December 1988

Comparative Introduction

1

Green Parties and Alternative Lists under Cross-National Perspective

Ferdinand Müller-Rommel

New Politics:
From Social Movements to Green Parties

In recent years, the term "new politics" has attracted the attention of many distinguished scholars, journalists, and politicians. Generally, it has been argued that the increased economic development and prosperity of advanced Western industrialised societies during the past decades has transformed the basic value priorities of succeeding generations. Some scholars describe this process as a transition from "old politics" values of economic growth, public order, national security, and traditional life-styles to "new politics" values of environmental quality, social equality, alternative life-styles, minority rights and participation. These new issue demands initially manifested themselves outside the established parties. Citizen action groups were formed in many countries across the Western world. The famous 1972 Club of Rome Report, *Limits of Growth* (which described the larger and long-term problems associated with environmental destruction caused by governmental environmental policies), together with the emerging general "fear" about the security provided by the nuclear deterrence of Nato and the expansion of nuclear energy programs were responsible for the formation of new protest movements and green parties in advanced industrial democracies.

Most of these movements emerged spontaneously on the local level as politically independent citizen-initiative groups. These groups were interested in single issues such as the provision of parks; they protested against urban renewal, new highways, or the construction of nuclear power plants. The citizen initiatives employed a variety of methods in seeking to influence policy decisions.

They mobilized public opinion via the unconventional political behavior characteristic of the earlier student movements, such as demonstrations and occasional sit-ins, information campaigns, and similar tactics. They also utilized local and national laws to obtain public access to urban renewal and construction plans, and to force compulsory hearings for those directly concerned. In many countries, the success of citizen-initiative groups concerned with local environmental issues led to the establishment of federal umbrella organisations in order to strengthen the political impact of the environmental movement nationally. For instance, the *Bundesverband Bürgerinitiativen Umweltschutz* (BBU) was founded in Germany in 1972, the *Amis de la Terre* was formed in France in 1971, the Swedish *Miljvardsgruppernas Riförbund* (MIGRI) originated in 1971, and the Dutch *Vereiniging Milieudefensie* (VDM) was formed in 1972.

In the mid 1970s, one particular issue became dominant in several European countries: nuclear energy. Heavily influenced by the oil crisis, most European governments decided to expand their nuclear energy programs. It was precisely the nuclear power issue, however, that demonstrated the need for organizing political movements at the national level, since energy problems could not be resolved at the local level. More and more local action groups in various countries formed nationally organized "anti-nuclear power" organizations as, for instance, the Organization for Information on Nuclear Power (OOA) in Denmark founded in 1974, The Committee for the Co-ordination of Regional Anti-Nuclear Power Initiatives (LEK) in the Netherlands (1973), the *Miljöverbund* in Sweden (1976), the Initiative of Anti-Nuclear Power Plants (IAG) in Austria (1976), and the Action against Nuclear Power (AMA) in Norway (1974).

In the late 1970s the environmental issue was joined by debate over the NATO dual-track decision on intermediate nuclear forces and the eventual stationing of cruise missiles and the Pershing II in Western Europe. This political decision created considerable solidarity among new social movements that crossed European national borders. Large demonstrations were held, along with illegal occupations of the proposed missile sites. Most of these activities were initiated by nationally organized peace movements.

In the early 1980s most citizen-initiative groups and new political movements looked for closer contact with the Social Democrats or other large, established left-wing parties. They expected those parties to act as an effective force against unlimited economic growth, the destruction of the environment, and the stationing of nuclear weapons. Major efforts were made to influence the nuclear policy of the Social Democrats and other Labor and socialist parties in Western Europe, albeit without much sucess.

For several reasons the larger leftist parties could not (or would not) respond adequately to the demands of the new political movements. *First of all*, in many European countries the socialist parties held governing power during the 1970s, precisely around the time that these nations underwent a crucial economic crisis with a subsequent increase in unemployment rates. The leftist governments were forced to work more closely with the trade unions and other conventional interest groups in order to manage the economic crisis. However, the trade unions in Western Europe are strong advocates of economic growth as a mechanism for improving the status of the working class. Since the socialists and other established leftist parties are, to varying degrees, dependent upon the electoral support of the trade union leaders and rank-and-file membership, an environmental or anti-nuclear power position by these parties would be directed against the trade unions´ economic policy. Therefore, the new politics issues brought up by political movements in the 1970s have not figured prominently in most socialist parties´ platforms or policy stands, although there were anti-nuclear and environmentalist factions in these parties. Now that many of these parties have moved into opposition, these new political groups have more influence on the programs of the left-parties.

Secondly, the hierarchical, bureaucratic organizational structure and the "catch-all" character of most socialist parties made it almost impossible for new political movements to implement any major policy change in a short period of time. By and large, Michel´s classic analysis of the "iron law of oligarchy" still contains a lot of truth about the internal life of socialist parties in contemporary Europe.

Hence, the negative experience of the followers of the new political movements with the established left-wing parties, as well as the perceived inability of political parties and other political institutions to come up with a fundamentally different policy approach, became the major reason for both the growth and the electoral success of green parties. These parties basically represent the demands of new political movements in the party systems of advanced industrial societies.

Electoral Strength of Green Parties:
An International Comparison
The political profile of green parties is predominantly related to the
new issues and the new style of political participation and
communication.

Most green parties follow an ideology that consists of strong
concerns with equal rights (especially for minorities), strong
ecological and anti-nuclear power thinking, solidarity with the Third
World, demands for unilateral disarmament, and a general left-wing
egalitarian disposition. Among others, green parties stand for peace
through unilateral disarment and a nuclear-free Europe; protection of
the natural environment through the introduction of transnational
pollution controls and more generally an effective environmental
policy directed against an unquestioned commitment to economic
growth. Green parties advocate an alternative life style through less
emphasis on material goods, more individualism, self-realization,
and self-determination. They display a more sympathetic orientation
towards the Third World, including a genuine sharing of wealth
between rich and poor nations, and help for poorer countries to
create their own self-sufficient economies free of financial
domination by the industrial nations. In sum, green parties introduce
a programatic and ideological thinking that differs significantly from
those of the established larger parties.

Most green parties display a strong preference for participatory
party organization. The organizational structure of most green parties
gives local party branches more autonomy in decision-making. It is
designed to give the grassroot a maximum chance of interest
articulation and, as such, an impact on policy formation within the
party (Poguntke 1987). This process of decentralization in decision-
making is seen to be the essential precondition of meaningful
participatory opportunity on all levels of the party organization,
because it distributes power to more units and makes politics more
transparent and hence intelligible (Müller-Rommel/Poguntke 1989).

Although there is some diversity in the programatic demands and
some variety in degree of participatory organizational structure
among green parties, they have consolidated in many party systems
alongside the traditional parties. However, their activities and their
electoral success vary considerably between countries and between
the local, regional and national levels within any one country. Green
parties clearly transcend frontiers of political systems and cultures,
and are found with similiar types of program and organization in

Canada, the United States, Japan, and Western Europe.

The first party with a clearcut "new politics" program was founded in the late 1960s in *New Zealand* under the name of the Value party. Since the electoral system in New Zealand requires a majority vote in a given electoral district in order to win a seat in the legislature, the Value party never gained any seats in the national parliament. Due to internal bickering the party vote declined in the mid 1970s. In 1980 the Value party declared themselves as a socialist party and faded away in the following years.

The first Green party in North America was founded in British Columbia *(Canada)* in February 1983. The Greens managed to field four candidates in the 1983 provincial elections, winning a handful of votes. Green party organizations in Ontario and some other provinces followed. With local co-ordination, 58 green candidats competed in the 1984 federal election. In the 1985 Ontario provincial election eleven green candidates were nominated. However, as in New Zealand and various other countries, the electoral system is biased in support of the established larger parties. The rule that a candidate must receive 15 percent of the vote in a constituency before being eligible for public funding helps the major parties to overwhelm new entrants to the political arena. Because of this rule the Canadian Greens have not as jet been able to win seats in any election.

In the *United States of America,* local green political organizations have sprung up around the country since the late 1970s, sometimes contesting in local elections and, occasionally, winning. Green or green-affiliated candidates have been elected to municipal offices in New Hampshire, Connecticut, Wisconsin, Michigan, and North Carolina. In 1987, there were 75 unaffiliated local green parties. Representatives of some of these local groups met in 1984 and decided to set up a national "green movement committee of correspondance." In 1987, more than 500 persons from all over the country came to the first national conference of the "American Green Movement". The participants, however, neglected to form a national green party in the United States.

In *Japan,* a national green party was formed in 1983. They participated in the 1983 local and national elections. Although the Greens could not gain any seats in the National Assembly, they sent several candidates into local parliaments.

The development of green parties in *Western Europe* is more advanced than anywhere else. Green parties exist in nearly all Western European party systems (see Table 1.1).

The first "Ecology List" in Western Europe to be organized on the national level was formed in *France* prior to the 1974 presidential elections. For the first time in French politics, the ecologists nominated their own presidential candidate. In 1977, three ecological groups formed the *Collectif Ecologie* '78 for the purpose of campaigning for the parliamentary elections. It was, however, not until January 1984 that the various factions among the *ecologists* and other new social movements founded the French Green party *(Les Verts)*. Electorally, the ecologists have been rather unstable over the past ten years. In the 1974 presidential elections, the ecological candidates polled 1,3 percent of all votes and held sixth place in the field of twelve candidates. In the 1976 cantonal elections, some local ecological groups obtained relatively high electoral results, and encouraged other ecologists to nominate candidates for the local election in March 1977. The ecologists, however, had not received the expected high amount of total votes. In the 1978 general election, the ecologists received the highest number of votes in Paris and in areas where there was strong local opposition to nuclear power stations. For the 1979 European elections, the ecologists formed a list called *Europe Ecologie* and gained 4,4 percent of the vote. In the 1981 presidential elections, the ecologists´ candidate obtained 3,5 percent of the poll, 3,1 percent of the total electorate, and ranked fifth among the ten presidential candidates. For the 1984 European elections, the French Green party and another moderate green list *(Entente Radicale Ecologiste* - ERE) competed for voters. Because of the electoral split neither of the two green organizations received the 5 percent of the vote necessary to send green candidates to the European Parliament. In the 1986 national parliamentry elections the Greens could only gain 1,2 percent of the vote.

Inspired by the electoral success of the French Greens in 1977, the ecologists in *Belgium* have formed two green parties (AGALEV for the Flemish and Ecolo for the Wallons). Although both parties campaigned in the 1977 and 1978 elections, it was not until the 1981 general election that they could win 4,8 percent of the vote and receive four seats in the national parliament. In fact, Belgium is the first country in Western Europe where self-styled representatives of green parties were elected into national parliament. In the 1984 European elections, the Greens in Belgium achieved another electoral breakthrough, winning two seats in the European Parliament. Ever since then, the two green parties became an established element of the party system in Belgium. They received 6,2 percent of the popular vote (9 seats) in the 1985 and 7,1 percent (9 seats) in the

1987 national elections.

In *Luxembourg* an "Alternative List" (AL) was founded in 1979 prior to the European and the national elections. In both elections, the AL gained 1 percent of the vote. Encouraged by the electoral success of the Belgian Greens in 1981, the followers of new social movements in Luxembourg - after a series of intensive and conflictive debates - founded a new green party in 1983 (The Green Alternative). In the 1984 European and national elections, the party won 6,1 percent and 5,8 percent of the vote winning two seats in the national parliament. Because of the "country-vote-proportional representation" for the European parliament, the Luxembourg Green party has no seats in Strasbourg.

The Greens in *West Germany* are by far the strongest group in Western Europe. It was not until March 1979 that the alternative political alliance (SPV) was first founded, primarily to contest the European elections of that year. Following their success in obtaining 3,2 percent of the vote, they made serious efforts to form a national party. After a series of lively conferences which demonstrated the differences among the various groupings, a party *Die Grünen* was founded in January 1980. Participation in the 1980 federal election resulted in a rather disappointing electoral outcome of 1,5 percent of the vote. In spite of this poor national performance in 1980, the green and alternative lists had between 1979 and 1982 more electoral success at the state *(Länder)* level. In March 1983 the Greens could increase their number of supporters to win 5,6 percent of the national vote and 27 seats in the national parliament. In the European election of 1984, the Greens gained an impressive 8,2 percent of the vote and received seven seats in the European Parliament. As in Belgium, the Greens in West Germany then consolidated themselves in the national party and parliamentary system. In the 1987 federal election, they received again 8,3 percent of the national vote. Because of this result, the German Greens presently hold 44 seats in national parliament.

In *Scandinavia* we find green parties - organized on the national level - in Finland, Sweden, and Denmark. The history of the Greens in *Finland* began in 1979 when they first nominated their own candidates for the parliamentary elections.They gained, however, only 0,1 percent of the national vote. From 1979 until 1983, the decentralized green *list* - which has not been established as a green *party* - increased its voter strength in local elections. In the 1983 national election the green list received 1,5 percent of the vote and - because of the proportional electoral system - won two seats in the parliament. In the 1987 national election the green list was able to increase its electoral success to 4 percent of the total vote.

In *Sweden* the *Miljöpartiet* was founded in 1981. According to a reliable Swedish public opinion poll, the *Miljöpartiet* should have gained around 4 percent of the national vote in November 1981. However, the electoral result in the 1982 general election was disappointing for the patry: they received only 1,6 percent of the vote and gained no seats in the national parliament. Since 1983, the Swedish environmentalists made efforts to establish closer ties to other green parties in Europe: In autumn 1984, the party changed its name from *Miljöpartiet* to Green party in order to be more attractive to new social movement followers at the 1985 national election. The electoral outcome was again very disappointing for the Greens. Because the Social Democrats adopted several environmental issues in their program for the campaign, the Greens only gained 1,5 percent of the national vote. In the 1988 national elections, the Green party received 5,5 percent of the total vote. Because of this result, the Greens currently hold 20 seats in the Swedish national parliament.

In *Denmark* a green party was set up in 1983, but did not receive enough support among the voters to appear on the ballot papers for the following national elections. In the local elections of 1985, however, the Green party won enough of the vote to elect several delegates to local councils. According to a national survey, 2,3 percent of the population was ready to vote for the Greens in December 1985. However, in the 1987 national elections the Danish Greens received only 0,2 percent of the total vote.

The forerunner of the present ecology party in *Great Britain* was formed in 1973 under the name People´s Party. In 1975 the party changed its name to Ecology Party (and later to the Green Party). In contrast to most other green parties in Europe the People´s Party and the later Ecology Party were not as strongly supported by the British environmental and peace movement. However, the Greens were the fastest growing party in Great Britain until the formation of the Social Democratic Party in 1981. The ecologists were quite successful in the 1976 and 1977 local elections. In the 1979 general elections the Green Party nominated 53 candidates and gained 1,6 percent of the vote where it contested seats. In the June 1979 direct elections to the European Parliament, the Greens nominated three candidates, who gained 3,7 percent of the vote in their constituencies. The general elections of 1983 and the European election of 1984 brought low electoral support which was a likely consequence of the British majority electoral system, where smaller parties stand hardly any chance of winning seats in the national parliament.

The green party in *Ireland* was founded under the name "Green Alliance" in 1981. The Irish Greens fielded seven candidates in the 1982 general elections and received only a small number of first preference votes. For the 1984 European elections, the Green Alliance nominated only one candidate in the constituency of Dublin where the party gained 1,9 percent of the vote. In the 1987 national election they could slightly increase voting support on the national level to 0,4 percent of the total vote.

In *Austria,* two green parties were founded in 1982: The Alternative List (ALÖ) and the Green Union (VGÖ). The ALÖ has established its strength at the local level and has used the grassroot network to gradually extend its electoral support in district elections. Both parties polled well enough to send green party members to the respective parliaments. In the 1983 general elections the Austrian Greens were not very successful mainly because of conflicts within and among the two parties. The VGÖ and ALÖ nominated separate lists and gained 1,9 percent and 1,4 percent respectively, of the total vote. With a united green list and an electoral result of 3,3 percent (VGÖ/ALÖ), the green parties would have been able to send seven delegates to the national parliament in 1983.Consequently, for the 1986 national elections both green parties formed an alliance and received 4,8 percent of the vote and 8 seats in the national parliament.

In *Switzerland*, the first regional green party was founded in Zürich in 1978. The party participated in the 1979 general elections with its own candidates list, and gained one seat in the national parliament. In the following years several green parties were formed in different areas throughout Switzerland. At the same time, alternative left-wing social movements developed in larger cities. In May 1983, most of the decentralized green parties founded the "Federation of Green Parties in Switzerland" (GPS) on the national level. One month later, some left-wing followers of the alternative groups established the "Green-Alternative List in Switzerland" (GAS). Both groups nominated their own canditates for the 1983 general election. The GAS won 3,5 percent and the GPS 2,9 percent of the national vote. In the 1987 national election the GPS could increase its voting support to 4,8 percent while the GAS polled again 3,5 percent. Currently, the Greens hold seven seats in the national parliament.

The foundation of local green lists in *Italy* dates back to 1980, when some small autonomous ecological groups nominated candidates for local elections in several Northern-Italian cities. The number of local green lists increased to 16 in 1983, and for the local administrative elections in May 1985 about 150 green lists competed with other parties for voters. On the whole, they won 2,1 percent of the total turn out in three districts where they nominated own candidates. Green lists in Italy gained a total of 141 seats in the representative assemblies: 10 in the regional, 16 in the province, and 115 in city councils. In June 1987 national election the *Liste Verdi,* a joint group of all green lists in Italy polled 2,5 percent and won 13 seats in the national parliament (Chamber of Deputies) and two seats in the upperhouse (Senate).

This cross-national overview has shown that green parties are at the level of voting support and parliamentary representation relatively small. However, boosted by a lively media interest, green parties have influenced many areas of political life, such as environmental awareness, nuclear policy and demand for disarmament among the mass public.

Political Relevance of Green Parties:
A New Conflict Dimension in European Party Systems

Although green parties exist in virtually all advanced industrial Western countries, their individual and collective political relevance has not been examined in any systematic or comprehensive way. While it is understandable that major parties have received privileged attention in scientific work (obviously because of their political visibility and role), there is currently sufficient political impact of green parties to challenge cross-national research on small political parties (Müller-Rommel / Pridham, 1990). In Western Europe, we find, for instance, growing and continuing disaffection with many established parties; declining system performance in the context of the economic recession with possible profound effects on party systems; evidence of fragmentation and electoral volatilitiy in several countries; and the emergence of new political issues opening the way for some restructuring of the political systems. Altogether, these features present a significantly different situation compared with the postwar period and one of sufficient duration in which green parties might have unprecedented opportunities.

Comparative work on European party systems has debated - though rather inconclusively - the "unfreezing" of long-standing cleavages. Support for the established parties is characterized by

Table 1.1

Electoral Results of Green Parties/Lists in National Elections in Western Europe*

	1978	1979	1979[1]	1980	1981	1982	1983	1984	1984[1]	1985	1986	1987	1988
Belgium[2]	0.8(0)	-	3.4(0)	-	4.5(4)	-	-	-	8.2(2)	6.2(9)	-	7.1(9)	-
West Germany	-	-	3.2(0)	1.5(0)	-	-	5.6(27)	-	8.2(7)	-	-	8.3(44)	-
Denmark	-	-	-	-	-	-	-	-	-	-	-	0.2(0)	-
France	2.1(0)	-	4.4(0)	-	1.1(0)	-	-	-	3.4(0)/3.3(0)[3]	-	1.2(0)	-	-
Finland	-	0.1(0)	-	-	-	-	1.5(2)	-	-	-	-	4.0(4)	-
Great Britain	-	0.1(0)	0.1(0)	-	-	-	0.2(0)	-	0.5(0)	-	-	1.3(0)	-
Ireland	-	-	-	-	-	-	-	-	0.1(0)	-	-	0.4(0)	-
Italy	-	-	-	-	-	-	-	-	-	-	-	2.5(13)	-
Luxembourg	-	1.0(0)	1.0(0)	-	-	-	-	5.8(2)	6.1(0)	-	-	-	-
Austria[4]	-	-	-	-	-	-	3.2(0)	-	-	-	4.8(8)	-	-
Sweden	-	-	-	-	-	1.6(0)	-	-	-	1.5(0)	-	-	5.5(20)
Switzerland	-	0.8(1)	-	-	-	-	6.4(6)[5]	-	-	-	-	8.3(7)	-

* percent of total vote and number of seats in national parliament

(1). Results in European Elections /(2). Results of AGALEV and Ecolo together / (3). 3.4 = Les Verts; 3,3 = Entente Radical Ecologiste / (4). Results of VGÖ and ALÖ together / (5). Results of GPS and GAS together

specific historically-rooted social milieu, whereby the structure of social conflict within a nation produces long-term and relatively stable political cleavages within the party system. Furthermore, the determinants of electoral choice could be traced back to basic social allegiances such as class, religion or regional traits (Lipset and Rokkan 1967). The end-result was largely a Left-Right pattern of partisan alignment.

Yet the emergence of new value orientations in Western Europe together with the foundation of green parties has produced a new dimension of conflict. This is because green parties direct their protest which is based on new values against left and right targets alike. As such, the Greens challenge the stability of the established political constellation by adding a "new" conflict dimension to the traditional left-right party system cleavage structure without breaking down the primary cleavage structures.

Ronald Inglehart (1979; 1984) argues that the traditional Left-Right dimension no longer adequately describes modern patterns of political conflict, because new political issues can no longer be regarded as expressions of Left-Right conflicts alone. The need to combat environmental pollution and to develop a peace policy is not, at least overtly, questioned by either conservative or left-wing parties.

Inglehart shows that the "valence issues" of the new politics are better placed on an establishment / anti-establishment scale than on a Left-Right one. Some sections of the population sympathize with the peace movement, squaters and social fringe groups. Others favour the police, the administrative bureaucracy; that is, the established institutions of the state defending the existing social order. In this context Inglehart holds that this new political dimension is partly an expression of the emergence of a sizeable and active minority giving priority to post-material values.

In examining the electoral behavior of this post-materialist minority, Inglehart found that these individuals heavily prefered left-wing parties. Initially this finding appears to confirm the thesis that voters are still in the habit of attaching their political ideas and demands to certain parties via terms like "Left" and "Right". In a comparative study, however, Inglehart und Klingemann (1976) showed that the designations "Left" and "Right" have largely become stereotypes for specifying political parties, and that the decision to vote for one of these parties is still closely connected with a party identification shaped by class and religion. According to Inglehart, it is precisely this inertia of established party loyalties and group formations which prevents the post-materialist value structure from taking full effect on electoral choice.

Following the logic of this argument, the new dimension of conflict should become more pronounced when green parties with new politics issues enter the competition for votes. Some studies on the Greens in single European countries have shown that green party voters are both highly interested and very active in politics. They view governmental policy more critically than the average voter and they are mostly without historically formed party identifications to one of the established parties. The new dimension of conflict within European party systems should, therefore, intensify when green parties increase their electoral success (Müller-Rommel 1990).

It has already been argued that green parties in Europe mobilize many followers of new political movements by making it possible for them to find rational expression for their views at the ballot box. Green parties thus serve as a political vehicle for those movement supporters whose grievances have been ignored by the larger established parties. Green parties also give assurance to their voters that they are doing something on a parliamentary level about the causes of their discontent. By making themselves the spokesperson of the discontented, green parties, however, additionally promote the process of change of party loyalties for older generations and prepare the way for increasing volatility within the party system.

On the other hand, green parties also affect political issues and the tone of political life by bringing controversial matters into the public debate. If the issues prove popular, they may well be adopted by one or more of the larger established parties, as larger parties in Europe currently seek to adopt some environmetal issues first raised by green parties. This leads to changes in the programs of major European parties.

It seems to be evident that green parties compete in the first glance with larger socialist parties. Both party types are committed to changing the political system. However, while socialist parties seek system change through reform policies addressing the traditional conflict between capital and labour, the green parties ask for a fundamental rethinking of the economic growth theory.

This process particularly affects the larger socialist parties. In most European countries, the Socialist´s rank-and-file members as well as party elites split into two groups: those with a traditional left-wing outlook who are concerned with the security of the working class and economic stability (the Old Left), and those with a new politics orientation who rather emphasize the quality of life, the nature of economy, and the extent of democracy (New Left). The "New Left" in socialist parties stands in competition with green parties regarding the "new politics voter", while the "Old Left" is still fighting along the old cleavage dimensions. The socialist parties are, therefore, trapped between two cultures, although only a minority of the electorate is on the new politics side. The majority in most Western European democracies stand in the center of the political spectrum. Whatever the socialist parties might be able to gain from the new left, they risk losing from among the old left voters. Consequently, the only viable strategy for the Socialists is to attempt some reconciliation of old politics (in order to integrate the majority of the Socialist´s voters) and a moderate version of new politics (in order to attract green parties voters). A radical realization of "new politics issues" is beyond the reach of the socialist parties.

In functioning as promoters of new politics issues, however, green parties offer radical answers to radical questions concerning ecological problems, military concerns, and the questions of democratic and civil rights. The success of green parties is nourished by radical issue positions that larger socialist and conservative parties are not able to take fully into consideration. It thus seems theoretically cogent and empirically substantiated to predict that green parties are here to stay as long as the political issues of new political movement followers remain on the political agenda and are not adopted by any established party.

Comparative Research on Green Parties:
A Terra Incognita of Comparative Party Analysis

In spite of their strong public support and their influence on the fragmentation of some party systems in Europe, green parties have not been studied systematically. While some research has been conducted on green parties in single European countries (see the references in this volume), there is hardly any cross national analysis on the Greens available in the literature (Rüdig 1985; Müller-Rommel 1982, 1985; Poguntke 1987; Kitschelt 1988). This might have something to do with the fact that the electoral success of the Greens is still a fairly recent phenomenon. On the other hand, there are also some other reasons for this lack of attention (Fisher 1980: 609 ff). First, the Greens are often seen as politically unimportant because of their size and their low electoral turnout. Second, most scholars focus their research on parties for which information is more likely to be available. Studying the Greens in

Europe creates definite language problems. Most manifestoes, programs, and party statutes of the Greens in single European countries have not been translated into English or another language. In addition, survey research data on green voters is not available in those countries where the Greens have only marginal electoral success. Furthermore, in official election statistics, the Greens are often grouped together with other small parties under the label "other parties". A third reason for the lack of research on the Greens is that green parties currently have no measurable consequences on national governments. Because of these three practical research problems, the contributors of this book are country specialists and native speakers who have access to a variety of information about the Greens in their home countries.

Several of the questions regarding the political relevance of green parties cannot be answered without a close examination of the "birth" and the "life" of these parties in each country. This is basically what the book attempts to do. Although we know that the traditions and the political culture of European countries as well as their political, social and economic problems are different, this volume will describe the main features of green parties on the basis of a common framework. The single country chapters deal with the development, the organizational structure, the electoral support, the government participation, and the programatic profile of green parties across Europe. Naturally, the picture that emerges is one of considerable variety: common themes are so to speak diffracted by the profound idiosyncrasies arising from a different cultural heritage or as a result of the existence of different problems.

The bulk of detailed information about single green parties, however, poses the problem of drawing comparative conclusions. What research on green parties needs is a common approach providing a framework for analysis on the basis of which it will be possible to summarize, incorporate and interrelate the various characteristics of green parties´ "birth" and "life". The two comparative essays in the third part of this book, therefore, offer a cross-national classification and analysis of green parties in Western Europe.

Case Studies

2
Austria:
The "United Greens" and the
"Alternative List/Green Alternative"

Christian Haerpfer

Development of the Green Parties

The transformation of new social movements (peace movement, women´s movement, anti-nuclear movement, etc.) into the organizational form of green-oriented political parties in the Austrian political system was accelerated and triggered by one political event in the 1970s, the nuclear power referendum held in November of 1978. That year saw the real birth of the green parties in Austria. One might say that what the Boston tea party was for the United States, the referendum of 1978 whereby the Austrian population decided to ban nuclear energy in Austria, was for the Greens of Austria. Most of the decisive meetings of green activists throughout the long and complicated process of the formation of green parties were always held in subsequent years, on the 5th of November a "holy day" of sorts for the green movement in Austria (Pelinka 1983).

Both green parties were founded as nationwide parties in 1982. The United Greens (VGOe; *Vereinte Grüne Österreichs*), a pure green reformist party according to the definition of this concept put forward by Müller-Rommel (1985: 491) was formed as a new political party in the spring 1982. Some months later, in November 1982 - in the midst of celebrating the anniversary of the referendum against nuclear energy - the Alternative List (ALOe; *Alternative Liste Österreichs*) held its founding congress establishing it as a new political party. This party is close to the type of an alternative green radical party, according again to the definition developed by Müller-Rommel. Hence, the year 1982 could be characterized as a crucial year for the transformation of the traditional Austrian party system after almost four decades as one of the world´s outstandingly stable party systems.

Concerning the electoral history of green parties in Austria, we must distinguish between three levels of analysis: the national, regional and local levels of green participation in the elections. The electoral history of the Greens is relatively new. It begins with the numerous electoral successes of 1982/83. The local elections of 1977 in Salzburg, the first Austrian elections with a green victory (5 percent for the *Bürgerliste*) were, before 1982 the first, but sole green signal to the Austrian party system, that the Greens were forming into a popular political movement - into actual political parties.Consequently, this sole victory did not impress the traditional parties at all (Fröschl, 1982). Hence, the following analysis is of time restricted to the five-year-period from 1983 until 1987 - a rather short period indeed, if compared to the forty years of electoral history of the Austrian Second Republic since World War II (see table 2.1).

The Austrian green parties participated for the first time in the 1983 national elections after failing to do so in the 1979 general elections. The latter failure was caused by the fact that after the triumph of the 1978 referendum, the multitude of grass-root groups were not able to establish an organization for the election campaign within a few months. The *VGOe* and the *ALOe* tried to form an electoral alliance, but personal and policy differences proved to be too great, so that both parties decided to participate separately. The green parties together got 3.3 percent of the total vote, which meant that both failed to achieve a parliamentary seat. A common candidature would have resulted in more than five seats. Nevertheless, the green parties were a crucial factor in the demise of the so-called "Kreisky-era", from 1970 to 1983 (the end of an era of socialist majorities in the Austrian *"Nationalrat"* and consequently, of socialist governments). The regional organizations of *VGOe* and *ALOe* then participated in the 1983 regional elections in Lower Austria and suffered a dramatic loss with a cumulative share of only 1.6 percent of the vote. In Lower Austria, a significant difference regarding the organizational structure of both parties could be seen. Whereas the national party of the *VGOe* had close links to the regional organization, the Alternative List in that region was completely autonomous from the national *ALOe*. We can see that the *VGOe* have developed organizational patterns which are very similar to those of the traditional parties, whereas the *ALOe* structures consist of separate units, which are independent actors at higher levels of party organization. (i.e. the national *ALOe* is no more than a meeting of all regional alternative lists with equal influence upon the decision-process).

Table 2.1
Votes and Seats for Green Parties in National, Regional, and Local Elections in Austria (1977-1987)
(percent of the total valid vote, number of seats in legislature in parenthesis)

	1983	1984	1985	1986	1987
National Elections:					
Presidential Elections					
Mrs. Meissner-Blau	-	-	-	5.5%	-
Parliamentary Elections (Nationalrat)					
VGOe (Vereinte Gruene Oesterreichs)	1.9%	-	-	-	-
ALOe (Alternative Liste Oesterreichs)	1.4%	-	-	-	-
Alliance of Green Parties:					
Gruene Alternative (VGOe + ALOe)	-	-	-	4.8%(8)	-
Regional Elections:					
Vorarlberg:					
Green Alliance: "GAL"	-	13.0%(4)	-	-	-
Salzburg:					
GABL	-	4.3%	-	-	-
DGOe	-	1.3%	-	-	-
Tirol:					
AT	-	3.6%	-	-	-
Styria:					
Green Alliance (VGOe + ALOe)	-	-	-	3.7%(2)	-
Other Green Parties	-	-	-	1.1%	-
Lower Austria:					
VGOe	1.0%	-	-	-	-
ALNOe	0.6%	-	-	-	-
Upper Austria:					
VGOe	-	-	2.2%	-	-
ALOe	-	-	1.7%	-	-
DgOe	-	-	0.4%	-	-
Burgenland:					
Green Alliance ("Gruene")	-	-	-	-	2.2%

(continued)

Table 2.1 (continued)

	1977	1982	1983	1987
Local Elections:				
Vienna:	-	-	-	-
ALW/Grüne	-	-	2.5%	-
WBU/VGÖ	-	-	0.7%	-
Salzburg:				
BL	5.6%(2)	17.7%(7)	-	10.1%(4)
Graz:				
AlG	-	-	7.0%(4)	-
Innsbruck				
AL Innsbruck	-	-	2.9%	-

Source: IKF-Elections Archive

The green parties had their first successes at two local elections in 1982 and 1983. The alternative list *"Bürgerliste"* got 17.7 percent in the Salzburg local elections, which brought them 7 seats in the local council and the green´s first executive post: municipal councillor for urban planning and environment. (Dachs, 1983) This post is still today the only executive post held by a green politician in the Austrian political system. In 1983, the local alternative list *(ALG)* received 7 percent of the vote and 4 seats at the local elections in Graz, another large Austrian city, (Merli/Handstanger, 1984). The greatest success for green parties at the regional level took place in 1984 when the first electoral alliance, between *VGOe* and *ALOe*, obtained 13 percent of the vote and 4 seats in the regional parliament at the elections in Vorarlberg. The case of Vorarlberg demonstrated the electoral advantage of green alliances and formed the basis of ongoing and continous efforts to create nationwide joint candidatures of green parties with the ultimate goal of forming a single, united green party in Austria; a topic which has been the issue of recent discussions within the green movement (Plasser/Sommer, 1985; Nick, 1986).

In 1985, three green parties, the *VGOe*, the alternative list *(ALO)* and a marginal third green party (*DGOe*; Die Grünen Östereichs), contested the regional elections in Upper Austria only to suffer complete defeat due to the splitting of green voters.In contrast 1986 marked the birth of a green parliamentary party following the general elections in November 1986 indicating again that November is a kind month for the Austrian green movement. Since the 1986 parliamentary election, the Austrian party system can no longer be described as "two-and-a-half-party system" *(SPOe/OeVe/FPOe)*, it is now a four-party-system, consisting of two major parties (social democrats and conservatives) in structural decline, and of two small parties with increasing shares of the Austrian electorate: the conservative protest party *FPOe* (Liberals) and the green alliance *("Die Grüne Alternative-Freda Meissner-Blau")*. The last months preceeding the 1986 elections representatives of the *VGOe*, the *ALOe* and numerous regional and local groupings of Greens met, in order to produce the candidature of one single green party as basis for a long-awaited success at the national level, a success already shared by green parties in local councils and regional parliaments.The negotiations between the *VGOe* and the *ALOe* collapsed nevertheless with all the vehemence of a greek tragedy into a deadlock. In the face of such a situation, a group of well-known representatives, the so-called *"Promis"* (Prominent public figures) of national, regional and local green parties, having previously demonstrated their ability to win elections, joined in a third "loose" association, the *Bürgerinitiative Parlament* (Citizen initiative parliament). Their aim was to achieve a green alliance with a political elite of a dozen "stars" as the dominating actors representing the green movement. Thus, the electoral success in 1986 was the result of such political action, the action of green hierarchy and not the result of painful negotiations steming from the party´s grassroots. The "BIP" (*Bürgerinitiative Parlament*) consisted of green party leaders from Vorarlberg, Salzburg, Graz and Vienna; most of them widely known veterans of green battles against the nuclear-power plant at Zwentendorf and against the hydroelectric power station at Hainburg, both events having been covered extensively by the Austrian media as well as winners of previous local and regional elections. The leading lady of the BIP, Mrs. Meissner-Blau, participated in the presidential elections of 1986 and received 5.5 percent of the vote, causing a second ballot to be cast between the socialist and conservative candidates. Encouraged by the latter green triumph, the *BIP* invited the *ALOe* and the *VGOe* to form an alliance in order to contest the general elections. This alliance came into being and was called *"Die Grüne Alternative - Liste Freda Meissner-Blau"* ("Green Alternative").The inclusion of the name of the green presidential candidate was intended to connect the presidential election campaign. Finally, the Green Alternative got 4.8

percent of the vote and thus obtained 8 seats in the Austrian parliament in November 1986. One structural advantage for the representation of a green party in the current Austrian parliament is that Austrian electoral law does not have a five-percent-barrier (like in West Germany, see Frankland in this volume), the only condition for obtaining a seat is to get a basic seat *("Grundmandat")* in the first step of the process of conversion of votes into seats in accordance with the D´Hondt procedure always as part of proportional representation permitted by the Austrian constitutional law. In 1986, a green alliance also received 3.7 percent of the vote and 2 seats at the regional elections in Styria. The last elections up to the present time have been regional elections in Burgenland where electoral defeat for a green alliance (2.2 % of the vote) was suffered. Local elections were also held in one stronghold of the Austrian green movement, in Salzburg, where the oldest and most successful green party, the Citizens List, won 10 percent of the vote and 4 seats in the local council. In comparison with the last Salzburg elections of 1982, this result means a decrease of seven percent in the green vote and the loss of the one executive post held by a green politician in Austria, resigning immediately afterwards from his political career. This election might be an indication that the long-term electoral base for green parties in the Austrian party system is not much higher than one tenth of the electorate.

The current situation of green political parties in Austria, primarily at the national level, could be characterized by the effort of the parliamentary party, the Green Alternative, to attract party members from the *ALOe* and the *VGOe* to join the Green Alternative which is - from their point of view - the only green party of the future. This process is successful as far as the *ALOe* is concerned, which is slowly approaching its own dissolution (e.g. in Vienna), but the *VGOe* is resisting these tendencies and is trying to remain a separate organizational entity with its own finances and its own hierarchical structure in analogy to traditional parties. Three of the eight green members of parliament are from the *VGOe* and they regard the parliamentary party simply as an electoral alliance, where the *VGOe* is but another independent partner.For the moment it appears as though the Green Alternative is the institutional successor of the *ALOe*, which now represents a type of alternative green radical party while the *VGOe* still remains as a second party with the characteristics of a pure reformist party.

Electoral Support

Throughout the 1970s, Austrian electoral behavior was characterised by a very high stability of voting patterns - the floating vote well under ten percent of the electorate. Party identification with the traditional Austrian parties was decreasing slowly, however, this process of smooth dealignment was not apparent at the general elections due to the pull of political leadership exerted by the Socialist Austrian prime minister Dr. Kreisky. Since the 1983 elections however, the floating vote in Austria has increased from nine percent to 17 percent in the 1986 general elections, thus indicating higher levels of electoral volatility. The potential for a green party was ten percent of the electorate in 1976 and, after years of steady, growing support, it can now be quantified to about one fifth of the Austrian voters. This twenty percent represents the widest potential for green voters and can only be achieved if the green party would offer a convincing party programme together with party personalities who are able to represent green ideas in public, and expecially on TV.

Concerning the extent of stability of the green vote one can state that the increasing volatility of the Austrian voters has its effects upon the green electorate. The comparison of the green vote at the general elections of 1983 and 1986 demonstrates that only fifty percent of the green vote consists of stable green voters with affective ties to a green party. About 35 percent of the green vote is a floating one with voters primarily coming from the Socialists and the Conservatives. The remaining 15 percent of the national green vote in 1986 consists of either new voters or of previous non-voters. Currently, the core group of green voters in Austria consists of three percent of the electorate; the second half of the green vote is volatile. As recent regional elections have shown, the green parties are forced to compete with the second small party in the Austrian party system, the liberal FPOe. The Greens must also attract a share of the large group of protest voters, who, being undecided, make voting decisions very late in the course of an electoral campaign. Thus, the Austrian Greens enjoy the benefit of the continous partisan dealignment existing in the Austrian party system since the early 1970s, at the cost, however, of being prey to an unstable and volatile group of supporters.

Concerning the impact of sociodemographic characteristics upon green voting, it is important to note that social class is not the basis of green partisanship. The influence of social class within the established parties, the Socialists and the Conservatives, is decreasing since the 1970s, but is nevertheless considerably higher than in other European party systems. Two dimensions are of central importance for green voters: the level of education and the age cohort. The third decisive influence is the urban-rural dimension. Thus, we are able to identify three basic sociodemographic characteristics of the green vote, education, age and the size of the community (see Table 2.2).

The *ALOe* can be labelled as a party of academics: 42 percent of the alternative vote have higher education which is a high percentage of the academic vote considering that 15 percent of the Austrian population are academics with tertiary education. The small impact of voters with compulsory education is reflected by the fact that only one quarter (24 percent) of the *ALOe*-vote consists of respondents with primary education, a group however, whose national share of the electorate is of 40 percent. Voters with a secondary level of education form one third (34 percent) of the alternative vote (National share: 45 percent). If one looks at Austrian voters with tertiary education, it is interesting to see that 11 percent of them support the *ALOe*, whereas only 4 percent of the general electorate could be described as alternative voters. Hence Austrian academics and persons with further education (secondary level of education) form the core group of the alternative vote.

The impact of education upon the *VGOe*-vote is similar to the pattern of the *ALOe*. Roughly one third (34 percent) of the support for the *VGOe* stems from voters with tertiary education (National share: 15 percent) and 27 percent of the *VGOe*-vote comes from persons with compulsory education (National share: 40 percent). The interesting difference in comparison with the *ALOe* is that respondents with secondary education display a 39 percent greater share within the *VGOe* than within the *ALOe*. The *VGOe* is obviously appealing to the tertiary and secondary levels of education. The Austrian academics support the *VGOe* with 25 percent of their vote.

The essential outcome of the analysis of the influence of education on green voting behavior is that one third of all Austrians with tertiary education (36 percent) have no affective ties with the traditional party system and support either the *VGOe* or the *ALOe*. The effect of this phenomenon is a dramatic loss of academics within socialist partisanship on the one hand, and a significant weakening of a former academic stronghold of voters within the Conservative Party *(OeVP)*.

The Austrian green parties are not only young in terms of their historical development, but also very young in terms of their electoral support. Almost 80 percent of the alternative voters (79.1 percent) are younger than 40! Generally speaking, one might say that the younger a voter is, the greater the probability will be of his voting alternative. The core group for the *ALOe* are voters under 25 years of age, they constitute 37 percent of the alternative partisanship (National share of that age group: 20 percent). The majority of alternative voters are to be found amongst Austrians between 25 and 39 years of age, which form 43 percent of the alternative supporters (National share of that age group: 29 percent). Only one fifth of supporters of the *ALOe* derive from age cohorts of above 40 years of age (National share: 52 percent). The distribution of the support for the *VGOe* is distributed more evenly along the age-dimension. One third of the *VGOe*-voters (31 percent) are Austrians under 25, another third (36 percent) comes from the age cohort between 25 and 39 years of age and the final third (33 percent) is to be found among the older political generations of above 40 years of age.

At the party system level, one can say that 24 percent of Austrian youth under 25 form the core of the green vote. If one considers that around 30 percent of this age group are non-voters, one might say that the established parties are only able to attract a minority of the Austrian youth. The Socialists, Conservatives and the Liberals have lost the absolute majority among the younger age groups of the Austrian electorate. The second stronghold for green parties are the age cohorts between 25 and 39 years of age. The latter, which might be labeled as the first post-war-generation, display a green share of 19 percent. The resignation of considerable parts of younger political generations (one fourth of the youngest and one fifth of the younger generation) with respect to the traditional organizations of interest intermediation and the increasing share of green voters and nonvoters among these age groups forms a considerable challenge to the Austrian political system.

The slow greening of the Austrian party system takes place primarily in urban areas. The typical green voter lives in a city and not in the countryside. The *VGOe* is more urban than the *ALOe*. The majority of *VGOe*-voters (48 percent) live in cities with more than 50,000 inhabitants. One third of the vote for the United Greens comes from the Austrian capital, Vienna (33 percent), which also happens to be the largest Austrian city. Another 15 percent of the *VGOe*-support can be located within towns of between 50,000 and 1 Million inhabitants. Interestingly, one further stronghold for the *VGOe* are small towns of between 5,000 and 50,000 inhabitants,

Table 2.2
Social Structure of the Green Vote in Austria, 1985
(in percentage)

Socio-Demographic Variables	VGÖe N=429	ALOe N=153
Education		
Primary	27	24
Secondary	39	34
Tertiary	34	42
Age		
15-24	31	37
25-39	36	43
40-59	22	12
60 and older	11	9
Type of community		
under 5.000 inhabitants	26	39
5.000-49.000 inhabitants	26	16
50.000-900.000	15	17
Vienna	33	28
Social class		
Working class	35	40
Middle class	45	44
Upper middle class	16	11
Farmers	3	5

Source: The data were drawn from a nationwide random sample survey on "Postmaterialism in Austria", conducted by *Institut für Konfliktforschung* (IFES), Vienna with the author as a principal investigator, in November 1985. A total of 3978 persons had been interviewed face-to-face. The number of cases for the VGOe was 429 (10.8%) and for the ALOe 153 (3.8(%).

where 26 percent support the Green party (National share: 22 percent). This might be an indicator that green ideas and support for green political parties are also slowly spreading to rural areas.

Support for the *ALOe* shows basically the same pattern with only slight deviations. The relative majority of alternative supporters (45 percent) comes from cities with more than 50,000 inhabitants. In Vienna, the alternative supporters form 28 percent of the *ALOe*-vote. The highly educated alternative voters show a peripheral pattern: they are stronger in regional centres (17 percent of the alternative vote) and, surprisingly, in rural dwellings with less than 5,000 inhabitants where 40 percent of the alternative partisanship can be found. As stated above, this seems to be the effect of the greening of local elites, even in very agrarian milieus. This phenomenon finds its political expression in the flourishing of citizen initiatives within rural areas throughout the 1980s. The basic outcome of the analysis of the influence of the urban-rural dimension on green voting behaviour is that 22 percent of voters in the Austrian capital, Vienna, and 22 percent of the electorate that lives in regional centres with more than 50,000 inhabitants, can be regarded as the core group of the Austrian green parties.

The impact of other sociodemographic dimensions, such as occupational status, social class and sex is considerably lower than that of education, age and size of community. They are secondary dimensions for the "green-vote" explanation, but, nevertheless, necessitate a short analysis. Social class, that is, the occupational status of a particular voter, is not the basis for green party vote in Austria. The absolute majority of voters in both green parties are not occupationally active as full-time working employees or employers. The voting share of full-time working persons is 47 percent in both green parties. One quarter (24 percent) of the alternative vote consists of college and university students. One interesting fact is that women with part-time jobs are politically "greener" than housewives, the latter showing no signs of green partisanship. The *VGOe* displays a similar pattern: 24 percent of *VGOe*-voters are either in the educational system or are working part-time. The basic outcome of an analysis of the occupational structure of green parties is that one third (33 percent) of all young Austrians in the educational system are voting for green parties. Furthermore, one fifth (22 percent) of all part-time employees vote green on election day, which indicates again that occupationally-active women are more politically inclined towards green partisanship than housewives.

If one looks at the social composition of the green electorate, as measured by the occupation of the head of a specific household, it shows that the Austrian green parties are not the parties of the middle class, but rather, that considerable segments of the Austrian middle class form the majority of the green vote. The *VGOe* is more middle class than the *ALOe* with 62 percent of its vote coming from either the middle class or the upper middle class. The relative majority of the voters for the United Greens (45 percent) are members of the middle class (National share of the middle class: 29 percent). The Austrian upper middle class constitutes 17 percent of the support for the *VGOe*. One third of the *VGOe*-vote (35 percent) stems from the Austrian working class, whereas farmers are a marginal group amongst green voters.The middle classes form a smaller majority for the *ALOe* with 54 percent, thus indicating that the *ALOe* is less dominated by voters from middle classes than *VGOe*. A relative majority of 44 percent from the middle class voters support the *ALOe*, whereas 10 percent of the *ALOe*-vote is recruited from the upper middle class. In contrast to the *VGOe*, labourers form 40 percent of the alternative vote, which seems to signal that the *ALOe* is attracting more green workers than the *VGOe*. Finally, one might argue that the so-called "new" middle class has found its political representation in both Austrian green parties, which is underlined by the fact that one fifth (20 %) of the Austrian middle class and 15 percent of the upper middle class constantly support the Austrian green parties. The middle class bias is more visible within the *VGOe*, which seems in effect to be the more bourgois party at the centre of the political spectrum, than among the voters of the *ALOe*. Voters for the *ALOe* are located more to the left on the left-right scale in the Austrian party system. These results are consistent with the typology developed by Müller-Rommel, a typology which differentiates between pure green reformist parties on the one hand and alternative green radical parties on the other hand.

Organizational Structure
The basic problem for green parties in the Austrian party system consists of the precarious relationship between the green social movement and green political parties that participate in local, regional and national elections. The voters and members of the *ALOe* and its institutional successor, the Green Alternative, dislike parties with hierarchical organisational structures like the traditional Austrian parties. Similar to its German sister party, the Greens in Austria heavily discussed the issue whether or not the green movement should adopt traditional party organizational structures. While the

ALOe considers the green parties in parliament as the political arm of the green movement, the *VGOe* are trying to build up organizational structures, which are very similar in nature to those found in the traditional Austrian parties. However, the endless discussions about the participation at forthcoming elections, about the choice of candidates, about the formation of electoral alliances and of party programs made it impossible to build up a stable organizational structure for the *VGOe* and the *ALOe*. The successor of the *ALOe*, the Green Alternative, is meanwhile trying to establish a party organisation from the basis of the green parliamentary party.

Programatic Profile
The development of party programs is neglected activity of both green parties in Austria. Since 1982, political discussions centered around the appropriate political organisation, the preparation of election campaigns and the placement of candidates for regional and national parliaments. One consequence was that the development and presentation of political programs was always planned as a last step during the campaign, which produced rather poor results in terms of detailed and consistent political programs. The scarce resources of both parties made it impossible to offer clear-cut election programs and tempted the *ALOe* for instance, to import party programs from the German Greens and to adapt them to the Austrian domestic situation. Nevertheless, it is still possible to identify basic political orientations of the *VGOe* and the *ALOe*/Green Alternative.

The party program of the *VGOe* aims to reform Austrian society and its politics in a pragmatic fashion. The focus of the political ideology of the *VGOe* is the individual person, the "citoyen". Traditional family structures should be supported in order to increase the opportunities of the individual, educational policy should further individual interests and abilities and personal rights should be extended as far as possible. This individual perspective has the consequence of demanding greater civil freedom and of demanding that the influence of the state should be reduced dramatically in social and economic policy. With regards to economic policy, the *VGOe* are asking for deregulation and privatisation. Approximately one third of the space within *VGOe*-programs is devoted to the protection of the environment through milder means of reform. The international dimension (e.g. Third World problems) is almost neglected and the peace issue plays a minor role in the party program of the *VGOe*.

The party program of the *ALOe*/Green Alternative supports the idea that radical and substantial changes are needed within the Austrian society and within its politics - their political ideology transcends the current shape of society. The central unit of political thinking is not a social class, but rests rather with the single individual in his or her specific context: at work, in school and in family. For the *ALOe*, the freedom of activity of the individual should be secured and widened by a more democratic participation at work, in school and in families. This includes more rights for children with respect to their parents, more rights for the students with respects to their teachers, more rights for employees with respect to their employers and finally, more rights for women with respect to their husbands. The policy options of the *ALOe* in the area of economic policy are leftist: they demand a stronger political control of the economy, the nationalisation of some areas of private industry, a basic income for everyone regardless of occupational status, 35 working-hours per week and absolute priority for public transport. As far as the protection of the environment is concerned, the main strategic emphasis is on the fight against large building sites (Power plants, highways, airports etc.) and private transportation. The *ALOe* is in general fiercely against the Austrian army and it is particularly projected against the build-up of the Austrian air force. At the international agenda, the *ALOe* is urging for the immediate termination of all arms production in Austria and for a Europe without nuclear weapons.

Henceforth, it is quite obvious that in the field of economic policy, that in the role of the state in society, that with respect to family policy, defense matters and with respect to the issue of abortion there are decisive ideological differences between both green parties. These differences exist - despite all efforts to build a united green party - and this consequently explains the existence of two green party electorates and of two green party elites.

Outlook

What are the prospects of the Greens in the Austrian party system? It is very difficult to assess the future development of the *VGOe* and the *ALOe*/Green Alternative five years after the formation of both green parties in 1982. Generally, the green parties have had electoral successes at the national, regional and local level ever since 1982. The main aim throughout recent years was to try to establish a national party and to build up nationwide organisation. In the near future, the green parties will develop strong local organizations covering all electoral constituencies in Austria. The electoral strength of the green parties is heavily dependent upon a coalition between *VGOe* and *ALOe*. Only three percent of the Austrian electorate are considered as stable green voters with affective ties to a green party. The simultaneous existence of a green reformist and a green radical party reduces the electoral chances for the green movement drastically. In the case of separate candidatures, the green vote is split with the possible effect that neither of them is able to achieve parliamentary representation. The bottom line of the discussion about the future of the Greens seems to be that the *VGOe,* as a green reformist party, could become an integrated part of the Austrian party system, with a considerable electoral basis, if given a broad acceptance by the media and the potential to participate in future party coalitions. The *ALOe*/Green Alternative has, however, only limited chances at elections in the long run and will likely remain a leftist outsider in the Austrian party system.

3
Belgium:
The "Ecologists" and "AGALEV"

Kris Deschouwer*

Development of the Green Parties

The history of the Belgian party system is a history of ever increasing fractionalization. The three so-called "traditional" political parties, the Christian-Democrats (CVP/PSC), the Socialists (SP/PS) and the Liberals (PVV/PRL) - each of them founded in the 19th century - have seen their electoral dominance constantly being eroded by new political parties. First there were the Communists (KPB/PCB), booking some electoral successes in the thirties and the forties. During the fifties and the sixties came the regionalist parties: the *Volksunie* (People's Union) in Flanders, the *Francophone Front* (FDF) in Brussels and the *Walloon Rally* (RW) in Wallonia. In the eighties the Greens appeared on the political scene. After the 1987 general election, there are 11 parties represented in the Lower House (the Chamber of representatives).

Although the fractionalization is rather high in the Belgium party-system, it is not only due to the uprise and relative success of new political parties. It is also due to the division of the country in two language-groups: a Dutch-speaking north (Flanders) and a French-speaking south (Wallonia). This duality has been the source of many political conflicts and crises. The problem is not simply a matter of language. There is a cultural division, with a predominantly Roman-Catholic north and a more secularized south. There is also an economic problem: the once dominating and early industrialized south is rapidly declining, and the economical dominance has now shifted to the north. The official language of the Belgian state created in 1830 was French.

*I would like to thank my colleague Patrick Stouthuysen, on whose research I relied very heavily in writing this chapter. He also made some useful comments on a first draft of the text.

However, today the two languages have equal status as the country´s national official languages.

Regionalist parties on both sides and in Brussels (a former Dutch-speaking city, made French by the massive immigration of French-speaking civil servants) have claimed and obtained a greater autonomy for the two regions and for Brussels. The point to be stressed here is the fact that this regional conflict was deep enough to cause a split in the three traditional parties. Belgium has no national parties left, only regional parties. There are two Christian-Democratic parties (split in 1968), two Socialist parties (split in 1978) and two Liberal parties (split in 1971). Only the Communists are still a national party, but they are no longer represented in Parliament.

This particular shape of the Belgian party system is important to notice, for it is the party-political background in which the Belgian Greens were born. As one could expect, they were twins. There is a Flemish party called "AGALEV" (Anders gaan leven - "For an alternative way of life") and a Walloon party called "ECOLO". They are not the result of a party split, but each of them has its own specific history.

The Flemish Greens: AGALEV

The Flemish AGALEV came first on the political scene (Stouthuysen 1983). Its roots go back to 1970. A teacher and priest (Luc Versteylen) in a secondary school near Antwerp, created a group in which he and his students were able to cherish three valuable principles: solidarity, sobriety and silence. The group met in an old brewery and it had nothing to do with politics. It was simply a rather religious inspired community, pleading for a revival of what they called "catacomb christianity", as opposed to "Koekelberg Catholicism" (Koekelberg stands for the official church of Belgium - it is the place in Brussels where a huge and rather ugly basilica is situated).

The members of this community quickly felt the urge to implement the values in which they believed. One of the first actions undertaken was the revival of a local primary school (in Massenhoven), condemned to disappear because of an insufficiant number of pupils. The group strived for the maintenance of the school and succeeded in reorganizing it. The (usual) educational values of achievement and competition were not stressed, but rather, tolerance and respect for the total individuality and personality of the children.

Several other (and smaller) actions were also undertaken since then, protesting mostly against the deterioration of the natural environment: against nuclear power plants, against new roads, against polluting factories, etc. The striking property of these actions was their playful style, aimed mostly at drawing the attention of the public. It made the movement grow, and this created problems for some members feared that in stressing the action element, the original contemplative aspect of the movement could possibly be lost. Some individuals then created the *Anders gaan leven*-group, still, part of the whole movement, but formally seperated from the action groups.

The real organizational problems, to which we will return later, arose when the movement decided to take its first steps into active politics. In 1974 the movement decided not to participate in the legislative elections, but rather to present so-called "green lists". These would consist of the names of candidates of different political parties, deserving the confidence of the *Anders gaan leven*-movement. This was not a very successful experiment, for the elected candidates of the green lists turned out to be loyal members of their own respective political parties.

In 1977 the group decided to present a list for the general elections held in Antwerp, the birthplace of the movement. The list was called "AGALEV", and was only a temporary creation which was to disappear after the elections, but it did not want to become a permanent political party organization. AGALEV polled 0.3 percent of the Flemish votes. In 1978, at the next general elections, it polled 0.7 percent.

The real breakthrough came with the first direct elections of the European Parliament in 1979. AGALEV polled 2.3 percent in Flanders at its own and at every one else´s astonishment. In 1981 it entered the Belgian parliament. The 4 percent of the Flemish votes were enough for obtaining two seats in the Lower House and one in the Senate. The local elections of 1982 were a further success: AGALEV now polled 5.6 percent of the votes in the municipalities where it presented lists. Without having made that explicit choice, the movement had become a real political party. Not everybody within the movement was very happy with this evolution, and a lot of internal discussions were to follow.

The Walloon Greens: ECOLO

For the green party in the south of the country, a different story must be told. The Greens in Wallonia walked a long and winding road before reaching the stage of becoming a real political party. Unlike their Flemish brothers, the Walloon Greens are a rather heterogeneous conglomerate of different movements and ideological factions. The history of their growth is not a linear one; and today, the party still is a more labile organization than AGALEV (Mahoux/Moden 1984).

The movement started from within the political arena. After the legislative elections of 1971 trouble arose in a local section (Namur) of the Walloon regionalist party RW when the party leadership did not accept the election of a local president, who then quit the party with some of his followers. They created *Démocratie Nouvelle* as a movement of "reflection and action", stressing the ideals of direct democracy and party self-governance. It presented a list for the 1974 elections, and polled 2.4 percent in the constituency of Namur. Links were made with several other organizations, for example with Amnesty International, the Young Christian Labor Movement (JOC), and the Christian Peace Movement. This combination of organizations presented a common list in Namur for the local elections of 1976, using the name *Combat pour l'Ecologie et l'Autogestion*. It polled 1.9 percent of the votes, obtained no seats, and soon disappeared.

A few months earlier, a Belgian section of *Amis de la Terre* (Friends of the Earth) had been founded by the initiative of some members of *Democratie Nouvelle* and of some members of an association for ornithological studies. It presented an explicit political program. In essence, very similar to that of *Démocratie Nouvelle* and of *Combat pour l'Ecologie et l'Autogestion*. The main themes were ecology and a better democracy.

At the next legislative elections, that is April 1977, ecological lists were presented in Brussels *(Ecolog)* and in a few Walloon constituencies *(Wallonie-Ecologie)*. The results were satisfying, but not spectacular, varying from 0.3 percent to 2.3 percent of the votes. The most important result of the election however, was the creation of *Wallonie-Ecologie* as a permanent organization in 1978.

At the end of 1978 the Belgian section of *Amis de la Terre* split into two fractions after long and bitter debates. A minority group, pleading for a complete autonomy of the local sections, founded the *Réseau libre des Amis de la terre*. This dissidence had subsequent consequences for the next elections in 1978: *Wallonie-Ecologie* presented candidates in a fewer number of constituencies than in 1977, and in Brussels there were two green lists: *Ecolog* (rather independent) and *Ecopol*, the latter with candidates of the minority fraction of the old *Amis de la Terre*.

Table 3.1
The Electoral Results obtained by AGALEV and ECOLO since 1978 in Belgium (percentages and number of seats)

	Flanders AGALEV	Wallonia ECOLO	Belgium AGALEV	ECOLO
Legislative elections (Lower House)				
1978	0.4	1.2	0.3	0.5
1981	4.0(2)	5.9(2)	2.3	2.2
1985	6.1(4)	6.2(5)	3.7	2.5
1987	7.3(6)	6.4(3)	4.5	2.6
European elections				
1979	2.3	5.1		
1984	7.1(1)	9.4(1)		
Local elections*				
1982	6.2	7.4		

* The percentage of the votes obtained in those municipalities where a Green list was presented
Source: Official Electoral Statistics

As it happened for AGALEV, the real breakthrough of the Walloon Greens came with the first European elections in 1979. Despite the internal conflict, a common list was presented, called *Europe-Ecologie*. The results were unexpectedly good. The party obtained 5.1 percent of the Walloon votes, the best score of all the European Greens. This unforeseen success was the immediate cause for the creation of a real and permanent ecological political party in Wallonia. It was created in March of 1980, and was named ECOLO.

This did not put an end to the struggles between the so-called "libertarian" and "institutionalist" fractions of the green movement in Wallonia. ECOLO is the emanation of the majoritarian institutionalist fraction, but at the 1981 elections, the other fraction presented a list called *Ecolos*. In Brussels there were as much as four different (francophone) green lists, one of which advocated a clearly extremist right-wing ideology. Only ECOLO presented candidates in every Walloon constituency. The 5.9 percent of the Walloon votes were enough for the two seats in the lower house. Ecolo thus entered the Belgian parliament at the same time as AGALEV. Its further electoral history follows the same upward road as AGALEV (see Table 3.1).

Organizational Structure

Like all the green parties, the Belgian Greens explicitly do not want to be "traditional" parties. They are looking for other and better structures to organize mass political participation. They want the more democratic society they strive for to be reflected in their own political organization. The Greens want to defy Michels´ iron law of oligarchy by combining organization and democratic control.

The urge for being a new kind of political party is not only motivated by this non-instrumental view of the party. There is also a strong "individualistic fundamentalism" attitude towards any kind of collective action. The idea is that an individual commitment can not be delegated to a collective entity, unless the collectivity can be directly controlled and be called to order at any time by the individual members.

Understanding and trying to avoid the trend towards oligarchy is not enough to succeed in creating a new style of party. As soon as a party grows, some permanent structures are needed and for the Greens this raises difficult problems and a lot of internal debates. As in other countries, the Belgian Greens had to face them.

AGALEV did not start as a political movement. It became slowly, and rather reluctantly, a political organization and a political party. When the *Anders Gaan Leven*-movement decided to present candidates for the legislative elections of 1977, the name AGALEV was chosen as a kind of joke, and AGALEV was explicitly meant to disappear after the election. The social movement did not change into a political party, but it temporarily invented one. In this set-up, the temporary political party was directly controlled by the social movement. The party had to ask the *Landelijk Beraad* (national congress) of *Anders Gaan Leven* for the authorization to participate in the elections.

This organizational set-up worked as long as nobody of the AGALEV-candidates were elected. In 1981 however there were suddenly three AGALEV-members in the national parliament. AGALEV could not simply disappear; it had to stay alive and to organize itself for political action in the parliament. The national congress of *Anders Gaan Leven* then set things clear by creating a formal separation between "Anders Gaan Leven" and AGALEV.

There still is an inspirational link (and a lot of personal links) between the movement and the party, but no formal one. This means that the party now has a permanent structure, and that it is no longer controlled by the movement. AGALEV has its own internal democratic control.

AGALEV adopted explicitly and deliberately a non-pyramidal structure. The decision-making power lies with the local sections, with the so-called "base-groups". There is no formal party leader and no one can speak on behalf of the party without having the formal authorization of the other members. This is the theoretical principle. Banning formal positions of authority however, does not abolish authority as such. Ludo Dierickx, one of the founding fathers of the party and member of the Lower House (member of the Senate since December 1987) is mostly considered by the public as the (informal) party leader.

An important step was made in 1986. The "Uitvoerend Comité" (executive committee), consisting of salaried employees, was granted a great part of political responsability. This may be considered as a qualitative change in the party organization. Paying participants for their work enables an organization to dissociate the organizational goal (the party ideology) from the motivation of the members to participate.

The story of the Greens in Wallonia specifically starts with a dispute on the organizational structure of political parties. A non-democratic decision by the leadership of the *Rassemblement Wallon* initiated the evolution towards a green political party. The issue of party organization was always present and it aborted many attempts to form a green party in Wallonia. While *Anders Gaan Leven* tried to find a suitable relationship between a social movement and its political or electoral branch, the Walloon Greens immediately went for a new kind of political party. It took them a few years more to succeed in creating one.

ECOLO is, as we described it earlier, the party of one (majoritarian) group within the Walloon Greens. It is the party of the "institutionalists", of those accepting the need for a relatively strong and disciplined organization, without however rejecting the need for democratic control. The minority did not and does not like formal organization. They fear the potential danger that such organizations may catalyse a loss of real democratic control. Even as the "institutionalist" wing of the Walloon Greens, ECOLO wants nevertheless to reduce delegated power to a minimum, workable level. There is no party president and no rigid executive structure.

Autonomy and self-control of the local sections are the keywords of party organization. All the important policy decisions are taken in the *Assemblée* (national congress) in which all the members can vote. This *Assemblée* elects for instance, the important *Comité d'Arbitrage*, which has the responsability of managing all internal conflicts as they occur.

As we have already stated, ECOLO faced and still faces quite a lot of internal disputes. There was, in 1986 the resignation of the member of the Lower House of parliament, Olivier Deleuze. He did not agree with the ECOLO-strategy of helping the labile majority of Christian-Democrats and Liberals in the Walloon parliament. Consequently, a very interesting debate followed, since Deleuze only quit ECOLO and wanted to stay in the parliament as an independent MP. ECOLO wanted him to "give his seat back to the party". Deleuze considered himself as mandated by the Belgian voters (which is formally correct), and not by the party on whose list he was elected. In claiming the seat, ECOLO acted very much like the other traditional political parties would have done. Finally Deleuze gave up his seat, and was succeeded by another member of ECOLO. This man, Jaques Preumont, was excluded from ECOLO a few months later for not obeying party instructions!

The "fundamentalists" are a minority in ECOLO. It surely is a less formalized and more democratically organized political party than the Socialists, the Liberals or the Christian-Democrats. However, on several occasions, it has proved that it is really an organized party, and not a loose association of political dreamers. The same is true for AGALEV, which seems to have less internal strife in being what it has become: a political party.

Electoral Support

The general pattern of green party voters is well-known: they are fairly young, well-educated semi-professionals or professionals, stressing non-materialist political issues like peace, democracy and protection of the natural environment. This group of persons are also the voters of ECOLO and AGALEV. Furthermore, the voters of both parties seem to be rather concentrated in urban centers: Brussels, Antwerp, Ghent, Liège, Namur. The urban concentration of the Green voters is not a typically Belgian phenomenon. It is the case for almost all the green parties in other countries. Poguntke (1987) suggests that this could be a spurious relation, caused simply by the concentration of the young and well-educated voters in the cities.

In Belgium, however, we tested this hypothesis with a multivariate model (for the AGALEV voters), and found that the urban characteristic was still standing as an independent and strong predictor of the green vote (Deschouwer/Stouthuysen, 1984). There is within the Belgian political context a fairly simple explanation for the greater success of the Greens in the cities. The Belgian society is reknown for being strongly "pillarized"; different subgroups (the two most important are the Catholics and the Socialists) live in highly segregated worlds. Each group consists of a closed network of social relations. Within each world, there is a variety of organizations, performing secular tasks (schooling, housing, leisure, newspapers, etc.) with a recognizable ideological or religious label. The political parties are an integral part of these pillars, and thus penetrate deeply into the social environment of the citizens. To quit a party is to quit one´s whole social environment. Pillarization is a structuration of society that consequently impedes political volatility.

This pillarization is not as strong today as it was earlier; completely separate realities do not exist anymore. The social and political control by the parties is still important, but it is loosing its strength. This is especially true in areas where social control is in general low: namely in cities. Moving from a rural area to a city opens new possibilities for an easier reorientation of one´s political beliefs. New parties find a very fertile soil in the urban areas. This is true for the Greens, as it is or was for the regionalist parties and for the extremist left-wing or right-wing parties.

The strongest pillar is the Catholic one and it is by far the dominant pillar in Flanders. One can safely expect the AGALEV voters to be deserters of the Catholic stronghold. As we saw earlier, AGALEV began as a religious movement, a movement protesting against the official Catholic Church. A large part of today´s green voters in Flanders have Catholic parents, while they see themselves either as "christians outside the Church" or simply as non-believers. AGALEV attracts the voters that formerly went to the Flemish Christian-Democrats. These Flemish Christian-Democrats have lost a great deal of their attractiveness for young voters. The Flemish Socialists have been trying very hard to convince young Catholics to vote for them, but so far they have not been very successful. It is only constituencies where the Socialists have really offered a young and dynamic image that they have succeeded in attracting young catholics. In those constituencies, AGALEV polls its worst results.

Progamatic Profile
The green ideology is also well-known - it is an aggregation of new political values stressing quality of life and quality of democratic participation. If the Belgian parties AGALEV and ECOLO are called "green", it is precisely because they share this ideology. Some of the elements of the ideology are stressed more heavily by AGALEV and ECOLO and some aspects of the ideology have a very special meaning within the Belgian political context, for instance, the political patronage.

It is a very common procedure for political parties in Belgium to interfere directly, at all levels, in the appointments of civil servants. The parties in power agree on the proportion of the nominations they will be able to control, and thus the candidates are selected in function of their political afiliation. This practice occurs at all levels, which in turn means that all the parties are in one way or another involved in the system. Only the very small parties, having no political power whatsoever remain outside of its reach.

It is therefore understandable that small parties protest against this political patronage. The new regionalist parties did so in the sixties, and the Greens do so today. Only the Greens, however, have "clean hands", and they seem to be determined to keep them clean. As we will see below, one of the demands made by ECOLO to accept the formation of a coalition to govern the city of Liege, was the immediate stopping of the political patronage in the local administration.

The Greens get a lot of support for this idea and especially from many competent and frustrated civil servants. Other parties also claim to have stopped the patronage. But, none of them has been very eager to put their words to action until now.

The quality of democratic political participation is another main concern of the green parties. They do not reject the system of representative democracy as a whole, but they want to give more chances to the individual citizen to express his political opinion and to participate directly in the process of political decision making. These ideas are translated into the demand for a more democratic internal organization of political parties and in the demand that political decisions should be taken on the smallest scale possible, for the small scale offers more possibilities for direct and real democracy.

In Belgium the above ideas have also led to the demand of the holding of referendums as procedures of more direct political decision making. As in all fragmented party-systems, where the government is always a coalition, and where the voters do not really decide which coalition will govern, the risks for largely spread feelings of political alienation are high. A feeling of political frustration is part of the motivation to vote for new and non-traditional parties. This is also true for the Greens.

But Belgium is, however, a typical "consociational" democracy, where important decisions are not taken by a simple majority vote, but by a large consensus. This "prudent leadership" in a highly fragmented country safeguards political stability. Majority rule would be very explosive, since a majority in one part of the country usually is a minority in the other part. This situation leaves little room for decision making by means of a referendum.

Another programatic feature of both green parties in Belgium consists of federalism. AGALEV and ECOLO want Belgium to become a real federal state. This is not a surprising demand for all the Belgian parties want a federal system to be instituted, and a first step towards its realization was made in 1980. Using the term "federalism" in the Belgian context may be misleading. When the other parties speak of "federalism", they want Flanders and Wallonia (and eventually Brussels) to be granted a large political autonomy, thus institutionalizing the cultural differences that exist between the two sub-national communities. Since the Belgian community is not a homogeneous one the organization of the state must recognize and reflect the existence of the Flemish and the Walloons. Federalism and nationalism are closely related.

This is not the meaning the Greens want to give to the concept of federalism in Belgium; they want to focus on democracy. Federalizing the country should be a process of political decentralization, and should not be the creation of two new centralized sub-states. The ideology of nationalism is rejected by both AGALEV and ECOLO; it is considered to be totally absurd in a country that must be prepared to become a part of a European federation. The Greens want the concept of nation-state to be dissociated from the concept of *Volk*, with its connotations of linguistic, racial or ethnic homogeneity.

The green voice in this respect has not been heard. Nationalism is a part of the ideology of all the important political parties, even if one should expect their ideology to be clearly internationalistic. In launching these new concepts (new in Belgium) of nation-state and federalism, the Greens place themselves outside the realm of the ongoing political debates. They stand almost alone. Ironically they are, as all the other parties are, divided into two factions: AGALEV and ECOLO have good mutual relations, but these are not good enough to create one Belgian Green party. Yet, they are still two of a kind.

Government Participation

The political relevance of a party is not merely a matter of its size. To assess the political relevance of a party, one must know the party system in which it acts. In this respect a different story can be told for the national, the regional and the local party system in Belgium.

The National Level

ECOLO and AGALEV participated at every legislative election since 1978. For both parties there has been a steady growth, although ECOLO did not progress very much after its immediate success (from 1.2 percent to 5.9 percent in Wallonia) in 1981. Since 1981 both AGALEV and ECOLO have a few seats in the parliament.

The Belgian system of proportional representation (system D'Hondt) makes it fairly easy for small parties to win seats, as long as their votes are relatively well spread over different constituencies. The electoral system does not, however, allow a Belgian party to win a 50 percent majority of the seats. Since there are only regional parties presenting candidates in only one part of the country, this is in fact totally excluded. The CVP (the Flemish Christian-Democrats) are always the largest party. In 1987 it polled 19.5 percent of the Belgian votes, and it obtained 43 out of the 212 seats in the Lower House. The Belgian government is always a coalition government of at least two Walloon and two Flemish parties. In this game of coalition formation, the "large" or traditional parties do not need the Greens or any other small party. These small parties do not have the slightest political relevance at the national level.

The Regional Level

Belgium is not really a federal state, although since 1981 some political autonomy for Flanders and Wallonia exists. There are no separate regional elections, but the elected members of the national parliament are all elected in one specific region, and as such, they automatically become a member of a regional parliament.

In Flanders the situation is almost the same as at the national level. The party system is fragmented, with no party having a possible absolute majority in sight. Coalitions must be formed, and can easily be formed without the Greens; AGALEV was never asked to participate in the regional government. From 1981 to 1985, the first four years of the newly granted political autonomy, the regional government was composed proportionally (this was a legally arranged transition system). Seven Flemish ministers were to be appointed, but AGALEV was too small to be able to claim one. Since 1985 the Flemish government is a coalition of the Christian-Democrats (CVP) and the Liberals (PVV).

In 1987 AGALEV campaigned with a program that was explicitly adopted as a project concrete enough to be realized through active governmental participation. The list of items on which AGALEV wants its views accepted by the partners of a possible coalition, is still too long and too stringently formulated to open any chance of participation in a national coalition.

In Wallonia the situation is slightly different. From 1981 to 1985 the same proportional system of government had to be adopted, thus excluding the too small ECOLO. After the 1985 elections, a very particular situation arose. The Walloon Liberals (PRL) and the Walloon Christian-Democrats (PSC) formed the regional governmental coalition, controlling just 52 out of the 103 seats in the regional parliament. Hence here, the Greens could play a role. Their three seats became very important. ECOLO offered to help the majority at the crucial votes, if the majority would occasionally accept some points raised by the Greens. This decision caused the resignation of Oliver Deleuze, one of the members of the regional parliament which had to carry out the decision. Ironically, the Liberals rejected the offer, and ECOLO always voted against the governmental majority! Oliver Deleuze could not, of course, come back.

After the 1987 elections, a similar situation can re-occur. The coalition of Liberals and Christian-Democrats has lost its majority in the Walloon parliament. However, several other coalitions are also possible. Most probably, the Socialists will govern with the Christian-Democrats, but this, of course, is not certain. If, at the national level, the (Flemish and Walloon) Liberals and Christian-Democrats will govern together, the Walloon Socialists could then take revenge by governing Wallonia with the help of the Greens. Together they control 53 seats.

The Walloon party system is different from the Flemish one. In Wallonia, there is a clear left-right cleavage, placing two almost equal blocs against each other. In this party system, a small party like ECOLO can possibly play a role that is far more important than what could be expected from its mere electoral size. ECOLO has undoubtedly real chances of governing in Wallonia in the near future. In Flanders, however, the Christian-Democratic center is too powerful to let AGALEV even dream of governing.

The Local Level

Local party systems can have very different shapes. The chances for green parties to play some political role are best at this local level. In some municipalities the Greens poll 10 percent or more, and this can mean that they are indeed often greatly needed to help a larger partner reach the majority.

At the local elections of 1982 (the only local elections in which the Greens have participated until now - the next local elections being in 1988) AGALEV polled 6.2 percent of the votes in the municipalities in which it presented candidates. It succeeded in concluding a coalition agreement in two municipalities: Schoten (near Antwerp) and Meise (near Brussels). A few months later however, everything turned for the worst. The coalitions collapsed because of the very stringent attitude of AGALEV, refusing any kind of compromise in implementing the local policy. New coalitions were then formed without them. In another municipality (Overijse near Brussels), Mark Dubrulle, the man who had led AGALEV to its first electoral victory at the European elections of 1979, also formed a coalition in which he engaged his party. The concessions he made were not wholly accepted by AGALEV and Dubrulle was consequently excluded from the party.

It is again ECOLO that offers a real example of political relevance. Since 1982 it governs the city of Liège, in a coalition government with the *Parti Socialiste*. Again it is the party system in Liège that gives ECOLO its political relevance, rather than the number of seats controlled by ECOLO.

Up until 1976 the city of Liège had been governed by a coalition government of Liberals and Socialists. When in 1979 a new Walloon Liberal Party was formed (the PRL), mainly on the initiative of Jean Gol (from Liège), the Liberals moved clearly to the right. This shift caused some embitterment within the socialist party of Liège. In preparing the 1982 local elections, the Socialists formed a cartel with some smaller regionalist parties, and presented a list called *Rassemblement Progressiste en Socialiste Wallon* (RPSW). The list was drawn up with the aim to win the absolute majority. As a reaction against this cartel, the Liberals and the Christian-Democrats (united in the national government) also presented a common list called *Union pour Liège* (UPL). The electoral campaign was very aggressive and hence, very polarized, leaving little room for the other parties such as the Communists and ECOLO.

The electoral outcome was dissapointing for the two protagonists: out of the 51 seats, the RPSW cartel got 23, and the UPL cartel obtained 21. ECOLO controlled 6 crucial seats and the Communist Party 1. Both groups invited ECOLO to form a coalition government and ECOLO chose the Socialists. The negotiations, however, did not cause much trouble. This is rather surprising, since ECOLO had a list of important and difficult demands. It wanted the city not to distribute any electricity produced by nuclear plants; it wanted to stop the political patronage in the local administration; it wanted the meetings of the city council to be broadcasted on local television; it wanted to foresee the eventuality of organizing referendums; and it claimed 3 out of the 11 seats in the local governing committee. Surprisingly, the Socialists accepted everything.

Today, after 5 years of this coalition government, the most striking observation is the very slow pace at which all political changes initiated by ECOLO have progressed. The Green party clearly overestimated the effective power of local government. In 1988, ECOLO will have to go back to its voters with only a very few items of its political program realized.

Outlook

In sum, AGALEV and ECOLO share the same ideology as the other green parties and have pointed out some of the very crucial aspects of the Belgian political system. Changing these aspects in the way they want, could have far reaching consequences. However, one should not forget that the Belgian Greens have almost no political relevance at the national level, and that even if they grow to obtain some 10 percent of the votes, they have good chances to remain what they are for a long time: friendly, sympathetic and politically harmless.

4
Denmark:
"De Grønne"

Suzanne S. Schüttemeyer

Development of the Greens

The development of the Danish party system sets it apart from most others in Western Europe and makes for anything but an ideal breeding-ground for "green" parties. Until 1960 four parties dominated Danish politics and were based on the class cleavages and the urban-rural divide. The Social Democrats drew their support from the working class, the Radical Liberals "from such diverse sources as the smallholders and the urban intelligentsia" (Borre 1977: 4); the Agrarian Liberals were the party of the urban middle class and the Conservative People's Party represented the farmers. The few existing smaller parties did not play any role to speak of in parliamentary politics.

This changed when the Communist Party split in 1960: The Socialist People's Party entered the scene and turned Denmark into a five-party-system until 1973. During that period the country could build on the post-war industrialization process and develop strategies for a welfare state. This gradually-emerging welfare society increased state expenditure and thus the individual's tax burden as well as creating a larger bureaucracy and with it a new middle-class. In 1966, when, for the first time after World War II, a "red" majority of Social Democrats and the Socialist People's Party was able to form a cabinet the voters grew so dissatisfied with the high bill for the welfare state that they turned to the bourgeois parties at the next election. Their coalition not only failed to meet the demands of less expenditure, lower taxes and a reduced bureaucracy but, on the contrary, aggravated these problems by adding even more taxes. When the issue of joining the EC deeply split the Danes in the early 70s, the discontent was complete and spread to the entire electorate (Borre 1985: 389).

The voters resorted to newly formed or "new-old" protest parties to produce what has been called the "seismic election" of 1973 which doubled the number of parties in the Folketing from five to ten. 40 percent of the voters changed their preference between 1971 and 1973.

Since then the Danish party system has remained fragmented, albeit realigned to a certain extent in the last decade (Borre 1985). This is not to say that a stable parliamentary majority can be obtained easily; indeed minority government is the rule in Danish politics. Although fragmented, the party system is not strongly polarized. The extent of class voting is declining "due to the unilateral erosion of bourgeois support within the middle classes" (Borre 1977: 20) and the country´s political culture shows "economic" or "pragmatic" orientations (Rubart 1984: 94f). But as the parties did not immediately find answers to the current problems of the 70s there was still considerable potential for protest (Andersen 1981; Fitzmaurice 1981: 96ff).

This protest has partly found its expression in the new social movements which emerged in Denmark as in other Western European countries in the second half of the 70s. As this happened after the fragmentation of the party system there were parties that were small yet effective enough, ideologically acceptable yet flexible enough to take up these issues (Poguntke shows the similarities between the "new left" of the 60s and the "new politics" of the 70s and 80s, 1987:380). It was the Socialist People´s Party and to a lesser extent the Left Socialists who became the political and parliamentary representatives of the new social movements (Müller-Rommel 1985: 41ff). Since the mid-70s their electorate consists of the young and better educated; half of their voters live in and around Copenhagen (in 1988 the Socialist People´s Party scored 13,0 percent overall but 23,9 percent in Copenhagen). It is these groups which prefer unconventional forms of participation and are opposed to centralized, hierarchical structures (Damgaard 1980).

The Danish Greens were founded in October 1983 - thus too late to take either political or parliamentary advantage of the new social movements which were already represented through the small leftist parties. The Greens did not compete in the subsequent general election of January 1984 but waited another two years before they ran their first campaign in the local elections in November 1985. They scored 2,8 percent of the vote - a result that was regarded as a promising start on the political stage. This assessment was backed by opinion polls just before and a month after the election which showed that the Greens would manage to clear the 2-percent-hurdle (the minimum requirement for representation in the Danish Folketing) if national elections were held at that time. But as early as spring 1986 they disappeared again from the survey tables (Gallup Poll, in: Berlingske Tidende, 6/4/1986) and when elections to the Folketing were actually held in September 1987 they had to content themselves with only 1,3 percent (30.000 votes less than in the local elections). Eight months later - the bourgeois cabinet of four parties had called new elections after the defeat of the Prime Minister on a security policy issue - the Greens had not made any headway. They again scored 1,3 percent and failed to enter the Folketing.

Electoral Support and Organizational Structure
The Greens are especially popular with the youngest age group among the voters. 51 percent of their electorate in the election of 1987 were between 18 and 29 jears old, and only ten percent were older than 40. They attract the better educated (44 percent with secondary, 44 percent with college education), and consequently they are a party of the cities. This pattern which stood out already in the local elections was confirmed in both national elections (for the demographic composition see Andersen 1988:410). It was in and around Copenhagen where they fared best (1988: City of Copenhagen 2,3 percent; Greater Copenhagen 1,7 percent). Roughly half of their total electorate came from that area. On the mainland however, i.e. the peninsula of Jutland which is largely rural, they scored only 0,9 percent - a result which could not even have been obtained if it were not for Aarhus, the second largest Danish city which lies in Jutland and where - in accordance with their urban character - the Greens were preferred by 1,1 percent of the voters. By and large, the green electorate resembles that of the Socialist People´s Party, and indeed 25 percent of the "green" vote in 1987 came from that party (Andersen 1988:411).

As to their internal structure it is noteworthy that their degree of organization is remarkably lower than that of other Danish parties (Kristensen 1980: 37ff). Party membership has declined in Denmark as in other West European countries due to a changing structure of communication between the parties and their voters as well as to growing dissatisfaction with the opportunities for participation which they offer and with their overall performance. However, this development is of only restricted importance as a good number of Danes is not opposed to party membership in principle and those who have left a party are not so completely alienated as to rule out future re-entry into a party (Kristensen 1980: 58).

While the Danish Liberals´ membership includes about one quarter of their electorate, the left wing parties´ degree of organization is lower; nevertheless, the Social Democrats come up to 14, the Socialist People´s Party to 7 and the Left Socialists to 4 percent of their electorate on average. With around 1.000 members and 45.000 voters "De Grønne" have recruited just over two percent of their electorate. This reflects certain characteristics of the "green" voters: urban and young, they are more independent and tend to reject organizational bonds and what seems to be any sort of an hierarchy.

This leads us to the internal set-up of the party. According to their own judgement the Greens did not score well enough in the elections of May 1988 because - among other reasons - they had to use too much energy to build up their internal organization; now they are established all over the country (Jyllands Posten, 11/8/1988). In contrast to many of the other competitors which have been characterized as *central-styrede massepartier* (Andersen 1982: 52) - in the comparatively narrow confines of the Danish political system - the Greens proudly claim to be highly decentralized. Their local organizations are independent when it comes to the selection of candidates and the formulation of policies. "De Grønne" do not believe in quota-regulations in order to enhance female participation but regard this arrangement which many of their sister-parties have adopted as a form of repression and discrimination.

Every four months a national conference is held in which each local party has one delegate per ten members. Although its decisions in policy matters would not be legally binding upon possible deputies to the national parliament the Greens claim that they feel a stronger obligation than other parties to listen to the "grass-roots". In general, as in their own organization, they want to bring about a decision-making structure which is as close as possible to those really concerned with the policies in question and their consequences. This principle which is put forward by most "green" parties sounds simple and convincing; it is in fact simplistic even under the conditions of a democracy as small in size as Denmark. Due to the growing interdependence of problems and the increasing network-character of societal and political structures it will rarely be easy to define precisely those immediately concerned.

Programatic Profile

"De Grønne" have very much the same programatic priorities as for instance their southern larger neighbours, the West German Greens. The four major features as laid down in their manifesto are: *Økologi, ikke-vold, direkte folkestyre, social sikkerhed* (ecological, free of violence, grassroot-democratic, social). They strive for a society which gives priority to the preservation of the environment and saves natural resources; for the causes of poverty and deprivation to be removed and social security to be granted as unbureaucratically as possible to safeguard the individual´s independence and self-esteem; for decentralized small units with wide-ranging autonomy and the frequent use of the referendum to ensure the direct influence of those concerned; and for internal domestic as well as international relations free of violence and domination which does not exclude self-defense and civil resistance (the latter is explicitly mentioned as often being the only remedy against existing systems and encroachments by the state).

Their program covers all sectors of society and the state, clearly distinguishing them from single-issue ecological counterparts in other countries or earlier forms of "green" parties. In this respect they have certainly profited from being comparative latecomers since they could learn from initial mistakes and difficulties of development encountered by their European sister-parties.

With regard to the Green´s competitors on the Danish electoral scene two issues in their program must be emphasized: the European Community and defense. "De Grønne" favour an unilateral disarmament of Denmark and the abolition of NATO and the Warsaw Pact. Since for them small is beautiful (apparently at almost any price) and as they characterize the present form of European integration as a centralized economic powerbloc which prevents effective campaigns against pollution, they consequently opt for Denmark´s withdrawal from the EC. Both this, and the opposition against increasing costs for military defence, had already been voiced by the Socialist People´s Party since the 70s - a party which has after all considerable parliamentary influence.

Outlook

The Danish Greens were established in a difficult political environment: First, the majority of the "protest vote" was already taken by small left-wing parties. There was no representation-gap to fill, not least because in Denmark - as Goul Anderssen assumes - the environmental issue is neatly divided along the traditional left-right dimension of politics: " `Green politics´ is `new politics´, but `new politics´in Denmark has been picked up by `old politics´" (Andersen 1988:411). Secondly, the Danish multi-party system supports the "lifespan" of these parties which are in fact the competitors for the "green" issues and clientele (Pedersen 1989).

Hence, there is hardly any scope in terms of issues and votes for the Danish Greens. They were too late to jump on the band-wagon of fragmentation in the early 70s and they failed to make use of the continued dissatisfaction as expressed in the new social movements of the late 70s. "De Grønne" will only be able to profit from the basically favourable, fragmented and unpolarized party system in Denmark, if new issues arise and if they are quick enough to exploit them.

5
Federal Republic of Germany: "Die Grünen"

E. Gene Frankland

Development of the Green Party

Proclaiming that they were neither left or right but in front, an ideologically diverse alliance of minor parties, green lists, alternative groups, and movement activists founded *Die Grünen* (the Greens) as a federal party in January 1980. Three years later, it became the first party in thirty years to challenge successfully the established parties by winning seats in the *Bundestag* (federal parliament). The Greens have represented a challenge in more than the sense of depriving the major parties of votes; they were launched as an "anti-party" party rejecting many elements of the postwar consensus of West German elites about the ends and means of politics. Many observers maintained that the Green party would disintegrate well before the 1987 federal election; however, the Greens were returned a second time to the *Bundestag* with significantly more parliamentary seats. Eight years after their launching, the Greens are represented at all levels of West German government and have held the parliamentary balance of power on a couple of occasions at the state level and on numerous occasions at the local level.

While it is possible to see the emergence of the Greens as evidence of a cross-national "post-materialist" transformation of generational values in Western Europe (Inglehart 1977;1981), it is also important to understand the Greens within the historical context of a changing party system in West Germany. One can identify at least five phases of change during its first three decades. First, there was the demise of several Weimar-like minor parties and the emergence of the "Bonn system" of the Christian Democrats (CDU/CSU), the Social Democrats (SPD), and the Free Democrats (FDP) during the early and mid 1950s. By 1961 all the minor parties had disappeared from the Bundestag and most of the Landtage (state parliaments). Second, prompted by the electoral successes of the CDU/CSU´s "catch-all" strategy, the SPD transformed itself from an ideological working class party into a pragmatic *Volkspartei* (people´s party) during the late 1950s and early 1960s. Not only were the two major parties often competing for the same voters with moderate programs and centrist symbols, but also the social profiles of their *Bundestag* deputies were becoming increasingly alike (Nagle, 1977). Third, in the late 1960s--following a transitional period of Grand Coalition between the CDU/CSU and the SPD, strong showings by the right-wing National Democrats (NPD) in *Land* elections, and strong protests by the APO (Extra-parliamentary Opposition) on the left--the Federal Republic experienced its first alternation of governmental power in Bonn from center-right to center-left.The *CDU-Staat* came under the control of the SPD-FDP coalition, whose reformist agenda faded as economic difficulties grew. Fourth, the early and mid 1970s witnessed the proliferation of extra-parliamentary, non-partisan *Bürgerinitiativen* (citizen action groups) focusing on specific local and regional problems neglected by the major parties. Polls indicated that more West Germans were actively involved in *Bürgerinitiativen* than were members of the major parties (Helm, 1980: 576). Fifth, during the late 1970s amidst evidence of growing disenchantment with all the established parties (Kaltefleiter 1980), the launching of new types of "parties" into local and *Land* (state) politics occurred.

As early as May 1977, anti-nuclear power groups in Lower Saxony were putting together green lists of candidates to contest local elections. In some *Länder* environmentalists joined forces with *bunte* (multi-colored) and alternative lists while in other *Länder* sharp left-right cleavages resulted in two or three competing lists (Hallensleben 1984). During 1977-78 such low budget efforts were successful in winning scattered local council seats; the efforts at winning seats in four *Landtage* were unsuccessful but brought the Greens increasing media attention. A heterogeneous alliance of green lists, minor parties, alternative groups, and *Bürgerinitiativen* activists (known as *Sonstige Politische Vereinigung "Die Grünen"*) contested the West German seats in the 1979 European Parliament direct elections. Though only 3.2 percent of the votes were won and no seats, the nationwide campaign added momentum to the efforts to from a federal green party to contest the 1980 election. Another strong boost came in October 1979 when the Bremen Green List won seats in the city-state´s parliament.

The Greens were launched in January 1980 as a party broadly based on ecological, democratic, social, and nonviolent principles by an alliance of parties, groups, and activists, even more ideologically diverse than had participated in the 1979 Euro-campaign. There was intense disagreement over whether members of other parties could simultaneously be members of the Greens. Many delegates feared that double membership would be an open door to communist groups whose entry would undermine the electoral appeal of the new party. In the end, *Land* associations were allowed to decide the issue in the interim on the basis of local circumstances.

Programatic integration proved to be much more difficult. Conservatives wanted to maintain a programatic focus on environmental issues while leftists wanted a broad program with radical policy proposals on a full range of domestic and foreign issues. Due to superior organizational skills, the latter prevailed in March 1980. Attempts at compromise in the following months were in vain; Herbert Gruhl, a former member of the Christian Democratic party in the *Bundestag*, and other prominent eco-conservatives eventually resigned from the Greens. The political consciousness of green supporters was rapidly changing. A national survey reported in *Der Spiegel* in November 1979 indicated that 72 percent of their supporters located the Greens ideologically in the middle, 22 percent on the left, and 2 percent on the right. Two years later, a survey found in terms of ideological self-classification that green supporters as a group were further to the left than the SPD followers (Harenberg 1982).

While the Greens were successful in winning seats in the March 1980 Baden-Württemberg *Landtag*, they were unsuccessful in the April 1980 Saarland and May 1980 North Rhine-Westphalia *Land* elections. A number of obstacles, particulary the polarization between the two Chancellor candidates Franz Josef Strauss (CDU/CSU) and Helmut Schmidt (SPD) in the federal campaign, left the Greens with only 1.5 percent of the votes in the October 1980 *Bundestag* elections. The party, however, continued to pick up new members and to win local council seats in the following months. During 1981-83, they won seats in four additional *Landtage*. In 1981 Gruhl and his allies launched a rival Ecological Democratic Party (ÖDP), which has failed to develop any electoral significance on the center-right.

The political opportunity structure has been more favorable for the success of a green/alternative party in West Germany than in other West European countries (Müller-Rommel 1982). To begin with, there was "a concentrated appearance of problems" (Langguth 1986:27), such as the environmental consequences of decades of intensive industrialization in a densely populated country. To which the SPD failed to respond because it shared the CDU/CSU´s and the FDP´s commitment to quantitative economic growth--and to nuclear power as the guarantor of future affluence. During the mid 1970s West German activists waged a passionately fought direct action campaign against nuclear power; frustrations turned many activists toward electoral politics where they were joined by those mobilized by concerns about environmental pollution. Because of the SPD´s lack of dynamism in the early 1980s, the Greens had the political space to broaden their appeal beyond environmental issues. The Greens became the *Öko-pax* party though they were only a small component of the heterogeneous West German peace movement. Similarly the Greens became the champion of the cause of women´s rights and those of diverse social minorities. Not sharing in the party elites consensus regarding NATO, the Greens could provide a focus for the successor generation´s striving toward a new sense of national consciousness, free from the guilt of 1933-45 and neutral between West and East.

There have however been institutional facilitators for the success of the Greens. The five percent threshold of West Germany´s proportional electoral system designed to deter small parties ironically has provided the incentive for environmentalists,feminists, pacifists, counter-culturalists, and autonomous leftists to combine forces and to hold together as a movement-party. In West German elections there are no required deposits for candidates and those parties winning 0.5 percent or more of the votes in state and federal elections qualify for public subsidies of campaign activities. The West German party system has developed as a "two-bloc" system with a limited number of coalitional alternatives; thus a small party (5-10 percent) has the potential for disproportionate policy influence. Finally, the federal system of West Germany provides opportunities for a new party to build up its resources,experiences, and credibility by holding seats in *Landtage,* which have noteworthy policy domains.

Organizational Structures

Prior to 1980, green activists were scattered through a diversity of political organizations. For example, Herbert Gruhl´s *GAZ* (Green Action Future) was a minor national party launched from above in 1978 seeking to emulate the functions and structures of the major parties. Gruhl´s critics were disturbed by his "authoritarian" leadership style and the reactionary values behind the GAZ´s environmentalism. At the other extreme was the Hamburg *Bunte Liste (BL)* which was an *ad hoc* electoral alliance of some 200 assorted grass-roots groups open to communist participation. The *BL* was conceptualized by its founders as a voters' association to get "the foot in the parliamentary door" in order to facilitate extra-parliamentary activities (Strohm 1978). Between the "left" *BL* and the "right" *GAZ* was the *GLU* (Green List for Environmental Protection) in Lower Saxony that developed as a fusion of pre-existing local green lists. The *GLU* differed from the *BL* in its self-conceptualization as a political party seeking the reform of parliamentary democracy from within to attain ecological goals (Troitzsch, 1980). Also noteworthy was August Haussleiter's *AUD* (Action Community of Independent Germans) as a long standing national minor party combining left and right themes, which Stöss (1980:319) describes as "populist conservatism". After failing to be accepted as the party for surging green activism, the AUD's leadership turned to coalition-building during 1979-1980.

In a formal sense, the organizational structure of the Greens established in 1980 does not depart from characteristics of modern mass parties which can be traced back into the 19th Century,i.e., formal dues-paying membership, local and regional branches,large national party congresses to vote policies, and smaller executive council and boards to administer party affairs (Blondel 1978:144). The highest organ of the Greens is the federal delegate assembly; between its meetings the federal steering committe *(BHA)* is the highest organ and can bind the federal executive board *(BuVo),* whose 11 members and 3 co-equal speakers provide collective leadership in daily activities. This framework is more or less replicated in each of the *Länder* with party assemblies (in some cases of delegates, in other cases of members), *Land* committees (in most cases) and *Land* executive boards. The basic unit of the Greens is typically the *Kreisverband* at the local level. According to the federal party charter, the local and *Land* associations are to have "the greatest possible autonomy" regarding program, finances, and personnel. In practice, the Greens do operate as a decentralized party organization whose local and *Land* associations reflect the greatest ideological and regional diversity of all the parties now represented in the *Bundestag*.

The concept of *Basisdemokratie* was advanced to differentiate the Greens'organizational thrust toward participatory democracy from that of the established parties, which were perceived as bureaucratic oligarchies. Party meetings at all levels are open to all members. Minorities are guaranteed the right to be heard in party meetings. While narrow majoritarian decisions are at times unavoidable, the optimal decision-making is supposed to be by consensus, after thorough venting of the issue at all levels. The sessions of federal and *Land* party assemblies generally have been characterized by vigorous delegate participation in deciding--or delaying--policy decisions rather than any formalistic ratification of the plans of party leaders. The Greens embrace the concept of *Imperatives Mandat*, which obliges the resignation of any deputy who would deviate from policy resolutions of the party assembly.

The founders of the Greens erected numerous barriers to hinder the development of a professionalized party elite which would utilize technical expertise and organizational resources to entrench itself. The simultaneous holding of a number of party offices or of a parliamentary mandate and a party office is prohibited. Party officers receive no salaries but may be reimbursed for some expenses by party assemblies. Short time limits are placed on the tenure of elected party leaders. Except for early years in Baden-Württemberg, the Greens have adhered to the principle of collective leadership.

To prevent the development of a class of professional parliamentarians who would concentrate power in the *Fraktion* (parliamentary group) at the expense of the party, the Greens established the controversial procedure of midterm rotation of parliamentary seats to those lower on the party list. Due to the negative experiences with midterm rotation in the *Bundestag* parliamentary group, the green federal party assembly in May 1986 voted to abandon the rule for those deputies elected in January 1987, who would be able to serve a full parliamentary session but then be ineligible for re-election. The Green Alternative List (Hamburg) and the Greens in Schleswig-Holstein have continued to require midterm rotation of *Landtag* deputies; other *Land* parties have abandoned midterm rotation.

Bundestag deputies are required to give up a large portion of their generous salaries to eco-funds, but the fact remains that they are full-time paid politicans. In 1983 the effort to subordinate the *Bundestag* parliamentary group to the federal party leadership failed because of strong objections not only from deputies but also from several *Land* parties (Schrüfer 1985:161). The media coverage of the *Fraktion* has eclipsed that of the *BuVo,* and the former´s full-time paid staff has been several times larger than the latter´s; the same imbalances show up in the *Länder* where parliamentary seats have been won. Power tends to be dispersed within most *Fraktionen* of the *Länder* because of norms of collective leadership, annual selection of parliamentary leaders, ingrained resistance to hierarchical structures, and intra-green factionalism.

Membership figures of the Greens are more indefinite than those of the established parties because of the party´s views regarding centralized data collection. The Greens had about 13,000 charter members in January 1980, more than the right wing NPD but less than communist DKP. Party membership has grown in eight years to around 45,000 which is roughly half the size of the FDP´s membership. Some Greens are sensitive to the trade-off between size and internal democracy, i.e., the larger the party grows, the greater the difficulty in keeping its structure participatory. Others point to the inability of the party to occupy all the seats allotted to it by local election results, e.g. in 1984, due to the shallowness of its membership pool. Langguth (1986:47) argues that the Greens are a "cadre" party because they have the highest ratio of voters to members--87:1 compared to 16:1 for the SPD in 1983. However, this arguments neglects the fact that activists of the green movement are not necessarily party members.

Only about 10 percent of the Green party´s total budget (DM19.7 million in 1983) comes from membership dues, less than a third of the figures for the SPD or the CDU (Langguth 1986:46-47). The largest portion of the Greens´ revenues (over half) comes from public subsidies apportioned according to the votes received in state and national level elections. Green *Fraktionen* receive additional public funding to support parliamentary activities--which amounted to DM 7.2 million in Bonn according to the 1984 annual report of the *Bundestag* Greens.

While small in numbers of voters, members and deputies compared to the major parties, the Greens have presented themselves as the parliamentary arm of much larger "new" social movements. From the outset, activists from social movements (feminist, peace, anti nuclear, consumer, animal rights, etc.) sharing the objectives of the Greens have been given the right to speak at party meetings and as nonmembers have been nominated and elected as parliamentary candidates of the Greens. Numerous policy study groups have been organized to provide inputs from movement activists and outside experts to parliamentary deputies for future programmatic developments. Though many active members of the Greens have backgrounds in local environmental initiative groups, the leadership of the roof organization, BBU *(Bundesverband Bürgerinitiativen Umweltschutz),* has maintained its distance from the Greens.

The views of the Greens have been an anathema for most of the trade union leadership-- a sentiment reciprocated by Rudolf Bahro (1986:11-22), a leading spokesman for ecological fundamentalists among the Greens in the early and mid 1980s. On the other hand, eco-socialists have sought to build up working relationships with progessive elements within the trade union movement. Among the active policy study groups federally has been the one focusing upon trade unions. So far there is little evidence of the Greens´wooing rank and file trade unionists away from their traditional ties to the SPD, though a symbolic breakthrough occurred in February 1986 when for the first time a trade union executive board member addressed a federal party assembly.

Electoral Support

Public opinion polls of the late 1970s indicated a potential electorate of 15-20 percent for a still hypothetical national environmentalist party. In the 1980, 1983, and 1987 federal elections and in the 1979 and 1984 Euro-elections, the Greens have fallen short of such support levels, though their share of the votes cast has increased over time. Since 1979 the Greens have won over 10 percent of the votes in *Land* elections on three occasions--Berlin (1985), Hamburg (1986), and Bremen (1987) (see Table 5.1).

Although their share of the votes has fluctuated, the Greens have managed to clear the five percent threshold and win seats in eight of eleven *Landtage* and to maintain their parliamentary presence in following elections. In contrast to the major parties, there has been disagreement among green prominents regarding the optimal percentage of the electorate that the party should seek to win. One view was that winning more than 6 or 7 percent would be more harmful than helpful during the early development of the Greens (Kelly 1982) while another was that the Greens should shoot for 20+ per cent of the votes nationally (Schmid and Hoplitschek 1985). So far the Greens have approached this level of support only in some local elections in cities with large university populations or districts environmentally impacted by large development projects, yet they have won sufficent votes to be represented in the majority of local councils during the 1980s.

According to an EMNID national survey in January 1983, only 12 percent of green supporters were stalwart voters compared to 64 percent for the CDU/CSU, 54 percent for the SPD, and 31 percent for the FDP. Recent electoral results would suggest that the core support for the Greens has grown; for example, the Greens received 7.0 percent of the district votes *(Erststimmen)* in the 1987 federal election despite the improbability of any green constituency candidate´s victory, which compares closely with their 8.3 percent of the party list votes *(Zweitstimmen)*. Under West German electoral law party list (second) votes determine the total numbers of *Bundestag* seats which the party receives. Direct plurality (first vote) wins in the districts are subtracted from those won on the party list

Table 5.1
Election Results and Seats of the German Greens in Parliament

Election	Party	Percentage of Votes	Seats
Bundestag			
04.10.1980	Die Grünen	1.5	—
06.03.1983	Die Grünen	5.6	27 *
25.01.1987	Die Grünen	8.3	42 *
Euro-Parlament			
10.06.1979	SPV Die Grünen	3.2	—
17.06.1984	Die Grünen	8.2	7
Baden-Württemberg			
16.03.1980	Die Grünen	5.3	6
25.03.1984	Die Grünen	8.0	9
20.03.1988	Die Grünen	7.9	10
Bavaria			
15.10.1978	Aktionsgemeinschaft Unabhängiger Deutscher (AUD) --Die Grünen	1.8	—
10.10.1982	Die Grünen	4.6	—
12.10.1986	Die Grünen	7.5	15
Berlin			
18.03.1979	Alternative Liste (AL)	3.7	—
10.05.1981	Alternative Liste (AL)	7.2	9
10.03.1985	Alternative Liste (AL)	10.6	15
29.01.1989	Alternative Liste (AL)	11.8	17
Bremen			
07.10.1979	Bremer Grüne Liste	5.1	4
	Alternative Liste (AL)	1.4	—
25.09.1983	Die Grünen	5.4	5
	Bremer Grüne Liste	2.4	—
13.09.1987	Die Grünen	10.2	10

(continued)

Table 5.1 (continued)

Election	Party	Percentages of Votes	Seats
Hamburg			
04.06.1978	Bunte Liste	3.5	—
	Grüne Liste Umweltschutz (GLU)	1.0	—
06.06.1982	Grüne Alternative Liste (GAL)	7.7	9
19.12.1982	Grüne Alternative Liste (GAL)	6.8	8
09.11.1986	Grüne Alternative Liste (GAL)	10.4	13
17.05.1987	Grüne Alternative Liste (GAL)	7.0	8
Hesse			
08.10.1979	Grüne Liste Hesse (GLH)	1.1	—
	Grüne Aktion Zukunft (GAZ)	0.9	—
	Grüne Liste Umweltschutz (GLU)	0.0	—
26.09.1982	Die Grünen	8.0	9
25.09.1983	Die Grünen	5.9	7
05.04.1987	Die Grünen	9.4	10
Lower Saxony			
04.06.1978	Grüne Liste Umweltschutz (GLU)	3.9	—
21.03.1982	Die Grünen	6.5	11
15.06.1986	Die Grünen	7.1	11
North Rhine-Westphalia			
11.05.1980	Die Grünen	3.0	—
12.05.1985	Die Grünen	4.6	—
Rhineland-Palatinate			
06.03.1983	Die Grünen	4.5	—
17.05.1987	Die Grünen	5.9	5
	Ökologische Demokratische Partei (ÖDP)	0.4	—
Saarland			
27.04.1980	Grüne	2.9	—
10.03.1985	Grüne	2.5	—

(continued)

Table 5.1 (continued)

Election	Party	Percentage of Votes	Seats
Schleswig Holstein			
29.04.1979	Grüne Liste	2.4	—
13.03.1983	Die Grünen	3.6	—
	Demokratische Grüne Listen	0.1	—
13.09.1987	Die Grünen	3.9	—
08.05.1988	Die Grünen	2.9	—

* plus 1 indirectly elected Alternative Liste deputy from Berlin in 1983 and 2 in 1987.

SOURCE: Dirk Cornelson, *Ankläger im Hohen Haus* (Essen: Klartext Verlag, 1986), pp.15-16 for 1978-1986 results. 1987-1988 data from electoral reports of Forschungsgruppe Wahlen (Mannheim).

side of the ballot. (In those rare cases when a party wins more district seats than qualified for by its list percentages, extra seats are added.) The second vote is the more significant, especially for small parties. In 1987 the FDP received 9.1 per cent of the second votes and qualified for 46 seats while it won only 4.7 percent of the first votes and no direct seats. There is evidence that a growing number of West Germans are tactically splitting their votes.

The *Forschungsgruppe Wahlen* finds convincing evidence over recent *Land* and federal elections of tactical voting by many of those who sympathize with the Greens (Berger *et.al.* 1987:280-282). In elections where the Greens are unlikely to clear the five percent threshold and the SPD has a chance of gaining a majority, these tactical voters vote SPD. Where the power question is not realistically at issue, these voters decide for the Greens.

The most striking social characteristic of the green electorate has been its relative youth. In the 1980 federal election, the Greens attracted about 10 percent of those 18-24 years old; in 1983 the corresponding survey figures were 13.9 percent and in 1987, 15.5 percent (Berger *et.al.* 1987b:262). However, the most supportive age group in 1987 was 25-34 years old (17.4 percent)--a finding which also turns up in recent *Land* elections in places as diverse as Hamburg (Saretzki 1987) and Bavaria (Schultze 1987). After the 34-45 years old group the surveys indicate that votes for the Greens fall off sharply! As in earlier elections, the Greens were supported by relatively more men than women in 1987, but among those under 35 years relatively more women voted for the Greens than men (Berger *et.al.* 1987b:262).

The educational level of green supporters has been found consistently to be high. For example, a national survey in 1982 found that of those with the *Abitur* 16 percent favored the Greens, 32 percent the SPD, 37 percent the CDU/CSU, and 12 percent the FDP (Harenberg 1982:37-38). A multivariate analysis of 1980 data by Bürklin (1981) indicates a powerful interactive effect between age group (young) and level of education (high) in explaining the inclination to vote for the Greens. Müller-Rommel (1985) found students to be the largest "occupational" category in 1980-83 green voter data.

Areal studies have regularly shown since the late 1970s that green (and *Bunte*) candidates have run more strongly in urban residential areas of the "new" middle classes (white collar employees and public officials) and more weakly where workers or the self-employed are concentrated.1987 national survey data indicate that low or middle level employees and officials were the occupational category (by the head of the household) most supportive of the Greens (10 percent) while unskilled workers were the least supportive (3 percent) (Berger *et.al.* 1987:267). Aggregate data analysis of the election reveals that the FDP and the Greens both had good results in residential areas of employees and officials, but this structural support for the Greens is more positively associated with urbanization (Berger *et.al.* 1978a:21). In 1987 the *Forschungsgruppe Wahlen* found overall a .46 correlation coefficient between district population density and the Greens´ share of votes compared to .36 for the SPD. -.52 for the CDU/CSU, and .04 for the FDP.

Religious identification also relates to support for the Greens. National survey data indicate that in 1987 12 percent of non-Catholic favored the Greens but only 6 per cent of Catholics, a wider gap than in 1983. Furthermore, among both Catholics and non-Catholics, the weaker the church attachment, the stronger the support for the Greens (Berger *et.al.* 1987b:268-270). Aggregate data analysis shows that in 1987 there was a negative correlation of -.20 between the Catholic percentage of district population and the Greens´ share of vote compared to -.52 for the SPD, .64 for the CDU/CSU, and -.17 for the FDP. In sum, since the late 1970s studies have provided a distinctive social profile of the greens electorate; it tends to be young, well-educated, white collar salaried, urban, and secular. These are the social characteristics which

Chandler and Siaroff (1986) find closely associated with "post-materialist" values.

Government Participation

Green, *Bunte,*and Alternative lists´ local councillors have had to decide upon working relationship with the established parties from the outset. For example, during 1979-1984, Bielefield Greens (formerly *Bunte Liste*) cooperated selectively with the minority SPD administration and jointly passed three of five budgets (Tolmein 1986:198). Typically the Greens have had greater affinity with the local SPD´s policy priorities though in isolated cases there have been alliances with other parties. Except for Oberhausen in North Rhine-Westphalia, Greens have steered clear of local alliances with the communist DKP (Tolmein 1986:191). Some SPD-Green alliances have been transitory while others have lasted an electoral period (e.g., Kassel 1981-1985) yet many SPD local parties still prefer to govern with the CDU rather than with the Greens.

Since the early 1980s the Greens (and Alternatives) have struggled with the question of power sharing at the *Land* level. In the aftermath of the 1981 Berlin election, the Alternative List refused to tolerate a minority SPD government, so power shifted to the SPD and FDP. However, in the months following the June 1982 Hamburg elections, the Green Alternative List (GAL) negotiated with the minority SPD government over a toleration agreement. Followers of the GAL admit that they went into negotiations with the SPD, realizing that it would never agree to the GAL´s uncompromisable demands and endeavoring to solidify the GAL´s identity on the left (Kraushaar 1983:139-146). The failure of negotiations brought about an early election in December 1982 in which the SPD regained its absolute majority in the city-state parliament.

Opinion within the federal party was sharply split over the "Hesse experiment" (1983-87) in which the *Landtag* Greens first informally and then formally tolerated a minority SPD government, suspended this toleration, and later joined a Red-Green government with an environmental minister and two state secretaries from the Greens. Despite vigorous opposition by radical ecologists in Hesse and by members of the *BuVo,* a series of *Land* party assemblies provided majorities for SPD-Green cooperation, which finally collapsed in early 1987 because of inter-party differences regarding nuclear power. In exchange for a stable majority for the SPD budgets, the Greens procured additional or new funding for assorted environmental, economic, and social programs. Also they could point to major pieces of legislation enacted regarding waste disposal, decentralized energy, and computer data protection by Red-Green majorities in Hesse. The majority *Realos* (realists) were eager to resume SPD-Green cooperation after the April 1987 in Hesse elections, but, though the Greens scored gains, the SPD lost so many seats that the CDU and the FDP could form the new government.

Saarland Greens rejected flatly the idea of a Red-Green coalition floated by SPD *Land* chairman LaFontaine in 1984. Toleration rather than coalition was also the strategy favored by the majority of North Rhine-Westphalia Greens in 1985. In both *Länder*, the Green party´s unwillingness to participate in government was portrayed as evidence of its "irresponsibility", which worked in favor of the SPD´s campaign. There was a real chance that the June 1986 Lower Saxony elections would result in a Red-Green majority. Lower-Saxony Greens announced the party´s intention to negotiate with the SPD after the election but to leave the format of the cooperation open in advance, yet clearly many Lower Saxony Greens were ready to consider a formal coalition.

After the November 1986 Hamburg election, the GAL´s deputies again held the balance of power in the city-state parliament. The SPD minority government chose not to negotiate any deal with the GAL and to govern on the basis of "changing majorities". At times the GAL voted with the SPD government and at times with the CDU opposition. Eventually the SPD opted for early elections in May 1987, which paved the way for a SPD-FDP coalition. The GAL´s setback in this election led to factional conflict between its minority which is serious about toleration as a working parliamentary relationship with the SPD and its majority which talks toleration but is committed to fundamental opposition to the SPD.

During the 1980s there have been prominent Greens in Baden-Württemberg who have advanced the idea of tolerating or forming a coalition with the CDU in Stuttgart. Such pronouncements have originated with the *Ökolibertären* (eco-libertarians), a small minority on the economic right of the green spectrum nationally rule. In other *Länder*, parliamentary alliances with the CDU/CSU are currently ruled out by even *Super -Realos*.

Public opinion polls since the early 1980s have shown repeatedly that solid majorities of green voters at the *Land* and federal level rank the SPD as their party of second choice and favor the SPD as a coalition partner (Roth 1985). However, among many of the most active members of the Greens there is a negative fixation on the SPD as an early movement-party which accommodated itself to the system. Furthermore, *Basisdemokratie* and coalitional politics, with its wheeling and dealing by parliamentary elites, are seen as incompatible. The faction of *Fundis* (fundamentalists) believe that long run success depends on sharpening not blurring the contours between the SPD and the Greens. On the other hand, the *Realos* (realists) faction has argued that the Greens must make themselves acceptable as a junior partner to the SPD since there in no other alternative if the Greens are to bring about policy changes in the near future. The issue of strategy toward the SPD became an overshadowing controversy in federal party assemblies during the mid 1980s. At the September 1986 federal assembly, a majority of delegates voted in favor of negotiations with the SPD if the 1987 election should produce a Red-Green majority in the *Bundestag*. SPD Chancellor candidate Rau´s centrist campaign of distancing the SPD from any cooperation with the Greens allowed *Realos* and *Fundis* to pull together during the federal campaign.

Programatic Profile

The Greens have never been the one issue party which early critics discounted them as; they have had policy stands on a wide range of domestic and foreign issues since 1980. The thesis of their *Bundesprogramm* (federal program) is that West Germany is in the midst of an ecological and economic crisis threatening the future of industrial societies. The symptoms of this crisis are environmental destruction and human exploitation; its roots are profit-seeking competition and quantitative economic growth. The *Bundesprogramm* maintains that "economic goals should only be realized within a framework of ecological necessities" and that the affected people should decide, "what, how, and where products will be produced." Not only do the Greens demand strict measures to preserve the environment, they also call for just distribution of goods and services to those socially disadvantaged, a guaranteed income for all, the gradual shortening of the work week with full pay, an end to sexual discrimination, and a host of other socio-economic changes. To accomplish this fundamental realignment of industrial society, decentralization and self-administration are espoused. For example, large corporations should be dismantled into self-managing units and small alternative companies should be promoted, yet clearly the state is not to wither away since many proposed policy changes would necessitate enhanced enforcement powers. The *Bundesprogamm* neglects the technical questions of implementation and advances a number of absolutist demands, such as the immediate shutdown of nuclear power plants.

In the *Bundesprogramm* the Greens maintain that "an ecologically-conscious foreign policy is based on nonviolence".

They oppose the insanity of the arms race and the folly of the strategy of nuclear deterrence. The Greens demand the removal of all Pershing II, cruise, and SS-20 missiles from Europe. Stockpiles of not only nuclear but also chemical and biological weapons should be eliminated. The Greens call for the dissolution of NATO and the Warsaw Pact and for the withdrawal of all foreign troops from Germany. In the meantime, they advocate nuclear free zones in Central Europe and the reduction of West German army. Ultimately conventional armed defense should be replaced by (non-violent) social defense. The Greens support the rights of national self-determination of Third World peoples. They oppose the superpowers´military interventions in Nicaragua and Afghanistan. The Greens advocate ending the world arms trade and increasing foreign aid for developing countries. An expanded role for the United Nations is called for by the *Bundesprogramm*. Since 1980 where foreign policy disputes have occurred, they have been between those who hold to absolutist demands and those who accept gradualism; the former have prevailed in Green party assemblies.

While there has been a high continuty of foreign themes in party programs, changing economic and political circumstances have placed the Greens under increased pressure to refine their economic policies. In January 1983 the federal party assembly approved a *Sofortprogramm* (action program) of short and medium run measures to counter the worst effects of industrial capitalism. The Greens support creation of jobs by shortening the work week and restricting overtime, ecological investments in such areas as energy and transportation, conversion of industrial production away from destructive products, support for self-help organizations, maintenance of social programs, and special training programs for the young unemployed. The *Sofortprogramm* proclaims, "The ecological and the social belong inseparably together." In 1986 the Greens attempted to demonstrate more clearly the practicality of their economic proposals by adopting an *Umbauprogramm* (reconstruction program) focused upon concrete steps within the 4-5 year time frame. It contrasts with earlier programs in its budgetary concerns with costs, trade-offs, and priorities and its nonideological eagerness to make skillful use of the entire range of state policy instruments from public ownership to pollution taxes in order to move toward the ecological, social, and democratic economy.

The Greens have been "the" feminist party in West Germany. From the outset, their programs have advocated full equality for women and have highlighted the special concerns of women in a wide range of domestic and foreign issues. Emancipation of women is seen as beginning within the party itself. In 1986 the federal party charter was changed to require sexual parity on the candidate lists of the Greens while leaving open the possiblity of all female lists as in Hamburg 1986-87. Women were given veto rights over policy resolutions particularly pertinent to their interests. At times green women have been split sharply between those interpreting feminism as pursuit of equality for women within the current system and others interpreting it as pursuit of an alternative system.

The Greens have been steadfastly "civil libertarian" in their programmatic development. From the outset, they have promoted the rights of social fringe groups--foreign workers, gypsies, homosexuals, handicapped, prisoners, and aged. Consistently they have stressed the right of free speech, the right of assembly, the right of conscientious objection to military service, and the right to be free of surveillance. In recent years the Greens have mobilized grassroots opposition to the federal census because of the opportunities for governmental abuse of the citizen´s right of privacy. There is consensus on such nonviolent civil disobedience, but there are intra-party differences on more active--and potentially violent--forms of resistance.

As a small new party, the Greens have produced numerous, often lengthly, programmatic documents at the *Land* and federal levels. Early programs generally resembled warehouse catalogs of demands, but more recently there have been attempts to integrate various policy proposals and to work out linkages between short term measures and long term goals. The diverse origins of the Greens has made programatic development challenging during the 1980s.

Outlook
Since the beginning critics have regularly predicted the imminent demise of the Green party. For example, the failure of the Greens to win *Landtag* seats in the May 1985 North Rhine-Westphalia election was presented by much of the media as the beginning of the end, yet since then the Greens have won *Landtag* seats in nine of eleven elections and have been easily returned to the *Bundestag*. Despite programmatic renewal, the SPD in opposition has been unable to co-opt enough green voters to keep the Greens outside parliament. Repeated wins in local, *Land,* and federal elections have clearly demonstrated that the Greens are not a "flash" party of protest but have developed a distinctive base of social support that has persisted despite particular cases of campaign ineptness. On the other hand, it is also becoming apparent that some sort of generational transformation of societal values is *not* going to sweep the Green party upward and onward in terms of electoral percentages,

regardless of how chaotic its image may be. Furthermore, as the meager gains made by the anti-nuclear Greens in the Lower Saxony 1986 election following the Chernobyl nuclear disaster indicate, future crises may not necessarily translate into landslides of green votes. Barring some deep party schism or major electoral law change, the Greens seem likely to win enough votes to remain the third or fourth force at all levels of West German party system into the 1990s.

As a political organization (inside and outside of parliament), the Greens seem to be in perpetual crisis, particularly at the federal level. The high profile of their intra-party conflicts compared to the major parties´can be attributed to the wide open character of the Greens´decision-making process and to be the lack of consensus among the *"Promis"* (prominents) about structural, programmatic, and strategic questions. However, the episodes of bitter factionalism (typically amplified by a hostile press) tend to obscure the facts that there are many active Greens who are neither committed *Realos* nor committed *Fundis,* that numerous substantive policy proposals enjoy cross-factional support, and that there is the general realization that the historic success of the Greens compared to the radicals of the 1960-70s has hinged upon their accommodation of a diversity of groups. As a "pluralistic" party, the Greens have survived and accumulated formidable institutional resources compared to other European green/alternative parties.

The "anti-party" party phase of the Greens appears to be over though the rhetoric lingers. The Greens have become an increasingly parliamentarized party despite themselves. Political protest is still intrinsic to the self-concept of the Greens, but there is also growing awareness of the organizational requirements for the full utilization of the opportunities in electoral and parliamentary arenas for advancing the party´s radical agenda. Parliamentary entry has already modified informally and formally various *basisdemokratische* procedures of the party. Programmatic initiative has been slipping away from "amateurish" party bodies toward "professional" parliamentary groups. The parliamentarization process, however, is limited by the pillar of *Basisdemokratie* that provides the counter-legitimacy of the Greens and is manifested as a gauntlet of party boards and assemblies, which in contrast to the SPD´s are hardly predisposed to ratify proposals from above.

Factional politics has clearly left the Greens with a "split personality" in the late 1980s most evident when the strategy toward the SPD is at issue. Polls have shown that strong majorities of green voters favor the party´s forming alliances and/or coalitions with the

SPD; however, the question has sharply divided both party activists and parliamentary deputies during the 1980s. At the *Land* level, though circumstances vary, the trend is for the majorities of party assembly delegates generally to favor toleration agreements-- in some cases formal coalitions-- when minority SPD governments emerge. The outlook for the 1990s regarding cooperation with the SPD at the federal level would be more complex given inter-party differences especially on foreign and defense policies. *Realos* would be prepared to "wheel and deal" in coalitional politics with the SPD while *Fundis* would be prepared to sabotage the endeavor with the splintering of the Green party as a distinct possibility. All this speculation assumes that the SPD reaches internal consensus that it should cooperate with the Greens federally; however, the Hamburg SPD-FDP coalition formed in 1987 suggests that a few years hence there just may be an alternative partner to the "irresponsible" Greens. In conclusion, during the 1980s, as a new small party, the Greens have played an influential role in policy agenda-setting in West Germany and are likely to continue to do so in the 1990s.

6
Finland:
The "Vihreät"

Jukka Paastela

Development of the Greens

In the late 1960´s and early1970´s, Finland experienced an outsurge of new left radicalism among its youth and among its student population. However, this period of Finnish political history was rather short lived. Although the Moscow oriented minority faction of the communist party rose to an ideologically dominating position among the politically active students, it was the inflexible Marxist-Leninist dogma that brought about the downfall of the new left movement in Finland. Unattractive to young people interested in social problems and in social change, it was clear by the mid-1970´s that radical leftism had seen its political demise in Finland (Hyvärinen and Paastela 1985: 13ff).

In the late 1970´s various alternative movements emerged. From the very beginning, these movements were very heterogeneous: one maintained a journal of oriental mysticism and a vegetarian restaurant while another movement was organized by disabled persons unsatisfied with the activities of the previous organization for the disabled. Existing at this time were also various currents of radical feminism. In 1979, an environmental conservation movement also made its appearence on the political scene when it rallied its efforts to protect lake Koijärvi; a lake serving as a sanctuary to an active and flourishing bird population. The activists, chaining themselves to the excavating machinery were partly successful in preventing any drainage work to be done upon the lake (Järvikoski 1981: 313ff). In addition to these groups, the anti-nuclear power movement was established in 1977. The main roots of the greens are to be found in all these movements.

In the municipal elections 1976 an ecological list in Helsinki was for the first time present at the polls in Finland. However, it failed to obtain seats in the city council.

Four years later, the Greens in Helsinki succeeded in getting 1,7 percent of the vote and one seat in the council. In the 1983 national election the various alternative movements formed a "green list" and received 1,5 percent of the total vote. On the basis of this result, the greens received two seats in parliament (out of 200). One seat was taken by the chairman of the organization for the disabled who was bound to a wheelchair. The other seat in parliament was given to the initiator of the environmental movement that was organized around lake Koijärvi. From 1983 to 1987, both green members of parliament were not very active with respect to parliamentary initiatives and speeches. They were not against parlamentarism but saw their chances for a relevant political impact as rather weak. In the 1987 general election the Greens received 4 percent of the vote and four seats in the national parliament. This result was unexpectedly low given the surveys taken before the election in which the Greens scored around eight percent.

Organizational Structure
Until 1987, the Finnish Greens had not established an officially registered party with a formal organizational structure. Instead, the various political movements had then to nominate various candidates for a "green list". This lack of organization created severe problems. Candidates were, for instance, elected all too often in chaotic meetings and had no "credentials" from any formal organization. They simply represented their own ideas and beliefs. This loose structure aroused much criticism and the majority of the "green list" followers agreed upon the necessity of establishing a formal organizational structure.

The main question in the debate about the proposed organizational reform was whether or not the Greens should found a registered party. The advantage of forming a registered green party lay in the fact that such an organization would receive financial subsidies from the state (more than $ 50.000 per member of parliament in one year). In September of 1986, the Greens held a congress where the question of organization was further discussed. The delegates could, however, not agree on one organizational structure. It was not before February 1987 that the Greens decided to establish a "Green Association" which was to be led by a "Green Commission". The "Green Association" consisted of nationally organized green groups such as the "Green Feminist", "The Environmental Policy Association" but also included various green groups on the local level.

This organizational model had, however, only an interim character. The 1987 parliamentary election was not as successful for the Greens as was expected and the failure to get more than four mandates was seen by many Greens as a result of organizational weakness. At the same time, however, the division of the Greens into two tendencies, the ecological tendency and the social tendency was further aggravated by the fact that two of the M.P.´s are representatives of the former tendency and the other two are members of the latter one. The leader of the ecologists, Eero Paloheimo, declared that the ecologists would form a party and M.P.´s of the social tendency also said that a party was needed. In February 1988 the "Green Association" decided to collect 5.000 names needed in order to register an association as a party. However, the ecological tendency and social tendency could not agree to act in the same organization. The ecologists then founded their own organization simply named "Greens", and thus began to collect names. In August 1988 the "Green Association" founded their own green party. This is not necessarily a catastrophe for the Greens because the two green parties can still form an alliance in the elections and thus reduce the effort of the electoral system which favours big parties. If they, however, cannot agree, the result may be a substantial decreasing of parliamentary representation. The observers of the green movement have been very astonished by the fact that the Greens could not agree upon uniform party organization. If we compare the speeches of the green members in the parliament, we find that their content is very similar despite the fact that the green members in any representative bodies are bound to any group discipline. In fact, the Green members of parliament generally vote in similar way. In Finland, the split of the green movement can only be explained by the difficult character of its central leaders.

Financially, the parliamentary group is dependent upon donations. The green members of parliament finance the activities of the parliament group and the salaries of a few staff members. In addition, every green member in municipal councils and upon municipal boards pays two to five percent of the meeting fee to the parliamentary green group. Because the Greens were not a registered party from 1983 to 1988, they have received no subsidies from the state and therefore have lost more than $ 100.000 a year.

Programatic Profile

Prior to the foundation of green parties, the followers of the Greens presented different programatic ideas in all of the constituencies.

Instead of a party program, the delegates of the 1985 national convention of the Greens agreed upon a list of four programatic demands. They claimed that sulphur emissions had to be reduced by two thirds; that no new nuclear power stations should be built; that the wood-processing industry must not be expanded and that everyone can decide for her/himself how much she or he works.

In the past three years, several attempts have been made to prepare a "green program"; the initiative was taken either by groups or by individuals. Most prominent were two program drafts which were formulated by local green movement activists. Both papers were widely discussed in the mass media.

In 1985, a local green activist from Turku introduced a rather detailed program which contained green ideas but also some traditional left-wing demands. The program was, however, too radical for the majority of the green movement followers. Another attempt was made in 1986 by a member of the Finnish nature conservation movement, *Pentti Linkola*. In the program he proposed that Finland should be transformed into a one-party state where the only party allowed would be a green vanguard party. (Linkola 1986) The public discussion about this 47-page long document was very emotional and very serious. In the leading daily newspaper in Finland, thirteen articles were published which reacted to Linkola's ideas.

This program was soon sold out in the largest bookshops of Helsinki and the public was then familiar with the basic argument. Although this "green program" was rejected by most debates as undemocratic and unrealistic, it might have had an impact on the unexpectedly low results that the Greens obtained in the 1987 national elections.

The Finnish Greens have had difficulty in reaching a unanimous agreement about a common program. In order to obtain a stronger identity, a program is needed. However, in launching a traditionally rather vague program, the danger of party-likeness grows. On the other hand, any clear and/or radical program produces sharply differing positions. It seems as if the Greens are in a vicious circle: whichever route they choose; there are many difficulties and there is a high degree of dissatisfaction.

Electoral Support

Finland is divided into fifteen constituencies. In the 1983 national elections, the Greens nominated candidates in seven electoral districts in the southern part of the country. Since those constituencies are the larger ones the Greens succeeded for the first time in obtaining two seats out of 200 in the 1983 national parliament. In the general elections of March 1987, the Greens polled four percent of the total vote and gained four seats in parliament - much less than the opinion polls predicted. It has been found that many potential green voters did not vote at all due, amongst other reasons, to the public discussions about *Linkola's* green program. The turnout in the 1987 national election was exceptionally low among the younger generation, which had an impact on the electoral results of the Greens. Surveys have, for instance, convincingly documented that fifty percent of the green electorate is between 18 and 30 years of age.

The supporters of the Greens are also higher educated. Nearly forty percent of them have passed the *matriculation* (graduation), whereas only nine percent of the total population has passed this examination. In addition, twenty two percent of the green voters earn more than $ 2.500 per month which links them to the minority of people who form the Finnish upper class. Among the farmers, the Greens have only marginal support, basically because there is a traditional agrarian party (the Centre Party) that represents the interests of the farmers in the national parliament. Interestingly enough, the Greens can better mobilize former left-wing than former right-wing voters. (Taloustutkimus 1985)

According to a recent study, the Greens have more women representatives in municipal councils than any other party. (Jalonen 1986) Furthermore, the green councillors are younger than their colleagues and also benefit from a fairly high education. Seventy percent of the green councillors have passed the *matriculation* and the amount of those who have a post-graduate examination is striking (see Table 6.1).

Hence, the green voters in Finland - as their counterparts in other European countries - belong to a group of young and higher educated people.

Government Participation

It is impossible to imagine that the Greens will participate in national government in the near future. Not only were the Greens probably the most passive group in the 1983-1987 parliamentary session. Their impact was also marginal because the established parties did not consider the Greens as a party with a clear and politically reliable program.

Even in those councils where the Greens managed to have a fairly high representation, they, nevertheless, acted as an opposition party.

Table 6.1
The Education of Green Municipal Councillors in Finland 1984

Education	Male	Female	All
elementary school	8.6	4.4	6.2
vocational school or course	2.8	9.9	15.3
secondary school	17.1	21.7	19.7
graduated from university	42.9	54.3	49.4
post-graduate examination	28.6	4.3	14.8
Total	100.0	100.0	100.0
(N)	(35)	(46)	(81)

Source: Jalonen 1986: 41f.

Quite often, green members of local councils tend to support the position of the communists, for instance, regarding their demands to establish public transport and municipal child care. In spite of these alliances on certain issues, the Greens always underline that they are ready to cooperate with all political parties on issues like "care for nature and environment", "social equality", "rejection of ostentative waste-making" and so on.

Outlook
The impact of the Greens on Finnish political life will depend on cooperation between the two green parties. So far, the Greens have increasingly affected the Finnish public debate on ecological questions. However, the political impact of the Greens is still rather low. As long as no other party shows any concern in picking up ecological questions in their national policy-making, the Greens will remain part of the Finnish political system.

7
France:
"Les Verts"

Brendan Prendiville*

Development of the Green Party
The French Greens are a relatively recent social and political
phenomenon. Spawned by the cultural revolution of May 1968, it
was not until January 1984 that a unified organization was born at
Clichy in Paris out of the fusion between the two principal political
ecology groups; the *Confédération Ecologiste* and the *Verts-Parti
Ecologiste*. This fusion was the result of a realization, on the part of
these two groups that after 10 years´ existence without much
headway the political ecology movement was heading in its structural
form at least, towards gradual oblivion (Nullmeyer F. et al. 1983;
Vadrot 1980). Having made an entry onto the political scene in 1974
with Réné Dumont, renowned agronomist and ecologist candidate, in
the presidential elections of that year (1.3 percent), the ecology
movement reached an electoral peak in the presidential elections of
1981 (its candidate, Brice Lalonde, obtained 3.9 percent) and an
extra-parliamentary success at Plogoff in 1980/81 mobilization
against the proposed nuclear power plant followed by its
dismantlement (Bridgeford 1978; Dupoirier/Jaffré 1980). The arrival
of the socialist government in power in May 1981 marked the end of
a period of radical extra-parliamentary action and the beginning of an
attempted institutional integration.

The birth of *Les Verts* was, in reality, a compromise on the part
of ecologist activists who, no doubt unconsciously, transformed a
somewhat diffuse ´social movement´ into a political party with the
consequence of precipating a loss of radicality and an increase in
institutional representation.

*The author wishes to acknowledge the contribution of Tony
Chafer who wrote the sections on the ecologist electorate and the
1983 Municipal elections and who helped with the organization of
this chapter.*

Up until 1984, the movement had led a somewhat shaky existence, leaning heavily on a wave of anti-nuclear activity in the world´s most nuclearized country. In 1985, nuclear energy represented 65 percent of electricity production in France.

Despite the failure to gain any concessions from the extremely powerful nuclear lobby in France, the ecology movement did manage through this extra-parliamentary action to construct an identity which has both served and detracted from its cause. It has served it in the sense that the presidential elections of 1988 revealed an electoral stability over the last seven years and it has detracted from it by creating an image of a movement whose principal motivation is the defence of the *natural* environment. In a country whose agricultural population still totalled 45 percent of the working population at the end of the Second World War, this image could be linked to an attachment to the land which remains a major feature of the French collective consciousness even if the aforementioned percentage is now in the region of 7.5 percent. However, such a limited naturalist platform of the ecological group, coupled with a remarkable lack of political success, has led to a difference of opinion within *Les Verts*. One faction wishes to develop a firm autonomous political strategy and the other would prefer to link up with sections of the Alternative Left in a form of ´Rainbow Alliance´, along the lines of the German Greens, and subsequently to establish a contractual form of political alliance with the institutional Left. This opposition can be seen, in part, as a reflection of the nature of the French political system within which *Les Verts* are forced to operate.

In founding the 5th French Republic in 1958, General de Gaulle was, ostensibly, motivated by a desire to avoid the political instability of the previous 4th republic. The electoral system devised toward this end was one which reinforced the monolithic, highly centralised character of the Napoleonic French state by allowing for an emotional but largely meaningless, first round vote and a decisive second round one. This means that in national elections, the institutional representation of minority parties is a virtual impossibility and goes some way towards explaining the constant uphill struggle of French ecologists.

Although the electoral system is less than favourable to ecologists, they nevertheless participate in the national French elections. The results of the most recent presidential elections of April 1988 suggest the basic electorate of the Greens is relatively stable.

The ecologist movement has participated in three presidential elections with three different candidates reflecting the previously mentioned turnover in leadership personnel: 1974 Réné Dumont, 337.800 votes, total: 1.3 percent; 1981 Brice Lalonde, 1.122.445 votes total: 3.8 percent; 1988 Antoine Waechter, 1.145.502 votes, total: 3.7 percent. One may wonder why ecologists decide to participate in elections which are so costly. The majority of activists are of the opinion that they are obliged to so in order to exist given that, politically speaking, the presidential elections represent the democratic pillar of the 5th French Republic. Another reason is the prospect of negotiating to advantage after a good first round score. In 1981, for example, the election of F. Mitterrand was followed by the cancellation of the proposed nuclear power plant at Plogoff.

As for the second round, the French electoral tradition is for first round candidates to "advise" their supporters on how to vote in the second round. Ecologist candidates have always refused to do this, maintaining that their supporters are adult enough to decide for themselves, even if their individual sympathies tend to lean more to the left/centre-left than to the right (R. Dumont, B. Lalonde): This position is, of course, designed to back up their search for political autonomy even if the majority of their supporters (60-65 percent) vote to the left in the second round (Cochet 1987).

In the parliamentary elections, ecologist candidates often had a small voting base: In 1978, the *Ecologie Collectif 78* received 2.2 percent of the national vote. In 1981, a group called *Aujourd´hui Ecologie* gained 1.1 percent of the total vote and in 1986, *Les Verts* were supported by 1.2 percent of the French electorate. In 1986, there were the first direct elections to a regional assembly in France which consequently renders any comparison difficult. *Les Verts* received 2.4 percent of the vote and sent three councillors into regional parliaments.

Since the inception of political ecology in France, local elections are the most decentralised elections and thus the closest to people´s lives and daily concerns. The *commune*, in particular, is seen by many ecologists as the starting point from which a social base could be built, and, as such, the municipal elections are given, in theory at least, top priority.

The ecologist movement has taken part in two municipal elections: In their first appearance in 1977, the local ecologist/alternative-left lists won 30 seats around the country. The total vote obtained was 270.000. In the 1983 elections, the results were generally lower than in 1977. Despite this smaller share of the vote the measure of proportional representation introduced by the

Mitterrand government for these elections was favourable to minority groups such as the Greens. The requirement for longer electoral lists caused some problems, but in general the new law allowed the Greens to have far more candidates elected than in 1977. 757 ecologists were elected to town councils in 1983 for a total vote of 147.884. The green vote declined most, compared to 1977, in the very large cities. Some of their highest scores were in small towns, and especially in the towns surrounding the Cap de la Hague reprocessing plant and the Flamanville nuclear power station near Cherbourg. Some good results were also obtained in Alsace, which has traditionally been a good area for the Greens (Chafer 1983: 11-16). By in large, one might argue that the Greens in France can be considered as a stable minority within the French political system.

Organizational Structure
Les Verts are organized along regional lines which is a reflection of their concern that society should be as decentralised as possible in order for social and political control to be more accessible to everyone. This is, of course, a worldwide tenet of the ecologist paradigm. Consequently, their national decision-making body (CNIR - *Counseil National Inter-Regional*) is one in which 75 percent of delegates are elected by autonomous regional sections of the party and 25 percent during the Annual General Meeting. The Executive College, which includes four spokespersons, is subsequently elected by the CNIR. This style of political control is designed to avoid an over-personalisation of political ecology; such potential over-personalisation being a latent phobia of the ecology movement reflecting, in many ways the perceptible anarchist strand of thought and practice which exists within its very character. This fear of the loss of control over the leaders has produced the popular ecologist sport of ´head-chopping´ the first victim of which was the 1981 presidential candidat, Brice Lalonde. That is to say that once an ecologist ´leader´ emerges, he/she is often considered as a potential danger to internal democracy. More recently, the minority leaders Y. Cocchet and D. Anger have suffered similar fates, and, given the French electoral system, not to mention Napoleonic tradition, this is a phenomenon which does not facilitate the task of political integration (Prendiville 1989).

With regard to the practice of internal democracy, perhaps the best example is the recent designation of the green presidential candidate. Similar to the American presidential elections, a series of ´primaries´ were held in each of the different French regions allowing each member to participate in the final choice.

The membership oscillates around the 1.000 mark and financial support is limited to subscription fees (wage-linked) and sporadic donations. Such a meager financial situation is aggravated by an electoral system which requires that 5 percent of the votes be obtained for expenses to be reimbursed by the state; doubtless, *Les Verts* remain envious of their German counterparts.

In their overwhelming desire to forge an independent political identity *Les Verts* have no structural links with other socio-political groups. However, joint actions around topical issues are the ´bread and butter´ of day-to-day ecology. Especially visible in the 1970s, during the height of the anti-nuclear struggles, was the collaboration with the *Confédération Francaise Démocratique du Travail*; an independent left-wing trade union. This joint action was interpreted, somewhat hastily, as the beginning of a reconciliation between the ecological and the workers´ movements. However, since that time, there has been little contact and little collaboration between them.

As for what have been called the new social movements, France has yet again a distinctive position amongst its Western European partners. Certain movements, such as the feminist and regionalist movements, which are still alive and well elsewhere in Europe, are now considered ´outdated´ in France. Feminism, for example, has been submerged under a cultural wave of American-inspired neo-liberalism and, even within ecologist circles, it is considered as being slightly *ringard* or *dépassé*.The social movements which have had the most durable success are those which deal with the socio-economic consequences of the developing crisis of Western civilisation; e.g. Third World, Fourth World, Anti-Racism. It is the latter of these three examples which has received the most media attention through the organization *SOS-Racisme*, and its charismatic leader Harlem Desir. Long before the leader of the extreme right-wing *Front National*, Jean-Marie Le pen, gained 14.4 percent of the first round vote in the presidential elections of April 1988, large sections of the French youth (i.e. 1st generation French and immigrant) had been the first to foresee the danger of racism rearing its head under the respectable guise of the *Front National*, and had mobilized themselves as early as 1983 in defense of the immigrant community. Within this general mobilization, *Les Verts* are certainly still present in their support although they are discreet in their active participation. The aforementioned and highly successful group *SOS-Racism*, clings to its stated political independence even if it is often considered to be close to the Socialist party and the various *collectifs anti-rascistes*, which bring together other minority parties, including *Les Verts*.

Subsequently, from December 1986 to March/April 1987, a wave of protest somewhat suddenly swept over French society some six months after the election of a right-wing government.

Without entering into a discussion of what constitutes a social movement and how it differs from a pressure group (Prendiville 1987: 19-24), these movements took everyone by surprise, including *Les Verts*, which is another way of indicating the virtual irrelevance of the latter to the former. *Les Verts* aspire to a new form of political action based on greater participation, one which would place them in the role of an institutional expression (*relais*) of wider social movements, as is the case in Germany. It can be said, however, that this is the case in present-day France.

Programatic Profile

There are three main pillars to the political program of *Les Verts*: *Autonomy, Solidarity, Ecology*. These three pillars underlie proposals in each of the different areas of analysis and reinforce the world-wide ecologist slogan of "Think globally, Act locally". This well-known slogan is a reflexion of ecologists' concern to make the links between individual/specific action and collective/global consequences, be it within a communal, regional, national or international context. In every major statement of ecologist beliefs, before or after the formal creation of *Les Verts* in 1984, the defense of life in its many forms unquestionably takes first place. From "Protect Life" (*Protéger la Vie*) in 1980, "The Choice of Life" (*Le Choix de la Vie*) in 1984, and "Reconquer Life" (*Réconquérir la Vie*) in 1988, the concern from which all others stem is that of the safeguard of the natural environment upon which the social environment depends. This is to say that in the view of *Les Verts*, the ideology of industrialism, in the East and in the West, now threatens the continuing existence of life upon our planet. Industrialism being a philosophy which equates growth with individual and collective fulfilment, the proposals put forward by *Les Verts* are thus necessarily social and economic.

The dominating theme of *Les Verts*' economic proposals stems from the fundamental criticism of the productivist economic model that industrialism has generated. Productivism is the system in which production is no longer a means to an end but a system in which production becomes an end in itself. This, of course, is a fundamental tenet in ecologists' eyes, since the major danger to planetary stability is the environmental pollution which the present day economic system has produced. Consequently, it is not simply the ownership of the means of production which is in question, but also the nature of those means; for ecologists, a left-wing nuclear power station does not differ radically from a right-wing one.

Les Verts and the wider ecologist movement have therefore always adopted a holistic approach to economic and social problems, even if their proposals have become more and more precise over the years with regard to form and content (Journes 1979).

Form: Any political movement in the 1980s has to tackle the problem of *unemployment* in order to remain credible. It is no use to simply criticize the place and conditions of work in Western society, pertinent as that critique may sometimes be. Detailed solutions must be put forward, and at the end of 1984 the Greens did this by proposing an economy based on work-sharing as a means of attaining two goals. First of all, they stated that in order to solve the problem of unemployment in today's computerized, robotized economy the result of the transition from industrial to post-industrial society (Gorz 1980), work-sharing was and still is the only *long term* solution if full employment is to retain any viable meaning at all. This, they asserted, would create a society based on a greater sense of *social solidarity*, which constitutes the second goal they wish to attain. However, in order to be effective, work-sharing must be accompanied by a substantial reduction in the working week. Such a proposal, coupled with the creation of a *guaranteed minimum social wage*, would create more free time for people to engage in other activities, not the least of which would be to participate in the running of society. Perhaps even more important in contemporary France, such measures are designed to contribute to a more harmonious society, given that unemployment is seen as one of the principle reasons for the recent rise of racism in the country.

Content: If the nature of the economy, based on greater social solidarity in the form of work-sharing needs to be changed, so does the content of the work in question. Ecologists see little point in creating more weapons simply to keep people working. The technological choices which shape society and which are made largely outside the political sphere need to come under collective scrutiny. As a corollary, such scrutiny would be meaningful only under a system of collective control upon the means of production. These two observations lead *Les Verts* to go a step further than traditional left-wing economic analyses by proposing a form of social, economic and environmental management, termed eco-management ("écogestion"). This form of economic arrangement would allow for workers *and* the people living in a given community who are exposed to the effects of industrial production, to make collective decisions with respect to what has to be done with these effects instead of simply confining these people behind the factory walls. The choices so made would be based on both social (type and utility of production) and ecological criteria (environment). The ramifications of such a direct economic democracy are vast and would only make sense, in the Green´s eyes, within the bounds of a society organized along more autonomous lines.

Les Verts´ policy on defense is, once again, based on a holistic approach to the problem. Their belief in political non-violence as a means of broaching conflict leads them to question the very nature of national defense along with its ideological root: nationalism. In this respect, Les Verts propose a policy of defense which attempts to reconcile internationalism and pacifism.

Defense, *Les Verts* maintain, is not simply an absence of war. It is, or should be, the reduction of international tensions that create belligerence. Any defense policy should therefore be based on a double strategy of non-alignment and greater cooperation with Third World countries. This insistence on relationships with the Third World stems from a concern that Western economic development, which is often at the expense of developing countries actually accentuates disparities between the two hemispheres and contains the seeds of potential future conflicts; not to mention ecological imbalance.

The development of economic self-sufficiency within Third World countries is considered to be a pre-requisite for greater political and economic stability between the industrialized nations and the developing world. Such self-sufficiency can be stimulated by intelligent aid, such as technical aid and education programs as opposed to the unloading of European food surpluses which serve only to increase the economic dependence of the former upon the latter. *Les Verts* are also opposed to the continuation of arms sales to belligerent countries (e.g. the gulf states Iran and Iraq) as a means of supporting the French economy.

Ecologists in France do not deny the need for national defense but they do insist on the need for one which is both morally and strategically acceptable. *Les Verts* refuse to accept a defense based on what they see as certain suicide. That is to say that France´s present policy of nuclear deterrence (*dissuasion*), instituted by General de Gaulle, exists in order to prevent a war breaking out by convincing the potential enemy (i.e. USSR) that it would not be worth the risk. The French deterrent is therefore an ultimate weapon which, if ever used, would invite virtual, if not certain, annihilation of `the enemy´. Such a scenario is morally unacceptable to *Les Verts*, as well as being considered strategically inefficient.

As a moral and strategic alternative to this ´final solution´, *Les Verts* suggest a defense which would render the enemy powerless in the face of popular non-violent resistance. The policy of Non Violent Civil Defense (*DCNV: Défense Civile Non Violente*) requires the active participation of the population in preventing the enemy reaching the ideological, economical and political objectives which justify his initial aggression. Such active participation needs to be planned and prepared in advance (organisation networks, acts of civil disobedience, refusal to collaborate, sabotage), but the principal motivation behind it is the need for the population to feel it has something to protect (i.e. culture, tradition) instead of simply delegating its defense to the army. Needless to say, such a strategy rejects the present French attempts to create a third nuclearised power wedge in Europe between the USA and the USSR.

Electoral Support

Very little research has been done on the green vote in France. An early study of the green electorate has not been followed by any further systematic analysis (Boy 1981). In his study, Boy concluded that green voters belonged politically to the centre, while their cultural values and attitudes brought them closer to the extreme-left. An example of this, cited by Boy, is that a much higher proportion (42 percent) of green voters than any other voters in fact rejected nationalism. At the same time, he found that a vote for the Greens was frequently linked to a reduced level of social integration; due to the fact, for example, that a high level of education within the green electorate led to high career expectations which were often not met in reality. In other words a contradiction existed, he suggested, between their high educational qualifications (and consequently high social expectation) and their relatively mediocre socio-economic status. The high level of education among many green voters was further confirmed by a more recent study of green activists which showed that over 30 percent of those interviewed worked in the fields of either education or research (Chafer 1984: 36-44). Boy also suggested that a vote for the ecologists was in part a generation phenomenon, associated with the post-materialist values of the "generation of´68". The empirical study by Müller-Rommel and

Wilke (1981) confirmed these findings. Given the emergence of the French green movement in the aftermath of 1968, it would be surprising if there were no link between the aforementioned generation phenomenon and a vote for the ecologists. It must, however, be said that their propensity to vote for the ecologists varies enormously, as it does among all generations, according to socio-economic status. Very few workers, for example, vote ecologist, while managerial professions are relatively over-represented among ecology voters. In general, however, the green electorate appears to be younger than that of the mainstream political parties.

Outlook

It is difficult to speak of success with respect to the French Greens. Twenty years after the movement of May 1968, from which so much of their cultural inspiration originated, and 14 years after their appearance on the political scene, 3.8 percent of the presidential vote does not stand as proof of outright success. The reasons for this *relative* failure are, perhaps, to be found in three different areas: institutional obstacles, philosophical themes, and political culture.

The *institutional obstacles*, already mentioned, are sizeable. They constitute the principal explanation of *Les Verts* themselves. The electoral system of the 5th French Republic eliminates political minorities in the first round of the elections both politically and financially by tapering the political contest down to a two horse race and by erecting a five percent threshold barrier in order to obtain any form of financial reimbursement. Secondly, the national media (press, television, radio) outside of campaign periods, when air time is officially alloted, practise a form of self-censorship by rarely inviting minority voices to be heard.

One of the underlying *philospohical themes* of a world-wide ecology ´vision´ is the fundamental importance of spiritualism in human activity. A spiritualism which is not necessarily religious in content, but one which allows for its possible inclusion; that takes into account the intuitive aspects of human nature which have been too long buried under our Western deductive rationality. This stress on the importance of intuition is to be found within the feminist tradition which has itself played a large part in the worldwide development of the ecologist movement.

In France this desire to correct the imbalance between an intuitive, spiritualist philosophical tradition, and a rationalist, deductive one has come up against two major obstacles. First of all, René Descartes remains alive and well in the French scientific (social and natural) field; which is to say that the philosophical traditions of rationalism and positivism leave little place for the intuitive aspects of human thought and action. Secondly, the "Vive la Différence" tradition between the French sexes, has managed to overcome the post 1968 shock waves. The feminist movement of the post 1968 period would no longer seem to be in fashion and the sexual stereotypes traditionally associated with French culture have begun to hold sway once again.

The study of *political culture* has stressed the importance of its presence in a political movement. Within the movement itself, it forms a kind of political map which provides a constant point of reference for activists. At the same time it defines the articulation between the specific political culture of a movement and that of the surrounding political environment. That is to say that a minority political culture does not exist in isolation, and this no matter how much it wishes to be "alternative". Political culture, therefore, is an important factor in the development of a social and political movement at two different levels: internal and external practices.

Internal: the theory and practice of social change is the key factor here. The French political ecology movement has, over its 15-year existence, had a permanent problem of over-theoretisation. The weight of the French intellectual tradition is such that in a political movement composed principally of an intellectual earning class, the temptation to theorise often too great. The time spent on internal redrawing of ecologist blueprints can become over-consuming, and, as activists at the highest level admit: "*Let us stop continually starting from scratch and rethinking the world, it's one of the reasons for our lack of progress.*" (Marimot 1987)

Coupled to this, perhaps, is the amount of time spent on defending the independent identity of ecology by activists. It would seem that *Les Verts*, at times, are prey to the exclusive practices typical of the aftermath of May 1968: the smaller the organization, the greater the isolation. That is to say that the *gauchisme* of the late 60s/early 70s has left a cultural heritage which remains present within *Les Verts* and, indeed, several representatives of its higher echelons have had direct experience of it.

On the level of internal practices there seems to be a problem of coherence. Let us examine just two examples: The ecologist movement, world-wide, stresses that a new form of political practice, more participatory and open with less mutual distrust and suspicion, is necessary if the ecologist movement is to make any headway. These laudible sentiments are not always immediately obvious to the observer. The AGMs and CNIRs of *Les Verts* do not always constitute the political reflection of conviviality which ecologists favour and, on the level of form alone, there is very often little to distinguish a meeting of *Les Verts* from those of other organizations: personal attacks, power struggles, and political manoeuvring are all but too prevalent.

Secondly, autonomy is one of the major tenets of ecologist philosophy. Central to this is the idea that citizens should have greater control over their social, economic and political destinies. In a country as centralized as France, this is in itself a major problem for *Les Verts*. Decentralization remains, nevertheless, a central pillar of ecologist philosophy. Therefore, there was great surprise during the 1986 parliamentary elections when the national spokesperson, Y. Cochet, stood in a constituency in the north of the country (Nord-Pas de Calais) when he himself originated from the West (Brittany). This episode, which created considerable internal friction, was seen by opponents within and by outside observers, as an example of the vestiges of a *centralist mentality* clashing with a decentralist ideology. Here the distance between theory and practice, as perceived by the external observer, raises its head.

External: no doubt the first decision to make is that of defining its existence as distinct from the surrounding political cultures, specific or dominant. The definitions are legion and often complementary. One of the problems of the French political ecology movement resides in the difficulty of fully distinguishing their "osmosis" from that of the alternative left. The aforementioned elements: ideology, practices, and theory often overlap between the two groups and it is sometimes difficult to distinguish an open-minded ecologist from an open-minded democratic socialist. Certainly the identity of the movement as an expression of environmental concern has been made in the French collective consciousness. However, their political particularity is insufficiently clear in the minds of people other than activists who are, of course, the people who need persuading.

With regard to the dominant institutional political culture, the 5th French Republic is one which divides the country in two at every national election. This form of division, as we have seen with regard to the institutional obstacle, leaves little room for minority voices to be heard. However, what the system also does is to form cultural patterns of behavior which, once internalised through a process of political socialisation, are not easily renounced. This process of socialisation is of course an obstacle to any radical movement. *Les Verts*, however, culturally extreme as they may once have been, have always fought the theory and practice of the extreme left in French politics. The paradox is that they adopt a position which within the cultural confines of the 5th French Republic, is absolutely a revolutionary one. They have done this, as a political party in the second round of the national elections, by refusing to take part in the tradition of giving their support to one of the two remaining candidates or alternatively, by establishing a political contract with them. This refusal is based on the understandable desire to create an independent political identity- an indispensable element in any specific political culture. The question raised, however, is whether such non-participation, which has the appearance of denying the existence of the dominant political culture, is the best way of achieving this independent political identity. An important supplementary factor concerning the external political culture within the 5th Republic, was the coming to power, for the first time in 1981, of the institutional left. When F. Mitterrand won the presidential elections of that year and the socialist party tidal wave followed in the subsequent parliamentary elections, the French political landscape took on a radically different appearance. The effect of the left´s victory was to demobilize the extra-parliamentary social movements which existed at that time, such as, for example, the ecologists and the regionalists.

As a final remark the phenomenon of political and social ´fads´ is worthy of note. This is, no doubt, a product of any strongly mediatised society, but coupled to the aforementioned intellectual tradition that persists in France the fashions which come and go with such speed (e.g. Feminism, "New Philosophers", Regionalism) represent a sizeable obstacle to the pragmatic necessities of a social and/or political movement with long-term aspirations. Indeed, *pragmatism* is a term which is now cited with some regularity in ecologist and alternative circles. The lesson of Germany is perhaps an important factor here.

In sum, the Greens have to face considerable institutional, philosophical and cultural obstacles in their quest for recognition. The size of these obstacles is particularly great in France for the reasons we have mentioned above. How far they will be successfull in overwhelming them still remains to be seen. Traditions die hard in what often remains, despite the political revolutionary tradition, a somewhat socially conservative country.

Some hope for the Greens lies in the recent election results of A. Waechter. This hope, is based on the experience of their German counterparts, even if the two national contexts diverge considerably. The analysis is that one of the reasons for the success of *Die Grünen* was the lengthy period of power held by the Social Democrats in national government. This experience of social democracy, coupled with an active tradition of citizen participation in local affairs and a greater balance betweeen intellectualism and pragmatism enabled the German *Die Grünen* to carve out a distinct political niche. The reelection of F. Mitterrand in May 1988 may have then opened up a similar possibility in France.

8
Great Britain:
The "Green Party"

Paul Byrne

Development of the Green Party

Britain´s Green party is the oldest in Western Europe, having been founded in 1973, and becoming a recognisable national political party by 1975. It operates within a political system in which some ten percent of the adult population (approximately three million people) belong to a pressure group directly concerned with environmental issues.

The Green party has changed its name twice in its brief history, something which is perhaps symptomatic of its uncertainty over its own role in British politics. Its first incarnation was the People Party, centred around the city of Coventry and dominated by a few charismatic individuals. After a token effort in the two general elections of 1974 (only putting up five and four candidates), the party started to hold national conferences and attempted to form a cohesive political programme. It quickly became clear that there were strong differences of opinion within the new party, the most serious being between those who adopted a broadly left-wing perspective - identifying capitalism, and the type of industrialised and urbanised life which it encouraged, as the root cause of Britain´s malaise - and those whose political philosophy had more in common with right-wing beliefs, their rejection of industrialisation leading them to advocate authoritarianism in both family and political life. (Rüdig and Lowe, 1986)

These disagreements led to resignations from both sides, and the party´s change of name in 1975 to the Ecology Party could not disguise the fact that its very existence was in doubt. It survived, however, not least because of the new leadership which arose from the ashes of the left-right dispute, and was allied to neither faction.

The predominantly young leadership sought to transcend the ideological disputes by formulating the party´s philosophy not in terms of its relationship to capitalism or socialism, but rather in terms of new alternatives - principally decentralisation and an end to the pursuit of economic growth, ideas which have remained central in the party´s ideology. This new approach sufficed to keep the party intact, but the general level of activity within the party declined and the electorate remained largely unaware of it. This situation persisted until 1979, when the party took the gamble of fielding 53 candidates in the general election (Rüdig and Lowe 1986:268). Although they realised that this would almost certainly result in all the candidates losing the financial deposit required by British electoral law, the party´s leaders thought that the (free) television election broadcast to which their number of candidates entitled them would be worth the financial cost. Events seemed to prove them right; although the party only won 1.6 percent of the vote in the constituencies it contested, the Ecology Party became nationally known and membership rose from a mere 650 in 1979 to around 6000 by 1981.

Media exposure was not the only reason for the party´s revival. Developments in public policy, especially on nuclear matters, also contributed to public awareness and interest. The late seventies saw a major public enquiry which eventually endorsed the proposal to equip the British nuclear industry with the facility to reprocess its own and other countries´ nuclear waste (the "Windscale Enquiry"), and a new Conservative Government which was committed to expanding the nuclear energy industry, fully supported NATO´s "twin-track" decision to update nuclear weapons in Europe and decided to update Britain´s "independent" deterrent by acquiring the Trident system. The Ecology Party did attract more support as a result of these developments, but far more people turned to single-issue pressure groups as a means of registering their concern or opposition. Environmental groups (such as Friends of Earth) took the leading role in contesting the expansion of the nuclear energy industry, and the Campaign for Nuclear Disarmament (CND) saw its membership explode from a few thousand in the late seventies to a peak of around 100,000 by 1982/83 (Byrne, 1988). Ever since its inception, the Ecology Party had tried to persuade such groups to recognise it as their party political representative albeit without success.

The beginning of the eighties was a time of optimism for the Greens. Although party membership remained below 10,000, it was now stable and large enough for the party to be credible as a participant in national politics. Despite its very small impact on the electorate in 1979, the party´s strategists took hope from signs that the two-party system in British politics was in decline. Fewer people were voting for the Conservative and Labour parties, and the rise of nationalist parties in Scotland and Wales had shown that people were prepared to consider different electoral alternatives.

This optimism waned, however, as the party was beset by tactical problems. Some of these came from within the party; among the new recruits were a substantial number who not only agreed with green ideology, but also attempted to "live out" this ideology by practising an "alternative" lifestyle - anything from organic farming to communal living, a common theme being the rejection of hierarchy, sexism and racism in all aspects of their lives. Whilst there was much respect within the Ecology Party for those who acted on the principle that " the personal is political", there was less sympathy for them amongst the leadership when it became clear that they had very different ideas on how the party should be structured and the tactics it should adopt. The practitioners of an alternative lifestyle wanted the Ecology Party to behave more like a new social movement than a traditional political party. For example, they argued for a completely decentralised structure (with no national party organisation, as such), intra-party communication to be effected by networking rather than formal structures, and for the party to become fully involved in the unconventional protest and direct action which the more radical single-issue groups were mounting. The party leadership was convinced that such developments would harm the electoral credibility of the party, and managed to resist most of these demands.

Tactical problems also arose outside the party, most notably those caused by the breakaway of the Social Democratic Party from the Labour Party, and the subsequent formation of the SDP/Liberal Alliance. The Ecology Party leadership were not only concerned that they had lost their status as Britain´s newest political party. They also anticipated that, by entering into an alliance with the Liberal Party, the SDP would halt the drift towards green policies which had been taking place among Liberal activists. The Liberal Party, with its commitment to decentralisation, community politics and electoral reform, had much more in common with the Ecology Party than either of the main parties. The formation of the Alliance, however, meant that if the Liberal Party was moving anywhere, it was towards the more centralised style of the SDP.

In short, the Ecology Party went into the 1983 general election facing considerably more competition than it had in 1979. On the "moderate" end of the spectrum, the SDP/Liberal Alliance was presenting itself as the only realistic alternative to the established major parties, and was actively seeking "protest votes" from those desillusioned with alternating Conservative and Labour Governments. On the more "radical" end of the spectrum, single issue groups (and particularly CND) were at the height of their success; they were singled out for attack by the Thatcher government (which arguably made them even more attractive to radical-minded people), and consequently received much more media coverage during the campaign than the Ecology Party. Given this, and the popularity of the Thatcher government´s stand over the Falklands conflict, it is not surprising that the Ecology Party once again failed to make an appreciable impact upon the electorate. The 106 candidates only managed to achieve an average of one percent of the vote where they stood; the best individual result was under three percent. Elections to the European Parliament in 1984 saw 16 Ecology candidates standing, but again they only polled less than three percent of the vote in their constituencies.

In 1985, the party changed its name to the "Green Party" in an conscious attempt to make more of an electoral breakthrough. It was to be disappointed; despite producing a television election broadcast of unprecedented professionalism, the party saw its 133 candidates still receive an average of only 1.4 percent of the vote in the seats they fought. Only ten of its candidates won more than 2 percent of the vote in their constituency; only one candidate managed as much as a 3.5 percent share of the vote. After over a decade of organisation and campaigning, for most of which they had been acknowledged as a national party, the Greens could only persuade just under 90,000 of the British electorate to support them - about the same number that CND was able to motivate into becoming paid-up members of their organisation. To understand this minimal impact, we need to examine the party´s policies, its organisation, and the opportunities which have been open to it.

Programatic Profile

Much of the Green party´s program is well known; opposition to nuclear energy and weaponry, a preference for renewable energy sources and conservation measures generally, a determination to eliminate pollution, the promotion of organic methods of agriculture, and so on. Less well known however, is the foreign policy advocated by the Green party. It reflects the philosophical commitment to self-reliance which is a recurring theme in Green party thinking.Whilst being in favour of international cooperation generally, the Greens would favour British withdrawal from the European Community (which, at least in its present form, is seen as undermining sound ecological principles), withdrawal from NATO and overall lessening of military and economic links with America. Although in favour of increasing aid to Third World countries, the Green party does not want to see such aid simply have the effect of bringing about mass industrialisation which would destroy the environment, traditions and cultural heritage of those countries.

Self-reliance is a concept which also underlies much of the party´s thinking on trade and economic policy generally. Present levels of international trade are seen as unnecessarily high and wasteful of energy and resources. The Greens would introduce tariff barriers to discourage imports, and give some protection to the domestic economy whilst it underwent a radical restructuring. The intention would be to encourage the growth of economic units which are much smaller than at present, but much more self-sufficient in energy and materials. The long-term aim is to move to a "steady-state, sustainable economy" which would operate within "an interlocking system of small communities each as self-sufficient as possible in the necessities of life and in its own management, the whole comprising the Nation" (Green Party Manifesto 1987, Section 2.3).

Unemployment would be tackled by work-sharing, job-creation via schemes to develop alternative sources of energy, more labour-intensive rather than capital-intensive enterprises and , on a more general level, encouraging people to re-think their ideas of what constitutes "employment" such that working on behalf of oneself or one´s community become valid occupations. The Greens would like to see the growth of an "informal" economy alongside the existing structure, in which barter and exchange between individuals, families and small communities becomes commonplace. Whilst such communities and practices were being established, the Greens would introduce a National Income Scheme, guaranteeing a minimum level of material security for all, although the party´s program is somewhat vague on how the tax revenue to finance this would be raised. The financial institutions and money system itself would be reformed.Community Banks would be created which would channel local savings funds into local small businesses and co-operatives.

The Green party would also like to see a commensurate scaling-down of the size of political authorities and institutions. The Greens would not just revive local government, they would make one of its lower-level institutions the keystone of their new political structure. They envisage the present district level of authorities as becoming the basis for new selfgoverning units. It is accepted that such small units could not be completely autonomous of each other, so provision is made for provincial and central levels of government as well. Matters like resource management and pollution control would be dealt with by national-level government, but the district units would have a large say in the raising and spending of revenue. It is debatable whether such a system, if implemented, might not well result in power drifting inexorably upwards to the provincial and national levels. The history of the relationship between central and local government in Britain this century would suggest that this is a strong possibility. It is indicative that even the Greens envisage much of the important decision-making on matters concerning health and education would probably have to take place at the provincial rather than district level. Nevertheless, the point to note in this context is the strong ideological belief in the benefits of decentralisation that underpins the Greens´conceptualisation of how Britain´s political system should operate.

As one might expect, the Greens are also strongly in favour of changing Britain´s electoral system, to put it on a more proportional basis. At their 1987 Annual Conference, the party decided to opt for the Additional Member System (similar to that used in the Federal Republic) as their preferred system. They would also take steps to guarantee individual citizens data protection and freedom of information. In this, as in much of their policy on health and education, their thinking is not dissimilar to that of the Labour Party. The main difference between the two is the persistent emphasis the Greens place upon decentralising and devolving all power and decision-making to the lowest and smallest possible level.

In short, the green ideology is visionary and idealistic. Some of its aims are very long-term. The manifesto argues, for instance, the desirability of using education and persuasion to effect a sufficient reduction in the birth-rate to reduce the total population from 56 million to around 35/40 million (this being the population level that could be sustained by a "self-reliant ecological society"), but admits that this could take a century to achieve. The party program contains so many new and different ideas that it is impossible to give more than an overview in this context.The main themes are a rejection of economic growth at any cost and the devolution of power in virtually all areas of economic, social and political life. Their philosophy is one which transcends not just the interests of one class or group in society, but also the nation itself. Their perspective is truly global, in that their arguments relate to the future of the planet rather than just the nation-state. At the other end of the scale,their concern for the planet leads them to stress the responsibility of the individual. The Greens believe that human activity must be scaled down to the level of the individual living and working within small, inter-connected communities, but with those individuals sharing a common sense of responsibility for the whole earth.

Organisational Structure

Like many new parties and movements, the Green party has devoted considerable time and energy to discussing its own organisation. It is over-simplification, but in broad terms the debate has centred around two schools of thought. On the one hand, there are those who see the function of the party as being a vehicle or catalyst for change in society. They argue that if the party is to compete in the contemporary political system, it has to adopt at least some of the organisational characteristics of its competitors, the existing national parties. In effect, they argue that the party has to have some kind of authority structure in order to produce a coherent programme, and the party machinery to fight elections around that programme - whilst providing, of course, for intra-party democracy as well. On the other hand, there are those who believe that the Green party should run its affairs in a way which mirrors the kind of society the party is arguing for. Consequently, they are strongly in favour of the party decentralising its decision-making as far as possible - indeed, in the early eighties, they were opposed to the very idea of a national party organisation.

This debate preoccupied the party during the early eighties, but the compromises reached then have sufficed to quieten dissent. Pressure for decentralisation has resulted in the local parties, organised at constituency level, being given a key role. Local party organisations have considerably more autonomy than their counterparts in any of the other national parties in Britain. Local parties can determine their own constitutional arrangements, subject only to general guidelines from the national party.Thus, for example, each local party can devise its own arrangements for selecting candidates for Parliamentary and local elections, the only requirement being that the procedure adopted is democratic and allows for participation by all local members. Local parties are grouped together into some fourteen national and regional areas, and area organisations can issue their own manifestoes for local elections, but in practice the local party remains the influential element.

Area organisations are important in one respect: they function as a channel for electing representatives to the national level organisation, the party Council, comprising 22 people. One representative is elected from each of the areas, four are elected by a postal ballot of the entire national membership, and another four members are elected by delegates at the Annual Conference. Individuals may only serve on the Council for a maximum of three years, in order to guard against the possibility of a few people coming to exercise a disproportionate influence. In theory, the party council has considerable power. It elects three chairpersons, who effectively become the party's national spokespersons, and appoints from its own members five national committees to coordinate the work of the party(Committee on annual conferences; media; party mangagement; political issues; elections). In practice, the influence of committees is minimal, largely because the party council is so concerned to avoid charges of fostering hierarchy and bureaucratisation that it delegates little decision-making to its own committees. The party council attempts to reach political conclusions by consensus rather than taking matters to a vote, which has proved to be a very time-consuming exercise. One problem the party council does not face is an abundance of resources. The Green party's total income is about £30,000 a year, almost all of which is derived from membership subscriptions and donations. It does not receive anything other than token donations from pressure groups (and very few of those), unlike Britain's other national parties. There is no provision for public funding of political parties in Britain unless they are represented in Parliament.

As the party Council (and the national committees) only meet four times a year, it cannot be said to be running the party on a day-to-day basis. Local parties retain considerable autonomy, and party council and national officials are often unaware of what is happening at a local level, let alone controlling it. As there is a wide measure of consensus among the membership about the basic values the party espouses, this lack of a centralised authority does not tend to cause serious problems over policy questions. Whether such a structure would remain intact if the Greens were to enjoy electoral success is open to question. There is a long tradition in British parliamentary politics that MP's cannot be directed by extra-parliamentary bodies, which would seem to be at variance with the Green party's attitude towards intraparty democracy. The party constitution does not include any reference to the expectations that would be of any help to green MP´s. Given the party´s electoral record, of course, such considerations remain hypothetical in any case.

Outlook

Two things stand out in any examination of Britain´s Green party. Firstly, it is very different from the other national political parties, both in terms of the extent of its visionary idealism and in the way in which it seeks to run its affairs. Secondly, it is in a very weak position in the competition for national political power. What we must consider now is whether there is a causal relationship between these two factors.

One can certainly argue that the radicalism of the Greens does not enhance its chances of electoral success. British society may well be considered "post-materialist"in comparison with other countries. However, the fact remains that the British electorate has for most of this century been faced with parties which stress materialist values, take a short-term perspective, and tend to be insular, prioritising domestic over foreign affairs. The Green party´s emphasis upon idealism, seeking longterm solutions, and taking a global rather than domestic perspective may be disconcerting to an electorate noted for its pragmatism and aversion to radical change. It must come as something of a surprise to the British voter to be confronted by a party which is actually arguing for a reduction in material standards of living. Moreover, to date the Green party has not been subjected to much comment from the national media. If it ever does attract such attention, it is unlikely that Britain´s national press will resist the temptation to highlight the more extreme or visionary aspects of the party´s programme. Ridicule of idiosyncratic personalities and casting doubt upon the practicality of radical ideas have been tactics which Britain´s predominantly right-wing press have used to considerable effect against both the Labour and Liberal parties in the past; they could certainly be employed against Britain´s Greens.

Even if the Greens were to moderate their ideology and image the structure and working of the British political system would still place major obstacles in their way. Britain´s electoral system is reknowned for discriminating against small parties, and especially so if such parties´ support is geographically spread rather than concentrated. Such electoral support as there is for the Green party comes from both rural and urban areas. Although it does tend to be greater in the South rather than the North, it is far too dispersed for the Greens to gain from the electoral system in the way in which the nationalist parties in Scotland and Wales have been able to. The experience of third parties in Britain's effectively two-party system suggests that it is necessary to obtain somewhere in the region of 30 percent of the national vote before the electoral system starts working in their favour - a target which must test the optimism of even the most committed green supporter.

Another inhibiting factor on the political opportunities open to the Greens is the existence, attitudes and status of the environmental pressure groups. The Green party is effectively competing with these groups (and especially the more radical of them) for people's time, energy and committment. It argues that "green-minded" people should join the party because it tackles root causes, whilst pressure groups are seen as concentrating only upon immediate problems. Even if one accepts this analysis (and the radical pressure groups do not), the Green party cannot pretend to offer much possibility of success at least in the short-term. Arguably this may not matter, as many of those who consider joining either the Green party or a radical movement like CND are motivated by moral reasons rather than pragmatic considerations. In Britain's present political climate-one which is dominated by the Thatcher administrations - anyone opposed to the Thatcherite style of government might well be tempted to compromise their ideals and work for a party which has some change of success at the national level, or a group which concentrates its efforts upon one particular problem area.

Having said that, there are reasons for the Green party to feel some optimism about the future.The impact of super-power agreements about nuclear weapons upon Britain's peace movement is hard to predict.It is however not impossible that it will lead to a decline in popular support for CND (as the problem may seem less pressing), and that people will devote their time and energy to the Green party instead. The merger at present taking place between the SDP and the Liberal Party could well result in the more radical elements within the Liberal Party becoming sufficiently disillusioned with the course the new party is taking that they would consider switching their allegiance to the Greens - this was certainly the hope repeatedly expressed at the Greens'1987 Conference.

Even were these developments to take place, however, they would still leave the Green party as a minor force in terms of membership and electoral support when compared to the more traditional parties. Such a situation is likely to continue unless either the British electorate overcomes its apparent aversion to "wasting" its votes on a party unlikely to win, or Britain's electoral system is changed - something which only the larger parties have the influence to bring about. Until then, the Greens can take some consolation from the way in which the major parties have changed their own programmes to reflect a greater concern for "green issues". The existing parties are conscious of the potential threat to their own bases of support that the Green party represents. The Conservatives know that many of their supporters do place a high priority upon conservation and protection of the environment. The Labour Party is equally aware that a significant part of its support comes from that part of the middle class which does not allow economic self-interest to wholly determine their political allegiance - and have attempted to head off the potential green challenge by modifying their own ideological stances. In this way, by its very existence, the Green party has extended the parameters of policy options in British politics. The idealism of its supporters is such that it is likely to survive as a participant on the national political scene even if this is its only concrete achievement.

9
Italy:
The "Liste Verdi"

Mario Diani*

Development of the Green Lists

The very first example of local green parties in Italy date to 1980, when some small autonomous ecological groups fielded candidates at the city council elections in four towns (Usmate, Mantova, Este, Lugo di Romagna). Their number grew to 16 in 1983, including the Alternative List for Other South Tyrol (Alternative Liste für Andere Süd-Tirol), a rainbow coalition set up in South Tyrol in order to challenge the conservative orientations of the dominating People´s Party (Süd-Tiroler Volks Partei). The Alternative List polled 4.5 percent of the vote in the province of Bolzano, with a peak of 8 percent in the chief town (DeMeo and Giovannini 1985; Del Carria 1986).

In their early phase, the presence of Green lists was rather sporadic, and limited in most cases to towns and villages with specific environmental problems. Between 1984 and 1985, however, delegates from several local groups active in the ecology movement and in other social movements, met in national conventions and decided to coordinate participation of the Greens in the local administrative elections of May, 1985. On that occasion, about 150 lists stood in the elections, 12 of which competed at the regional level. On the whole, they polled 636.000 votes (2.1 percent of the total voters in the electoral districts where they competed), gaining

*Some sections of this article draw upon a paper I gave in the workshop "New social movements and the political system" during the ECPR Joint Sessions held in Amsterdam, April 1987. I wish to thank the participants in the workshop for their helpful comments. A grateful thank goes also to Roberto Biorcio (University of Trento), who kindly agreed to show me his data about the green activists and voters before their publication.

141 seats in the representative assemblies: 10 at the regional level, 16 at the provincial level, and 115 at the city councils level.

The result improved slightly in the June 1987 elections for the national parliament, when about one million voters (2.5 percent of the total, with peaks over 6 percent in several urban areas) elected 13 green representatives to the lower assembly (Camera dei Deputati) and two to the higher (Senato).

Although the rise of the green lists has been paralleled by a growing ecology movement (Diani 1988; Biorcio, 1988c), it would be misleading to view this as the sole explanation for the Greens' success. In fact, many other factors must be taken into account, among them, the presence of potential leaders, or "political entrepreneurs", able to mobilize potential support for green issues; the characteristics of the electoral system; the absence of real competitors in the political system.

Through the social movements of the 1970s a political counter-elite has emerged (leaders of grass-roots groups, members of "alternative science" committees, journalists in alternative medias, radical intellectuals) (Melucci 1984). Their integration into a wider political and cultural' elite has not always been easy, especially for those who refused to join either the traditional left parties or the Workers' Democracy party (*Democrazia Proletaria* - DP). Such a persistant lack of legitimation may have caused some of them to seek institutionalization in the classic electoral channel.

Several opportunities have facilitated their effort. The first one concerns the relative "openness" of the Italian electoral system. Very close to a pure proportional system (imperiali quota system), it allows even small and loosely structured parties a good chance to gain seats, provided they are able to reach a full quota in at least one electoral district. This makes participation in the elections particularly appealing to parties and lists originating from social movements, as such quotas are easiest to reach in the metropolitan districts (Milan and Rome) where social movements have their deepest roots.

The opportunities for new parties are usually wider if there are no substantial competitors in the political arena. This has been the case with the Italian Greens too, as no major party has shown concern for ecological issues except recently - which does however not qualify them as reliable representatives of ecological demands. Indeed, the Radical Party (*Partito Radicale* - PR) and Worker Democracy are the only real competitors for the Greens, being the only political groups to have paid long term attention to environmental problems. More precisely, the former would be expected to attract support from potential green voters who are most concerned with environmental issues, whereas the latter would appeal to green sympathizers who pay more attentions to social and political themes. Some scholars have even analyzed the Radical Party as an early example of the Italian green party (Müller-Rommel 1982; Rüdig 1986). On the other hand, it must be stressed that both the Radical Party and Workers´ Democracy are only partial competitors of the Greens. The Radicals concentrate their efforts on the national elections, paying much less attention to the local ones, green lists where they fought their first large-scale battle in 1985, and the most uncertain one. Actually, activists from the Radical Party have often made a significant contribution to the creation of the green lists. Only in a few cities, among which Turin is the most important, did conflict occur between the radicals and other green activists, resulting in two competing parties at the polls. Generally speaking, the Radical Party is a far less dangerous competitor for the Greens than Workers´ Democracy, whose local branches are much stronger and more widespread. The ecological commitment of this party has steadily grown in the last years, ranging from antinuclear campaigns to legislative action against hunting. Nevertheless, the stress they put on the role of the party and on a marxist approach deprives them of the support from those sectors of the green constituency who are most moderate and/or fed up with traditional party politics.

A look at the Italian experience suggests the existence of a twofold connection: one between the green lists and the current ecology movement and one between the lists and wider social movement sectors (peace movement, women´s movement, alternative movement). The same electoral programmes provide evidence of the Greens´ intention to represent both environmental concerns and other social and political issues. As is the case in other European countries, Italian Greens have campaigned for the rights of the more deprived sectors of society (youth, disabled people, prisoners); for grass-roots democracy and people´s self-government; against the development of the "warfare" state, nuclear weapons, etc.

Data from a national sample of green activists is consistent with this finding (Biorcio 1988a). For the large majority of the lists´ members (85 percent), the support paid to green politics is just the last step in a long-lasting political career, mostly spent in loosely structured groups fostering unconventional patterns of political participation. Fifty percent of the lists´ members belong to environmental groups. Although most overlapping memberships favor political ecology groups (33 percent of the sample are also active in the League for the Environment), a significant share (19 percent) are involved in more traditional organizations like WWF or Italia Nostra.

It is also possible to make a socio-demographic comparison between green activists and activists in the ecology movement (Diani and Lodi 1988). The movement and lists´ activists are quite similar in gender, occupation and education, although the latter are much younger, probably due to weaker support the Greens have among the more traditional sectors of the movement. Indeed, the socio-demographic features of Italian green activists confirm that the rise of green parties in Western Europe is related to the growth of a new, young and well educated, middle class, which has largely been influenced by "post-green party values". They are, therefore, more inclined to commit themselves to unconventional issues, cross-cutting traditional political cleavages, such as peace and unilateral desarmament, or environmental protection. In spite of the wide support that the green lists get among activists of the ecology movement, and in spite of the socio-demographic affinity between their respective constituencies, the reaction of the main environmental associations to the creation of the lists has been less than enthusiastic. Indeed, when the debate arose about the opportunity for the ecology movement to field their own candidates at the local elections in 1985, the biggest organizations refused to lend support, still allowing their members to engage on an individual basis. The only exception was the "Friends of the Earth", who played an important role in the formation of the lists. Meanwhile, the most established groups like Italia Nostra and WWF were particularly explicit in refusing the Greens any legitimation as representatives of the movement, and treating them as any other political party. The League for the Environment showed a stronger interest without, however, taking an official position.

The cautious attitude of the established organizations toward the lists makes it hazardous to consider the latter as the "political branch" of the former; however, that does not seem to affect negatively the creation of specific local alliances, which often involve even the most traditional groups. In fact, a more detailed analysis of the network structure of the ecology movement shows that the position of the green lists is not marginal at all (Diani 1988). On the contrary, green lists are often involved in fruitful cooperations with ecology groups and associations.

Electoral Support

The distribution of electoral support for the Greens does not differ significantly, when the results of the administrative elections are compared with those of the national polls, which were held two years later. In both cases, voters from northern and central Italy were much more sympathetic to the Greens than voters from the South, where in 1985 only ten representatives (out of a total of 141) were elected to local councils. No parliamentary seats were won in the South in 1987. Support for the Greens seems to be positively related to standards of socio-economic modernization and urbanization. The largest share of the vote has in fact come from the metropolitan areas (Turin 3.8 percent, Milan 4.4 percent, Rome 3.8 percent) and from smaller, but even more affluent towns with developed economic structures (e.g. Trento 7.3 percent, Vicenza 5.7 percent, Mantova 5.8 percent) (Manconi 1985; Gentiloni and Zamboni 1987).

According to the analysis of electoral flows (Biorcio 1988b), most green votes have come from people who had chosen either the radical, the socialist, or the republican party in the previous elections (1983); a smaller share came from former supporters of Workers´ Democracy, whereas the contribution from both the communist and the democratic-christian constituency was rather poor. These findings suggest that the Greens have proved much more able to attract "opinion voters", whose electoral behavior shifts according to their evaluation of specific issues, than "committed voters", whose choice is highly stable, being influenced by identification with a specific political subculture (Parisi and Pasquino 1977).

In terms of socio-demographic variables, the green voters seem rather similar to the green activists: they are over represented among young and middle class people, active in the tertiary sector (see Table 9.1). On the other hand, they seem to cover a much wider spectrum of political and social opinions than the activists. Whereas the latter generally consider themselves leftwing, the former look much more moderate. In contrast to the activists, the voters also have a positive attitude to traditional opponents of the social movements such as institutions, the church and employers´ associations (Biorcio 1988b).

The findings suggest that green voters only partially overlap with voters of the parties that could be seen as "potential competitors" (Radical Party and Workers´ Democracy): whereas about three quarters of people voting for either DP or PR are also likely to vote for the ecologists, the opposite holds true for less than one third of green voters (Biorcio 1988b). We can conclude that, at least as far as electoral choices are concerned, the cross-cultural nature of

Table 9.1
Socio-Demographic Background of Green Voters in Italy, 1986 (in percentages)

Socio-Demographic Variables	Would surely vote for the Greens	Might vote for the Greens
Gender		
Male	2.5	34.1
Female	2.7	35.3
Occupation		
Housewives	1.9	30.4
Retired people	1.3	25.6
Unemployed	2.2	47.2
Farmers	0.0	26.5
Manual workers	2.0	34.8
Shopkeepers/Craftsmen	2.2	33.1
Students	10.8	54.6
White collar	4.0	41.0
Teachers	10.3	62.9
Professionals/Managers	0.0	36.2
Education		
Primary School	0.7	24.9
Secondary School	4.1	40.7
High School	3.8	45.2
University	6.3	50.0
Age		
18-24	5.0	47.4
25-34	4.2	42.6
35-44	2.3	36.2
45-54	1.6	32.2
55 and older	1.4	25.0
The whole sample	2.6	34.7

Source: Biorcio (1988b)

ecological issues seems to have proven effective in mobilizing a heterogenous constituency, which would be hard to place on a strict left-right scale. In fact, the moderate political background of this constituency differs greatly from the leftist background of the activists. Thus, a political alliance is created between radical and moderate sectors of society which is rather unusual, if not totally new, in the Italian political arena, while being quite common in northern Europe countries.

Organizational Structure

Local green lists are usually similar to rather unstructured grass-roots groups, at least partially relying on other groups and associations for organizational support. There is no formal membership and anyone can participate in the local open meetings where decisions are made. The lack of formal rules has sometimes been harshly criticized by moderate sectors of the lists as well as by activists close to the Radical Party, on the basis that a loose organizational structure may be exposed to the domination of an "active minority" (i.e., of the restricted number of people either able or willing to spent most of their time and efforts in the lists´ activities) (Lodi 1988).

At the national level, the constitution of the official Italian Green party is very unpopular among activists, who prefer by a large majority a federative solution (71 percent vs. 6 percent, see Biorcio 1988a). Even the formal constitution of the Italian Federation of Green Lists, which occured in November, 1986, has been opposed by some sectors of the movement, who consider it as a threat to the autonomy of local lists. Regional lists have two official representatives in the federation, whereas city and provincial lists have one. Only appointed representatives have the right to speak and vote in the periodical meetings, although passive attendance is open to anyone. A coordinating committee with 11 members has also been set up, whose one-year mandate is meant to provide the lists with a permanent representative body able to coordinate national campaigns. Due to the sudden crisis of the Italian government and the call for new elections one year before schedule, that committee has in fact organized the Greens´ electoral campaign, once again under the criticism of those who charged it with acting as a factual leadership of the lists. (To be fair, it must be emphasized that only one out of 11 committee members gained a seat in the Parliament).

After the good electoral result of June 1987, the Greens are now facing some new political dilemmas which have relevant organizational implications. First of all, debate about the nature and future of the Federation is once more intense, as several local lists and influential members are strongly opposing the decision, taken by the national meeting of the Federation held in December, 1987, to become the only legal representative of the *Liste Verdi* in Italy. That decision is viewed, in fact, as the first step towards the foundation of a formal "Green Party".

The use of the impressive amount of money (several million dollars) which is going to flow into the movement´s cash, thanks to the law about public funding of political parties, is another crucial point. Up to now, the green lists have operated on the basis of a very tight budget (e.g., the whole 1987 electoral campaign cost no more than 150.000 dollars, which is the usual amount for a single ambitious candidate in a governative party). While it is not yet clear who will be appointed to manage such a large sum of money, it seems certain that it will not be used to build up bureaucratic structures; on the contrary, national scale single-issue campaigns will probably be financed, as well as the creation of an ecological scientific institute, in order to encourage research on environmental topics.

Last but not least, a relevant organizational dilemma concerns the role of the parliamentary group, and its relationships to the lists. In order to prevent the insurgence of any bureaucratic control over it, no formal links have been established between the Federation and the green MPs. The latter will work in full autonomy, only being held accountable to their voters and the wider ecology movement. On the other hand, they will not be allowed to act as the official representatives of the green lists, either.

The looseness of organizational structures in the green lists has surely facilitated coexistence between different sectors of the lists, and prevented the rise of factionalism. Impressive quarrels have nevertheless occured from time to time. Besides the organizational dilemmas emphasized above, another relevant debate concerned the choice of candidates in the elections, which sometimes resembled the widespread sectarianism of the social movements in the 1970s. A first conflict opposed the male majority to the female activists, who urged a 50 percent presence of women among both candidates and representatives. Although that plea was far from being fully satisfied (women were in fact about the 30 percent of total candidates), it was successful in recalling the issue of a "women´s question" within the green movement (Ingrao 1986). Another disputed question was whether priority in the lists should be given to grass-roots activists of the movement or to prominent figures of the environmentalist culture, who had not given any previous contribution to the lists. Once again, sectors opposing any centralizing tendency criticized decisions to choose candidates without a specific political background in the green movement. Both administrative and national elections eventually sharpened the disagreements between the libertarian sectors of the green lists and those activists who feel closer to the league for the Environment and to the traditional left. The former considered the massive presence of members of the League in the green lists as a hidden effort to submit the green movement to the strategy of the Communist Party (it must be recalled that the League for the Environment was until recently a branch of ARCI, the mass cultural organization jointly run by the Communist and the Socialist Party). Meanwhile, the latter charged the sympathizers of the Radical Party in the lists with longing for hegemony over the green movement. In spite of these conflicts, however, splits occured only in some local elections in 1985, which I have already pointed out above.

Outlook
The rise of green lists in Italy may be seen as the product of a set of factors, including the growing concern for environmental issues among public opinion, the characteristics of the electoral system and the lack of real competitors among existing political parties. No explanation could prove fully satisfactory, however, without considering the role of a small group of political entrepreneurs. Indeed, the Greens were able to exploit successfully the positive configuration of the political opportunity structure, in spite of the fact that the strongest and most established organizations in the ecology movement at first refused to support, and sometimes even opposed the creation of green lists.

While it would be hazardous to draw any conclusion about the impact of the Greens on political institutions and the political system as a whole, we can point out that impressive changes in the relationship between the ecology movement and the lists have recently occured. All the most important ecology associations except Italia Nostra have for instance made a joint public statement in March, 1987, urging the Greens´participation in the forthcoming national elections.

In order to explain this shift, we can assume that the two-years experience the Greens had in local institutions has made the persisting centrality of political parties within the Italian political system more evident to the ecology movement associations. Whereas in other Western countries political demands may be channeled through either political parties or pressure groups, in Italy the role of the latter is more limited. The only relevant exception is the Trade Unions and employers´associations. More specifically, Italy lacks a tradition in the field of "public interest groups", pursuing universalistic and collective goals. This is also emphasized by statistics on formal membership in environmental and ecological associations: the total membership of the main organizations does not exceed 1 million in Italy, compared to 3 million or more in Germany and Great Britain (Poggio 1983; Lowe/ Goyder 1983; Rucht 1987; Diani 1988). At the same time, political parties have extended their role as far as undertaking functions traditionally performed by interest groups or other organizations.

Due to the unusual relevance of party politics in Italy, the Greens´decision to run in the elections has been met with more media response than any previous mobilization by ecology groups and associations. The global impact of the ecology movement on public opinion has consequently increased. At the same time, the ecology movement as a whole is now identified with the green lists. Many activists in the ecology associations are now aware of such identification, and more inclined to cooperative efforts with the lists. They may still be critical of the original decision to participate in political elections, but now that green lists exist in Italy, they feel that any future success or failure of such lists will reflect on the ecology movement as a whole. For these reasons, wider and wider sectors of the movement consider a more intense presence of established ecology associations vital. What patterns of relationship between the ecology groups and the green lists will prevail (federation, informal cooperation, etc.) is now a subject for open debate in the next years.

10
Ireland:
The "Green Alliance"

David M. Farrell*

Development of the Green Alliance

In December 1981 a Dublin-based teacher, Christopher Fettes, founded the Ecology Party of Ireland (*EPI*). Fettes already had a long background in activities relating to ecological and naturalist concerns. By the early 1980s he was of the opinion that interest groups were not a sufficient means of affecting change in public and (especially) elite opinion. Ecological parties were emerging in many European countries and it seemed an opportune time to set up such a party in Ireland. A minority coalition government had been elected in June 1981 which looked like falling at any moment (Penninan and Farrell (1987). The new party could have some hope of influencing events either through having some candidates elected and holding the balance of power, or, more realistically, by putting ecological issues high on the public agenda and thereby affecting changes within the established parties. In the event things moved much faster than anticipated. The government fell in February 1982, before the *EPI* had had time to adequately develop a campaign organisation. The party fielded no candidates; instead, a leaflet was issued informing voters "you will certainly have the opportunity to vote for our radically sane policies on future occasions".

Such an occasion was to arise quickly. The government elected in February 1982 was again a minority government and it fell in November of the same year. The *EPI* fielded seven candidates in this election, winning a disappointing 0.22 percent of the total national vote (1.26 percent in the seven constituencies with *EPI*

*This chapter is based on interviews with several individuals from the Green Alliance, particularly Christopher Fettes, Paul O'Brian and Maire Mullarney, and on some access to documents. The Department of the Environment was most helpful in providing electoral data.

candidates). However, this bad result has to be seen in the context of the three elections which had been held in eighteen months. Under such circumstances the voters would most likely support the established parties in the hope of achieving some form of governmental stability. In short, 1982 was not an ideal year for launching a new party. The *EPI* was quite a centralised organisation, comprising a central committee and a system of branches in several urban locations around the country.

In 1983/1984 the *EPI* was completely reconstituted, with a new organisational form and a new name, Green Alliance (which is an English translation from the Gaelic *Comhaontas Glas*). Essentially the new party is different from the old only in organisational terms; the policies have not so much changed as developed. In 1986, a split occurred within the Green Alliance between the majority of members who sought to promote ecological and related concerns and a smaller group of activists who held more forthright anarchical standpoints: for example, they were against the idea of the Green Alliance as an "organisation"; they also pushed for greater recourse to "alternative" forms of political expressions. Inevitably, this group left the party.

Organisational Structure

The Green Alliance has a very decentralised organisational structure. As the title suggests it consists of an alliance of various green groups (currently ten) located throughout the country, but particularly in the Dublin area. Each of the groups has its own constitution and operates quite independently of the centre. The requirements for a group wishing to affiliate to the Green Alliance are: a subscription fee, approval of the Alliance fielding candidates in elections and adherence to the party`s principles (dealt with below). The party`s aim is to be as decentralised as possible. There is very little central apparatus. The headquarters is a tiny, cramped office located appropriately enough in a potential "development zone" in Dublin. The staff are volunteers. The party is financed by private donations and from a small levy on the individual groups. There is no central list of members; one "guesstimate" puts current membership at about three hundred.

The decision-making process is designed for a small organisation: there is a heavy emphasis on "consensus" as the basic organisational principle. Green Alliance representatives readily agree that some changes would be necessary were the organisation to become larger. Each individual member has a say in the design of policy.The pattern is that an ad hoc working group (which could be a local group) forms to draw up some policy proposals over an issue, inviting input from the membership as a whole. Successive drafts are then circulated to the various groups who discuss them among themselves and try to reach some consensus. Any one group can veto a proposal.

The party has several officers - this is largely to fill legal requirements for being recognised as a political party in Ireland (Chubb 1983: 107-8) - which include a treasurer, a European representative, the editor of the party`s newsletter (currently Christopher Fettes), and three "co-ordinators". None of these individuals is formally in charge of the party; there is no party leader. The central administration of the Green Alliance is the Council which meets on average every two months. This is made up of one delegate from each of the groups (plus an observer) and the officers who are *ex officio* members. To date the members of the Council have been nominated without election.

The Council is not a decision-making body, except on such administrative matters as require quick decisions (e. g. whether to only serve vegetarian food at a party convention). It is there to represent the interests of the individual groups. All decisions on policy and constitutional matters are taken by the party membership. The highest level of decision-making is the National Convention of all party members which occurs bi-annually, each time in a different location around Ireland.

The party`s activists tend to be young, university-educated (from the humanities and the sciences), middle-class, and increasingly male. There are some connections with interest groups in related areas (e.g. Campaign for Nuclear Disarmament - CND; or the Irish Peace Council). By the nature of the background of many activists there is little attraction towards close co-operation with the trade unions. In most cases the only relationship with interest groups occurs through overlapping memberships (e.g. with Earthwatch or Friends of the Earth).

Electoral Support

The first election fought by the new Green Alliance party was for the European Parliament in 1984. Fettes was nominated as the party´s only candidate in the Dublin constituency and won a respectable 1.9 percent of the vote. The party`s first major election campaign was to come a year later, the 1985 local elections. The party ran thirty-four candidates in urban areas throughout the country (twenty-eight of these in Dublin constituencies), winning 0.55 percent of the vote

(2.26 percent in the thirty-four constituencies with Green Alliance candidates). This was more than double the November 1982 vote achieved by the *EPI*. The party also succeeded in having one candidate elected to an urban district council in Co. Kerry.

The Green Alliance`s first general election campaign was in February 1987. The party contested nine of the country`s forty-one constituencies (running six of their candidates in Dublin constituencies) and got 0.40 percent of the national vote (1.79 percent in the nine constituencies). This was a drop from their 1985 result. However the 1985 figure was bound to have been somewhat inflated as it was a mid-term election with many voters taking the opportunity to register a protest vote. The 1987 result represented more accurately the base vote of the Green Alliance (see table 10.1).

The party`s vote is too small to allow analysis of survey data, so any consideration of the sociodemographic characteristics of Green Alliance voters can at best be only cursory. The only point which can be made with some certainty is that the party`s vote is largely an urban one, due to the fact that the party fights campaigns almost exclusively in urban areas.Some clues as to the characteristics of Green Alliance voters are provided by the Irish electoral system of proportional representation by the single transferable vote. Under this system voters can indicate preferences for all candidates on the ballot paper regardless of party, transfering their vote from candidate to candidate. An analysis of transfer patterns indicates several features about the Irish voter, such as the degree to which he votes exclusively for one party or the expression of coalition preference by the direction in which votes transfers from party to party. In this case, an examination of transfers from eliminated Green Alliance candidates can indicate something about the type of voter attracted to the Green Alliance. The data which give a breakdown of Green Alliance transfer patterns in the 1985 local elections and the 1987 general election provide evidence to support the Green Alliance claim that it represents neither side of the ideological spectrum of left versus right. In both elections the voters tranferred quite evenly between parties on the centre-right (Fianna Fail, Fine Gael and the new Progressive Democrats) and parties on the left (Labour and the Workers Party). The fact that the parties on the centre-right received proportionately more votes than parties on the left (38.5 percent versus 31.5 percent) probably reflects their overall dominance of the centre-right over the Irish party system (Gallagher 1985). There are two other features about Green Alliance voters: First,they are not very "exclusive": in 1985 only 11.4 percent of Green Alliance votes did not transfer to any other candidate; in 1987 that had dropped a bit lower to 9.8 percent. Second, in both elections the plurality of voters transfered either to Fine Gael or to Labour, the two parties which have formed coalition government on five separate occasions. This suggests, at the least, a certain compatability in support between these two "established" parties and the Green Alliance.

Table 10.1
Electoral Results for the Irish Green Alliance in the 1987 General Elections

Constituency	No. of candidates	No. of 1st preferences	% of first preferences
Dublin North	1	1061	3.12
Dublin North-West	1	504	1.46
Dublin South	1	1377	2.40
Dublin-South-East	1	1094	2.86
Dublin West	1	587	1.14
Dun Laoghaire	1	929	1.67
Kerry South	1	708	2.13
Limerick East	1	241	0.49
Wicklow	1	658	1.43
Total for country	9	7159	0.40

Source: Official Electoral Statistics

Programatic Profile
Section two of the Green Alliance`s constitution sets down the party´s basic principles which can be summarised as follows: environmental protection and the conservation of natural resources; decentralised decision-making; the urgent need for world peace; and the redistribution of wealth to the Third World. The party´s policies have been developed in line with these principles. There already are a large set of policies, but there are some gaps. For instance,a working group is currently trying to formulate the party´s overall economic policies which will have as a main role the function of demonstrating that the Green Alliance cannot be classified as "leftist" or "rightist".

In the 1987 election the Green Alliance produced a party program summarising much of their policies, only a sketch of which can be given here. On the economy the party proposed: each individual should be guaranteed, without conditions, a sufficient basic income; a move towards labour-intensive, locally-based industries; organic farming; the breaking of bank monopolies; tax equalisation; and a rescheduling of Ireland´s national debt. The party´s social policies included: educational reform to increase learning outside of school; positive discrimination for Gaelic speakers and the teaching of Esperanto; greater concentration on preventive medicine and nutritious diets. The Green Alliance argued that in society emphasis should be on decentralisation to individual or community level, with the encouragement of co-operative organisations. Civil rights should be promoted by such means as reduced discrimination, reduced sexism and a freedom of information act.

The Green Alliance´s international policies are derived from the party´s emphasis on consensus: in Northern Ireland people should be encouraged to discuss the issues fully prior to voting on a *range* of alternative solutions to the crisis (they wanted to get away from the "either/or" scenario which traditionally characterises Northern Irish politics); Ireland should be more forthright as a neutral country; disarmament (no mention of unilateralism); and wealth redistribution to the Third World, with an emphasis on self-help. Finally, the party´s ecological policies are much as would be expected: anti-nuclear; anti-pollution; energy conservation and alternative sources; urban conservation; a ban on animal tests; and the encouragement of ecological modes of transport.

Outlook

The Irish case, so far, is one of a green party without a support base. There is an active organisation which fields candidates in elections; a committed set of volunteer workers who run a national headquarters; and a steady output of policy documents. The one element missing is a ready electorate. It cannot be emphasised enough that the Green Alliance is a very small party. Their vote has risen since 1982, but only gradually. Public awareness of the party is still very small. Therefore, the main strategic emphasis is on increasing overall awareness whether at the local or national level. But there are many obstacles in their path which can be grouped into four broad categories: electoral, organisational, institutional, and environmental.

The Irish electoral system, on a scale of proportionality, lies in-between the British plurality system and the list systems used in other European countries (Gallagher 1987a). As such, smaller parties are not treated quite as fairly as in continental European countries. The Green Alliance also has some organisational features which - while probably not so far an obstacle - could cost them some votes. For instance, the lack of a party leader prevents voters from identifying with one aspect party image; it could also hinder media focus. Furthermore, the emphasis on consensual decision-making does not augur well for a smooth-running campaign machine.

Institutionally speaking the party is not helped by the peculiarities of the Irish party system. For some time Irish party politics has been characterised as "without social bases" (Whyte 1974). There is some recent evidence suggesting changes (Laver *et.al.* 1987). Nevertheless, the undisputable fact is that the left-right dimension does not readily fit the pattern of party division in Ireland (Sinnott 1985b). For instance, in 1987 the parties of the centre-right won 83.3 percent of the vote; those of the left got 10.1 percent - a not so uncommon result in Ireland. In this context, the Green Alliance´s claim to be transcending left-right divisions in society does not stand out as especially unique. Another institutional point has to do with whether there is the potential for the Green Alliance to attract floating voters. An examination of the Irish voter in the early 1980s suggested few signs of increasing volatility (Marsh 1985). By 1987 this had changed and the election saw some dramatic shifts in voting patterns (not least the remarkable 11.9 percent vote for the Progressive Democrats in their first election)(Gallagher 1987b) yet, the Green Alliance did not benefit.

Finally there is irony that the Irish case, on environmental grounds, is not one well suited for a green party. Traditionally, Ireland has never had a strong industrial base. The country skipped the industrial revolution moving rather swiftly in the 1950s and 1960s from an agricultural to a service economy. As a result the country is, environmentally, relatively well off. This is not to deny the existence of great concern over such issues as city conservation, smog scares, and river pollution. However, in comparison with other countries Ireland does have quite a clean environmental slate. As for nuclear power, a proposal to build a nuclear generating station in the late 1970s met with considerable public protest and was subsequently dropped when both the ending of the oil crisis and a downturn in the Irish economy caused a reassessment of the country´s energy needs. Today the anti-nuclear protests are directed against British stations which are said to pollute the Irish east coast.

Significantly, these disputes have been taken up by the Irish government.

In sum, the prospects for the Green Alliance do not look good in terms of vote percentages. There are, however, indications that environmental issues are receiving greater attention by Irish politicians and in that sense at least something of a "Green" message is being promoted. Whether this has resulted from pressure by the Green Alliance remains open to question.

11
Luxembourg: The "Greng Alternative"

Thomas Koelble

Development of the Green Party

The Luxembourg green party, *Dei Greng Alternativ*, was founded in June 1983 to provide the various protest movements (ecology, women`s and foreign workers rights, peace, anti-nuclear) an electoral option at the 1984 national and European elections. In Luxembourg these elections are run concurrently and naturally the national elections take precedent.

The party scored an impressive 6.1 percent election result in its maiden voyage into party politics. The party contested two of the four electoral constituencies. Luxembourg has a proportional representation system with four electoral constituencies in which the parties put up lists of candidates. The election result was sufficient to give the party two representatives in the 64 member Luxembourg parliament. This equals the performance of the Communist Party which has contested elections since the 1920´s but has proved singularly incapable of exploiting the severe economic crisis prevailing in its electoral bastions in southern Luxembourg. It is precisely in this southern region as well as the urban central constituency where the Luxembourg Greens contested the election.

The emergence of the *Greng Alternativ* was preceded by the efforts of numerous citizen initiatives in the ecological movement to oppose goverment plans to introduce nuclear power plants to Luxembourg during the 1970´s. In 1979 a list of environmental activists contested the elections under the label of *Alternative Leescht - Wiert Ich* (Alternative List - Defend Yourselves - AL WI). They gained only one percent of the vote. It was obvious to the activists that some form of party organization would be far more effective in the electoral arena. Although Greng Alternativ is not an extension of AL-WI, many of its candidates and members were active in the AL.

By 1985 the party had 120 dues-paying members (Rüdig 1985:61).

The political and economic context in which one has to place the emergence of the Luxembourg Greens is one of political consociationalism and economic corporatism. With the structural crisis of the dominant steel industry (Arbed Steel is the biggest employer and foreign currency earner in this tiny state) this political and economic system of consultation has been eroded (Hirsch 1986). The *Greng Alternativ* is as much a protest against environmental damage and industrial policies in Luxembourg, as it is a protest against the corporatist decision-marking process.

Luxembourg´s party system reflects the division of the population into a socialist, liberal and catholic camp (Hartmann, 1979). The catholic party has represented mainly rural interests and has been able to hold some 30 percent of the vote throughout the years since World War II. It is the pivotal party in Luxembourg´s government formations. The party stands for a "social market economy" along the lines of the West German Christian Democratic Union (CDU) where the state via welfare and other transfer payments is used to deflect the costs of economic adjustments on affected social groups. The formation of either liberal-catholic or catholic-socialist or even grand coalitions has been an expression of remarkable political stability. Only the communist party has been excluded from political power by the larger parties.

In economic matters, Luxembourgs´ capital, labor and the state developed a corporatist system of consultation (Hirsch 1986). In return for labor restraint, capital and the state provided the workers with rising wages, social security programs and extensive work benefits. But as the economic crisis of the steel industry in Luxembourg deepened, this trilateral accommodation started to disintegrate because increasingly the union membership had to carry the burden of industrial adjustment. By the late 1970´s it was no longer possible for the goverment to keep indigenous unemployment low by restricting the influx of foreign workers. By 1981 the "Tripartite Committee " found it impossible to agree upon the needed economic measures to both shut down uneconomic plants and reduce the socio-economic impact of largescale unemployment.

In a small economy such as Luxembourg, the crisis of one major employer is a national crisis. Once Arbed Steel was in trouble, the political authorities realized that other means of employment had to be found. This meant attracting new businesses and work to the region. Through a variety of measures such as taxbreaks and cheap loans for new firms, highways and offices buildings, the government attracted employment opportunities. This strategy worked, but it also brought with it dislocations, especially since many of these new projects were placed in previously residential, rural or semirural settings. Not only were established communities disrupted some of the new technologies were opposed on the basis of their intrinsic danger. The attempt to bring the nuclear industry from France and West Germany to the duchy sparked popular unrest.

Organizational Structure

The *Greng Alternativ* is a party which seems to have not only copied much from the Green party in Germany, but has also learned from its counterpart´s mistakes. The party insists on the rotation principle for its representatives and functionaries. The assumption is that if representatives are rotated out of office and replaced by other members, the party will avoid the establishment of a political oligarchy which works to maintain its own rather than the interests of the movement it is supposed to represent. All party meetings are open to all members. However, the party does not sport the divisiveness of its German counterpart. Internal divisions are met with statutory regulations requiring minority opinions to be published next to the majority decisions. The minority position will be publicized as long as it does not contravene the five basic principles of the party which are that the party represents "ecological, social, solidaristic, radical democratic, and peaceful " political aims.

The party consists of a national level (National Convention, a Full Convention and an Extra-Ordinary Convention), a local or regional level and the disrict level. The National Convention consists of all party members and is the highest decision-making authority. Its meetings are open to the public but only party members have a vote. The stated aim of the convention is to provide a forum for all views in the party to be aired. Decisions can be made if one third of the members are present and are taken by a three-fifth majority. If there are less than one third present, decisions can only be made if they are taken by 3/5 majority, are then written up and sent to all party members. If ten percent of the members then protest the decision, it has to be discussed again at the next National Convention. Decisions are binding to the entire party.

The Full Convention meets four times a year. It debates a particular issue or policy area which has been prepared by either the coordinating council or a working group in one of the local or district organisations. An Extra-Ordinary Convention can be called by the coordinating council, ten percent of the membership, a working or local group.

The local sections of the party correspond to the communal electoral constituencies. If there are too few members in a particular area, then a regional section can be set up. In densely populated areas where the party has more members, local sections may be further divided. The local or regional sections are asked to elect a committee to administer the section. The sections operate in autonomy but have to respect and act upon National Convention policy lines.

The most important organizational level is the district. The district convention elects a presiding committee which administers the district while the convention is not in session. All members of the party living in the district have voting rights at the district convention. The district convention elects representatives for the Coordination Council of the party and decides upon the party list of candidates for the communal and national elections. Its major task is to support the functioning of the local sections and making sure that each local section is represented in the delegation to the coordination council. The number of delegates to the council is determined proportionally by the number of members in the district.

The Coordination Council is the party´s administrative center and represents it to the electorate as well as making sure that democratic methods are maintained. It consists of the delegation from the districts with full voting rights and a delegation from the members of parliament which has consultative voting rights. A treasurer with full voting rights is elected by the National Convention. The Council supervises the finances of the party and administers them in conjunction with the local sections.

The party also sports a number of working groups in which topics are discussed and eventually presented to the National or Full Conventions. But perhaps the most important feature of the party is its internal distribution of organizational power and the relations which are supposed to exist between party representatives, the functionaries and the members. The party not only rotates representatives and party functionaries, it stresses the importance of participation. Members are encouraged to participate at as many of the party meetings as they can manage to avoid the evolution of a party oligarchy. Of course, such a development really does depend on the activity of the membership and its longterm willingness to attend party meetings.

Parliamentary representatives are under obligation to provide the party with their parliamentary salaries. The party then pays them a fixed salary which fluctuates with the wage index. Extra monies are given to representatives with dependent children. Parliamentary representatives are further bound by Convention decisions and are subject to an "imperative mandate". They are not to follow their own policy preferences but those of the party.

Programatic Profile

The main policy plank of *Dei Greng Alternativ* is of course environmental protection. The party claims that damage to the environment has arisen from the production process and only if industrial production is geared towards ecological products and production techniques can the environment be saved. The greens link deforestation, air, water and noise pollution to a common source - industry - which, in their view, needs to be reformed. The ailing Luxembourg steel industry is seen as both a source of problems as well as opportunities by the *Greng Alternativ*. They argue that the industry could be made very competitive if it turned to a diversification of its products and if these products were either produced ecologically or even promoted ecological production methods in other industrial branches.

Not unlike the realist wing of the West German Greens, the Greens in Luxembourg place a great deal of emphasis on the profitability of ecological products and production methods. This is not an anti-industry party per se, it opposes certain types of industry and production methods. The largest section of the election manifesto produced for the 1984 elections is therefore concerned with the steel industry and possible ways of overcoming its crisis. The reason for this emphasis on ecological production is the argument Greens are always confronted with : since ecology is expensive for industry (putting filters into chimneys f.i.), it will drive industry away from the areas where the ecology movement makes it impossible for them to produce. No industry means unemployment. The Greens want to suggest that it is possible to have ecological production and economic profitability, albeit in an economy which produces for the local market.

Ecological concerns are also at the heart of the *Greng Alternativ´s* opposition to building projects such as a planned highway through the duchy to attract traffic from the South of Germany to Holland. Not only do the Greens object to the highway because it will involve the destruction of woods and farmland, but also because it will increase air pollution through increased traffic.

The Greens propose to introduce lead-free gas and a reduced speed limit on the duchy´s "autobahns". They advocate a much greater emphasis on urban planning to avoid urban sprawl and the destruction of villages and communities to make way for new ventures.

The Greens oppose nuclear power plants - both in Luxembourg as well as on its borders such as the French plant Cattenom - and other plans for largescale power generators, arguing instead that decentralized power generation on a communal scale might be a more effective way of producing sufficient energy through the use of sun, wind and water generating devices and conservation. Further, ecological production techniques are viewed as a step towards a more " gentle" and "peaceful" approach to life in general. Just as the *Greng Alternativ* opposes violent protest, it also opposes a production system which creates aliention (a form of violence in the Green view) among the workforce. As the *Greng Alternativ* municipal election manifesto of 1987 puts it : "Social and economic processes cannot be based merely on the logic of competition and the necessity for economic growth. Betterment of life can only be achieved by solidary action and cooperative interaction, not by egotistical thinking, domination and consumption " (1987 : 15).

Much of *Greng Alternativ´s* election manifesto deals with questions of democracy and liberal freedom, including women´s rights, local democracy, the rights of foreign workers to vote and animal rights. Women´s rights are a major issue for the Greens. The party list consists of 50 percent female candidates and at all meetings, men and women take turns speaking. The foreign worker issue is another important topic in Luxembourg because of the large numbers of foreigners working in its industries. A major proportion of Luxembourg´s labor force is either Italian or Portuguese. Foreigners would be able to vote if the Greens had their way. In line with its democratic principles, the party proposes constitutional amendments which would make the referenda compulsory. Instead of elected politicians deciding on all issues affecting people´s life, those affected would get to vote on whether an industrial plant could or could not be built in their neighborhood.

Outlook
Given that the established parties have done rather well forming coalitions with one another, it is unlikely that the *Greng Alternativ* will be asked to join a government coalition. Its two seats are of no particular consequence currently and unless the party gains

significantly, it does not possess even blackmail potential in the parliament. Further, it is unlikely that the conservatives will ask the *Greng Alternativ* to join a coalition since the party happens to stand for the abolition of the monarchy and the seperation of church and state. This plank makes the party an unlikely partner for a catholic party and community which still administers its own parochial schools.

The party attaches as much importance to local representation as it does to parliamentary seats. Given the slim chance of governmental involvement, this strategy is advisable. At the local level the party has better possibilities, especially if its electoral base is concentrated and proves to be stable and mobilizable. Much of the party program is concerned with local politics such as urban planning, opposition to building projects (including nuclear power plants), education and above all the demands for decentralization and democratization of decision-making.

It is too early to tell whether the Greens in the Luxembourg are a success or failure. If we measure success in terms of votes and government participation, success is currently quite limited. If we measure it in terms of raising public consciousness about issues of the environment, local planning, industrial policy, womens´ or foreign workers´ right, then the *Greng Alternativ* is very successful in Luxembourg politics.

12
Sweden:
The "Miljöpartiet de Gröna"

Evert Vedung*

Development of the Green Party

The Green party in Sweden was founded in September 1981. However, a few local green and alternative parties were already founded and gained some electoral support in several communities throughout the country in the 1970s. The alternative party formed in 1979 in the country`s capital, the Stockholm Party, captured three seats in the municipal election in the fall of that year as well as substantial national media coverage.The first local environmentalist party was formed in Ängelholm in the southernmost province of Scania in 1972. Later, similar parties were founded in Båstad, Sollentuna, Halmstad, Borgholm, Falkenberg, and Stockholm. Of crucial importance for the development of the Greens was the issue of nuclear energy. The anti-nuclear movement may be regarded as part of a more general anti-nuclear wave sweeping across the Western world in the 1970s. Crucial for the formation of the Green party in Sweden, however, was the way this issue was handled by the peculiar Swedish system of political institutions, particularly the Center Party in government between 1976 and 1978, and the Social Democrats, the Liberals, and the Moderates in the 1980 referendum.

*During the composition of this paper, I have received help from several people. Sherri Berman, graduate student of Harvard on visit in Uppsala, has provided important linguistic and substantive suggestions. Åsa Domeij, Uppsala, and Jill Lindgren, Stockholm, both of the Green Party, have been patient interviewees. Robert Harmel, Texas A&M contributed some comparative insights as a discussant at the International Political Science Association meeting in Washington, D.C. in September, 1988. Kerstin Göransson and Agnet Berglund, Uppsala University Data Centre, have cheerfully assisted in the machine-drawing of the figure on the parties in the opinion polls. To all of them, I wish to extend my thanks. - The article was finished in November, 1988.

To understand more clearly how this issue was perceived among Swedish environmental activists, it is helpful to provide a brief overview of the traditional Swedish five-party system (Vedung 1988). The Swedish five-party system has been "frozen" since the end of World War I. It has become exeptionally one-dimensional. Parties tend to align themselves along one ideological scale, the well-known left-right axis.

Figure 12.1
The Established Swedish Parties on Left-Right Dimension

Socialist Bloc			Non-Socialist Bloc		
Communist Party			People's Party		Moderate Party
LEFT	+	+	+	+	+ RIGHT
		Social Democratic Party		Center Party	

The left-right conflict dimension concerns the economic struggle between capital and labor, employers and employees, the bourgeoisie and the proletariat. To put it very crudely, left-wing parties pursue Socialism, right-wing parties Capitalism. The former aspire to use the resources of government to hamper what is considered to be economic exploitation of workers, strengthen the position of consumers against producers, and ameliorate the lot of tenants in relation to their landlords. The latter maintain that there should be a limited role for government in the economy because public intervention impedes the natural play of market forces, reduces freedom of individuals and inhibits their initiative and incentive to work. The fragmentization of the five-party system is mellowed by another standing feature of Swedish politics: the alignment of the Communists and Social Democrats into a Socialist bloc and the three remaining parties into a Nonsocialist bloc (see Figure 12.1).

Another outstanding property of Swedish politics is the strength of the Social Democrats and the relative fragmentation of the political right. While the right is divided into three competing parties of almost equal support, the left consists of the huge Social Democratic party and the tiny Left-Party Communists.

The Social Democratic dominance of the executive branch is a fourth tenet of modern Swedish party politics; since the Great Depression of 1929, this party has almost alone controlled the executive branch of government. Nearly every national cabinet between 1932 and 1976 has been dominated by the Social Democrats.

The rise of new environmental and ecological concerns in the late 1960s and early 1970s placed the ingrained patterns of the Swedish party system under stress. In particular, Sweden´s nuclear energy program "(allegedly the largest in the world on a per capita basis)" unexpectedly became a subject of deep public controversy in the spring of 1973. The relative positions of the parties on the nuclear issue strongly diverged from the standard Socialist-Nonsocialist cleavage. Not only hereditary foes such as the Social Democrats and the Moderates but also the People´s Party came out as advocates of nuclear energy, while the Communist Party and the Center Party, which initially supported the nuclear energy program,became decidedly anti-nuclear between 1973 and 1975. It might be suggested that the sharp nuclear-antinuclear controversy added weight to a latent growth-ecology cleavage in Swedish party politics at the elite level. A new political situation thus arose, characterized by a growth-ecology dimension alongside the traditional left-right dimension of conflict (see Figure 12.2).

The nuclear power conflict, which helped create the growth-ecology dimension generated tensions in the two traditional left-right partisan blocs. While there is no doubt that the left-right cleavage remained the predominant one, the nuclear energy conflict produced disturbances in the two-bloc constellation, pitting Communists against Social Democrats, and Centerists against Liberals and Moderates (Vedung 1979a: 169ff; Vedung 1979b; Vedung 1980: 109ff; Vedung 1981).

Figure 12.2
The Two Main Dimensions of Sweden's Party System 1975-1978

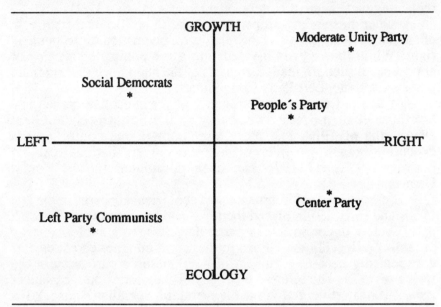

Elsewhere I have argued that the nuclear-antinuclear confrontation might be conceived as part of a more comprehensive growth-ecology dimension. This line of struggle concerns the rift between those espousing a political world view that generally emphasizes the benevolent impacts of continued, sustained material growth - higher employment, better housing, more high-quality nutrition for lower prices, faster and more comfortable transportation, higher standard of living in general - and those embracing a belief system which cannot accept detrimental side effects of continued growth. These side effects include the ruining of wilderness through the buildings of roads and highways, the harvesting of forests, the construction of hydroelectric dams, and mining. Other effects include the destruction of fertile agricultural lands by the expansion of cities and construction of airports; the destruction of natural habitats for wildlife through the drainage of wetlands, and threats to human health through the use of fertilizers, biocides, and pesticides in farming and forestry.

This obviously differs from the traditional left-right dimension as the issues involved do not concern the distribution of wealth or influence among those who have more and those who have less. Instead, the growth-ecology dimension covers issues regarding the level and type of welfare while debate along the left-right dimension concerns the distribution of welfare among different sectors and members of society.

In the 1976 national election campaign, the doggedly antinuclear stance of the Center Party leader, Thorbjörn Fälldin, elicited support from numerous members of the environmentalist grass-root movements, which surfaced around 1970. Fälldin's repeated promise - or prognosis - that nuclear energy would be phased out by 1985, contributed to a political sensation: the Nonsocialist forces captured a majority of the seats in Parliament and the Social Democrats were ousted from government. As a consequence, a three-party, center-right coalition cabinet was formed. This government was unprecedented in modern Swedish history. For the first time, a three-party Nonsocialist majority government was formed.Within the environmentalist movements, it was hoped that the Center Party would do everything in its might to phase out nuclear power. However, only supported by 24 percent of the electorate, the center party leadership felt compelled to compromise with the other two, pronuclear Nonsocialist parties so as to seize upon this unique opportunity to place the Social Democrats firmly in opposition. In the following two years, the party leadership chose to compromise time and to save the three-party, Nonsocialist coalition. Some progress was made for the anti-nuclear cause. However, nuclear energy was far from dismantled - in fact, not even its continued growth was brought to a decisive end. Although the three-party coalition eventually dissolved on the nuclear issue after a paltry two years in office, the Center Party's two-year-long inclination to compromise seemed to have damaged its credibility, with the no-nuke groups.

Early in 1979, the political situation regarding nuclear energy changed radically in Sweden. After the "Three Mile Island" incident in March, the pro-nuclear Social Democratic leadership announced that it would take a more cautious approach to nuclear power. It agreed to the old demand of the Center and Communist parties for a referendum on nuclear power. The other parties followed suit. The national referendum was to take place after the parliamentary elections in September 1979.

Held on March 23, 1980, the referendum offered three options. It ended up with a defeat for the anti-nuclear movement: option two received 39 percent of the valid vote (see Figure 12.3) (Holmberg and Asp 1984; Johansson 1980).

Figure 12.3
Options in the 1980 Swedish Nuclear Referendum

Option 1: (Moderates)
Nuclear power is to be phased out... To reduce our dependency on oil,... at most 12 reactors which are now in operation, completed or under construction are used. There must be no further expansion of nuclear power (Percentage of valid vote: 18.9).

Option 2: (Social Democrats/People's Party)
Nuclear power is to be phased out... To reduce our dependency on oil,... at most 12 reactors which are now in operation, completed or under construction are used. There must be no further expansion of nuclear power.
The main responsibility for the production and distribution of electricity must be in public hands. Nuclear power stations and any other future installations of importance for the production of electricity must be owned by the State and the municipalities (Percentage of valid: 39.1).

Option 3: (Center Party/Communist Party)
"No" to the continued expansion of nuclear power.
The phasing out of the six reactors now in operation within a period of, at most, ten years. (Percentage of valid vote: 38.7)

Although the Center Party was in government since 1979, it failed to act as an intermediary capable of linking anti-nuclear grass-root opinion and national decision making. The failure of an established anti-nuclear party to affect any substantial change in Sweden's nuclear energy policy while in government was certainly a major factor behind the emergence of the new green party in Sweden.

Organizational Structure
From the very beginning, the Greens wanted to create a party with a less top-down bureaucratic structure than that of the established parties. Strong emphasis was placed on participation. Opportunity for everyone to participate in societal decisions was a prime principle

embodied in the new party structure. The idea of rotation was also important. The rotation principle manifested itself in the concept of politics as a side occupation - as opposed to a full-time profession. While everyone should be encouraged to participate, no one should participate full-time or for all of one´s life. A third idea was division of labor. Too many functions were not to be centralized into one structure or in one person.

The internal structure of the Greens reflects these guiding principles. Decentralization, local influence, direct democracy, and diffusion of power are key words in their theory of political organization.

The party organization is three-tiered, with local, regional, and national structures. The borders of the local organizations - called local departments - coincide with those of the municipalities, whereas regional organizations are formed in each of the 28 constituencies for elections.

The "party congress", the highest national decision-making body of the party, convenes once a year. This is often compared to other Swedish parties, where congresses are held mostly at two- or three-year intervals.

The "party congress" designed in accordance with two principles of representation. The principle of geographic distribution is reflected in the by-law stating that each of the 28 regions are permitted to send two delegates to the party convention, irrespective of the size of the region´s party membership. Additionally, each local department of the party may send one delegate per hundred members. Thus, a local department of 15 members will send one, a department with 610 members seven delegates to the national "party congress". Being a deputy for more than three years is strictly forbidden.

Not only may motions to the congress be submitted by local departments and regions, but by individual members as well. Motions are processed by congressional committees, the composition of which clearly reflects the antihierarchical spirit of the party. Members of congressional comittees are not appointed by the congress itself, e.g., by a vote of majority. Instead, deputies decide by themselves what congressional committee they want to join. Again, the intention is, of course, to enhance the opportunities for grass-roots to influence party leadership.

The remaining national decision-making bodies of the party, including the "national council", and the four "national committees", also exhibit anti-hierarchical tenets both in their internal structure and external relationship to one another.

The "national council", the highest decision-making body between the "party congresses", is composed entirely in accord with geographical principles of representation. Irrespective of the size of party membership, each region sends one deputy to the "council". This means that the "national council" is neither appointed by the "party congress" nor responsible to it.

At the beginning, the "national council" had to convene once every third month. In 1987 this was reduced to at least twice a year. Members of "national committees" have a right to be present and participate in the deliberations of the "council". However, they have no right to vote due to the adoption of a strict rule stating that no one is allowed to be a full member of more than one national body at a time. Again, the idea is that power should be delegated to the regional deputies and not centralized in the party´s national representative bodies (Berva et.al. 1983).

Another organizational feature is that the power wielded by executive committees in the established parties is formally divided , in the Green Party, between two bodies: the "political committee" and the "administrative committee". While the "political committee" lays out the general policy of the party, the "administrative committee" manages the economy. Appointed by the "party congress" both committees consist of five to eleven members, elected for one year at a time. No one is allowed to be a committee member for more than six years and one quarter of the membership is renewed every year.

Leading members of the Greens argue that this division in top management sets their organization apart from established political parties where policy making, as well as economic power, is concentrated solely in the executive branch.

However, the most striking characteristic of the whole organizational structure of the Greens is the absence of a party leader in the traditional sense. This is because party activists firmly believe that leaders of the established parties are entrusted with too much power. They maintain that this is especially true of parties in office. Party leaders exert strong influence not only on substantive policy issues and economic matters, but on political appointments as well. For example, they determine who will be included in delegations to the Council of Europe, the Nordic Council, the United Nations, and in the most visible national policy commissions, as well as appointed to the boards of administrative agencies. The greens assert that the concentration of power in the hands of party leaders creates a conformist top-down political climate within the parties.

At the outset, leadership was collectively held by the eleven members of the "political committee". Convenorship (a notion which was preferred to leadership or chairpersonship) rotated. "Convenors" and "Deputy convenors" were elected by the "committee" only for three months at a time. After this brief period, they had to resign and be replaced by other members of the "committee". Convenors were responsible for practical matters with respect to "committee" meetings. However, they did not necessarily act as chairpersons during the session. Through this rotation arrangement, the founding fathers and mothers of the Green Party hoped to dissipate influence among all members of the Political Committee and impede the emergence of a strong and self sufficient party leader.

However, after the disappointingly weak election in September 1982 there was a clear tendency to elect convenors for somewhat longer periods, up to one and a half years. The reason for this adjustment was to facilitate communication with the media. Greater longevity among party spokesmen would make it easier for journalists to find the proper speaking partner and enable the Greens to present a more consistent picture to the mass media and the public.

In 1985, the system was modified. The convenorship institution in the "political committee" was retained, and the length of stay in this position now varied. It might be for one meeting, or it might be for one year. The role of the convenor was and still is considered strictly administrative. The convenor is responsible for preparing the agenda for committee sessions as well as for the dissemination of minutes from the meetings. The convenor might also act as chairperson in the meetings, but this is not necessarily so. From time to time, other members can also act as chairpersons.

The real innovation of the 1985 modifications was the introduction of a system of spokespersons, alongside the convenorship. Since 1985, the Congress each year elects two spokespersons for the party, one woman and one man, neither one of which are required to be members of the "political committee". This has, however, so far, never occurred.

It is important to note, however, that the spokespersons are strictly regarded as middlemen between the party and the media, not as party leaders. For instance, they do not chair "political committee" meetings as do ordinary party leaders.

Another tenet, designed to impede authoritarian tendencies within the Green Party, is the equality of sexes. For all four national committees the gender ratio must be six women to five men. This rule has been introduced to impede male dominance.

Electoral Support

Since 1981 the popular support of the Green Party exhibited a puzzling pattern. While faring surprisingly well in opinion polls, particularly between elections, and capturing a substantial amount of seats in municipal assemblies throughout the country, the party has failed to gain representation in the national parliament.

In the 1982 and 1985 national elections the greens attracted respectively only 1.65 and 1.5 percent of the votes and, consequently, have received no seats in Parliament.

However, the party fared much better in municipal elections which are held on the same day as the national elections. Ingemar Wörlund and Svante Ersson (1987) have shown that in one municipality in the 1985 election, for instance, the party gained 13 percent in the municipal election but only two percent in the national election. In several other municipalities, it gained between six to seven percent in the municipal election but only between two and three percent in the national election. In 1982, the party gained 167 seats and in 1985 240 seats in municipal assemblies across the country.

Table 12.1
Swedish Green Party Turnout in 1982 and 1985 in Municipal and National Elections

1982 Municipality	Municipal election %	National election %	Difference
Ovanåker	6.3	3.1	3.2
Haninge	5.8	2.3	3.5
Nynäshamn	5.2	2.7	2.5
Lund	5.2	3.3	1.9
Höör	4.8	2.3	2.5
Lerum	4.8	2.4	2.4
Öckerö	4.7	2.1	2.6
Båstad	4.6	1.9	2.7
Jokkmokk	4.2	2.4	1.8
Hedemora	3.9	2.6	1.3

(continued)

Table 12.1 (continued)

1985 Municipality	Municipal election %	National election %	Difference
Nynäshamn	12.8	2.3	10.5
Lund	3.1	6.7	3.6
Strömstad	6.4	2.4	4.0
Borlänge	6.2	2.4	3.8
Vingåker	6.2	2.8	3.4
Lerum	6.1	2.1	4.0
Höör	6.1	2.3	3.8
Borgholm	5.9	1.8	4.1
Tanum	5.9	2.5	3.4
Karlstad	5.8	1.9	3.9

Source: Wörlund and Ersson 1987: 7ff

Table 12.1 presents the voter turnout for the Greens in its ten best municipalities. Interestingly enough, a substantial part of those voting for the Greens in the municipal elections abandoned the party in the national elections.

Why did the Green Party win only 1.6 percent of the total vote in 1982 and a paltry 1.5 percent in 1985? Why did the Greens not pass the four percent mark and win seats in Parliament when they managed rather well in the municipal elections and made strong showings in the opinion polls before the elections?

First of all, we may note that green voters are very volatile. Sören Holmberg and Mikael Gilljam (1987) found, that Green Party voters exhibited the lowest party loyalty. Only 39 percent of those who voted for the greens in 1982 cast their votes for them again in 1985. This compares with 63 for the Centerists, 70 for the Communists, 71 for the Christian Democrats, 72 for the Moderates, 83 for the Liberals, and 87 for the Social Democrats.

Of those who abandoned the party in 1985, 28 percent went to the People's Party, 13 to the Social Democrats, 5 to the Communists and the Moderates, and 5 percent did not vote at all. Almost none of them transferred to the traditional environmentalist party on the

Swedish scene, the Center Party. The Greens gained very few voters from other parties in 1985. The most important addition - eight percent - emanated from the group who in 1982 did not vote (Holmberg and Gilljani 1987).

Some explanation for the Greens'low percentage in the 1982 and 1985 elections can be found in three institutional obstacles in the Swedish political system, working against the ascendancy of newcomers to the national, parliamentary scene: the funding, media, and constitutional barriers.

The *funding barrier* i.e., the rules of eligibility of the party financing program inaugurated by the national legislature in the late 1960s, has obviously disfavored the Greens. Since the level of public funding received by each party is proportional to the number of seats held by it in Parliament, only parties that have won representation in the legislature are eligible to full participation in this scheme. In order to gain representation, a party must attract four percent of the national vote. This obstacle to public funding is quite important since the extent of public financial support is substantial. The signifiance of this barrier is strengthened by the fact that the public subsidy programs established by counties and municipalities also only support represented parties. While the seat threshold in counties is only three percent of the total vote and there is no percentage hurdle at all in local elections, the financial rules still work to substantially disfavor beginners who start from scratch (Gidlund 1983: 11 ff., and 269 ff). Differences in regulatory regimes of public funding, then, may carry some weight in explaining why the Greens drew much less support in national than in municipal elections.

It is obvious that the Greens have been disadvantaged by the *media barrier*, i.e., the rules governing the allocation of time on Swedish public-service radio and television. Only parties that have passed the constitutional barrier - the four percent hurdle - and consequently have gained seats in parliament are permitted by the Swedish media authorities to participate in the specially designed election programs. This does not imply that small parties are entirely barred from appearing in the media. They may receive coverage in newcasts where, instead of the quota system, common rules of newsworthiness are applied. However, this means that small parties are excluded from an important sector of programs that enjoy considerable popularity among the Swedish public. This is all the more important since the Greens have a weak party press. The rule-system expounded above was implemented in the 1982 and 1985 elections. Before the 1988 election, the rules were somewhat changed in favor of the Greens.

These explanations suffer from a serious weakness: They cannot explain the puzzling variations in the support of the Greens in 1982 and 1985. They cannot explain why the Greens were comparatively strong in the polls between the elections and performed relatively well in the municipal elections but failed in parliamentary elections. There is one factor, however, that can illuminate these discrepancies. This explanation may be called the "No-Comrade-Four-Percent" factor.

The Swedish constitution contains a four percent hurdle to national parliament which seems to function as an invitation to strategic voting, that has disfavored the Greens, but favored for instance the Left-Party Communists. The phenomenon of Communist gains from strategic voting - jokingly called "Comrade Four Percent" in Sweden - must be understood as a function of the self-inflicted role of the Left-Party Communists in Swedish bloc politics as a reliable supporter of Social Democratic governments in critical situations in the national parliament. Usually, the three Nonsocialist parties have more seats in Parliament than the Social Democrats alone. From 1973 to 1976 and 1985 to 1988, for instance, the Social Democrats had 43.6 and 44.7 while the Nonsocialists had 48.8 and 47.9 percent of the national vote. But thanks to the Left-Party Communists - who amassed 5.3 and 5.4 percent, the Social Democratic government were able to remain in office. Should the Communists fall short of the four percent mark and lose their foothold in the national parliament, the Social Democratic governments would, in all probability, have to resign as well. This creates an incentive for particularly left-leaning Social Democratic voters to cast their votes for the Left-Party Communists in order to keep them in parliament and thereby secure a Social Democratic government; thus blocking the formation of Nonsocialist governments.

Strategic Social Democratic voting is facilitated by the fact that, having already been represented, the Communists have actually proven their ability to pass the four-percent hurdle. Although the Communists may be very low in the preelection polls, a strategic vote for them does not, then, become a wasted vote in the sense that they would not reach the limit.

For the Greens on the other hand, strategic voting produced by the four-percent barrier seemed to work against them in 1982 and 1985:

First, the fact that the party had never passed the four percent threshold is an obvious handicap. A vote for a tiny party, hitherto never represented in parliament, would be a wasted vote, for this party would, in all probability, not be able to obtain the four percent minimum which would allow it to enter parliament.

Secondly, there was no bloc factor helping the Greens in this situation. Contrary to the Communists, the Greens have consistently refused to be included in any of the two traditional Swedish political blocs. Instead, they have argued that they will take a stand from issues to issues in parliament. This means that voters who wished to support one of the partisan bloc were discouraged from supporting the Greens.

In actual parliamentary work and between elections, the significance of bloc politics is usually less noticeable. During non-election periods, consultations, negotiations, and so called "broad agreements" across the bloc line are common. This less rigid climate favors the Greens, enabling them to increase their support in opinion polls. During election campaigns, bloc politics and the concomitant issue of who will form the next government usually occupies a much more dominant place. This disfavors the Greens, who were viewed by the public as rather unpredictable with respect to what kind of government they eventually will support. Voters who have supported the Greens in the polls tend to return to their traditional bloc stalls on election day.

Finally, the elections of 1982 and 1985 were dominated by worries concerning Sweden´s deteriorating economy and the role of the public sector in the welfare state. Neither the Greens nor any other party succeeded in doing what the Center Party had achieved in 1976: making environmentalist issues a major theme in the campaign. Environmental concerns were clearly overpowered by left-right issues in the 1982 and 1985 campaigns.

Epilogue: The 1988 National Election

In the 1988 national elections, the Greens crossed the four-percent barrier and entered parliament. The party cleared the hurdle with a safe margin. It gained 5.6 percent of the vote and received 20 seats in national parliament.

Why did the party pass the famous four-percent hurdle in 1988? The *salience of environmental issues* on the political and media agenda seems to have been an important factor. Never before have environmental concerns dominated a Swedish electoral campaign as they did in 1988. Before and during the campaign, the Swedish people were flooded with news about poisonous algae, forests and lakes damaged by acid rain, milk contaminated by dioxin, and most of all, a sudden seemingly inexplicable surge of dead seals on the West Coast.

Another contributing factor may have been distrust in politicans, which means cynicism for traditional politics and politicians. In early summer, the so-called Ebbe Carlsson affair was aired daily in the media. Ebbe Carlsson, a private citizen, was commissioned by the Minister of Justice, Anna Greta Leijon, to pursue secret investigations into the Olof Palme murder case. After a political thunderstorm, the Minister of Justice was forced to resign. This event by itself and the public parliamentary committee hearings that went on for weeks afterwards probably strengthened the scepticism of politicans by the Swedish people. This favored the Greens who denounce the idea of professional politics and want to turn politics into a field for amateurs and laymen. There is certainly an element of system protest underlying the success of the Greens in 1988.

In addition, there was a lack of competing concerns of a right-left character. The economy was booming. Jobs and unemployment were of little concern. Expect for some skirmishes on the People's Party's tax reform plan there was no great substantive issue dividing the Socialist and Nonsocialist bloc. The mass media could concentrate on environmental issues and the Ebbe Carlsson affair. This helped to give the Greens higher marks than ever in the opinion polls well before the election. In sum, the situation before the 1988 election was much better for the Greens than it had been in 1982 and 1985.

13
Switzerland:
The "Green" and "Alternative Parties"

Andreas Ladner

Development of Green and Alternative Parties
In the early seventies the authorities of Neuchâtel, a city in the French-speaking part of Switzerland planned a motorway along the lake right through town. A petition drive aimed at stopping the project was unsuccessful, and a referendum at this stage was impossible. Since there were no remaining possibilities for preventing the project from outside government, opponents of the motorway moved to send their representatives to the local parliament and to fight against this motorway from the inside. At the communal elections in spring of 1972 the motorway opponents gained 8 out of 41 seats in the parliament and became the third-largest party behind the Free Democratic Party *(FdP)* and the Social Democratic Party *(SPS)*. The motorway project along the border of the lake was cancelled and the *Mouvement populaire pour l' environnement (MPE)*,the first green party in Switzerland, was founded. It united, among others, people from the Free Democratic and the Social Democratic Party. Another ten years passed before a green party was established on the national level.

In the mid seventies another green party appeared on the political scene. In the French-speaking canton of Vaud, affiliates of the *Ecole polytechnique fédérale* in Lausanne founded the *Groupement pour la protection de l`environnement (GPE)*. In 1979, the *GPE* was to become one of the first green parties in a western society to send a representative to a national parliament.

In 1978 a green party was established in the German-speaking part of Switzerland (*Grüne Partei des Kantons Zürich, GPZ*), to some extent with the conviction that environmental matters should not be left to extreme right- or left-wing parties.

Just prior to this, a group from the extreme right had announced that it would present a list of candidates with a green program at the national elections. On the local and cantonal levels the left-wing POCH, a party rooted in the student movement of 1968, had also been quite active in ecological matters. With the establishment of a green party at the political centre, the fragmentation of the green forces was about to begin (Geschwend 1986).

In the years preceeding the national elections of 1983, concern about ecological problems increased dramatically. Green parties of many different political persuasions appeared in various Swiss cantons and gained considerable support in community and cantonal elections. With a sharp eye on the new constitution of the national parliament, the green politicians attempted to bring all these groups under a common roof and to found a green party similar to that in Germany (Rebeaud 1987). Despite efforts to minimize conflicts through exclusion of nationally organized parties from the constitutional meetings, e.g. the right-wing Alien-Party (NA), the Independent Party (LdU) and the parties on the extreme left - the Progressive Organisations of Switzerland (POCH) and the Socialist Workers Party (SAP) the task proved to be impossible.

The differences between the moderate and the radical groups appeared to be too fundamental to resolve. Purely environmental concerns stood against more utopian ideals regarding the future of society. Another crucial point involved both parties´ positions towards the army, an institution which is well-integrated in the Swiss economy and politics, and is socially much more accepted than in other countries. The split between the moderate "cucumber-greens" (green inside and outside) and the radical "water-melon-greens" (outside green and inside red) inevitably took place. The more moderate groups which were united into the *Föderation der Grünen Parteien der Schweiz (GPS)* wanted to be active within the existing political and social system, whereas the more radical and alternative groups were in favour of fundamental social changes and formed the *Grüne Alternative der Schweiz (GRAS)*

Both parties showed quite disappointing results in the 1983 elections. With 1.7 percent of the vote, the moderate *GPS* gained two seats and came to a total of three representatives in the National Council, the radical *GRAS* achieved 0.8 percent and remained without a single seat. The National Council is the larger of the chambers in the national parliament. In this house each canton is allocated a certain number of seats based on its population. The smaller chamber, the Council of States (*Ständerat*), has only 46 seats (two per canton). Here the elections are held according to the "majoritarian principle" (*Majorz-System*), by which the winning parties receive all the seats and the losing parties are not represented. Smaller parties have little chance and usually are not represented here.

As the 1987 national elections commenced, the time for fundamental changes in party politics seemed to have come. Acid rain and environmental catastrophes in Chernobyl and in Basel (release of a chemical cloud), raised environmental consciousness. Green parties from both wings, but especially the moderate *GPS* had been very successful in local and cantonal elections. Particularly in the large agglomerations such as Zurich, Bern and Geneva they became a major political force.

Again, in anticipation of the national elections, the green parties attempted to consolidate their national organisations. The green *Föderation der Grünen Parteien der Schweiz (GPS)* tightened its name to *Grüne Partei der Schweiz (GPS)*. The alternative green parties gained support from the left-wing parties who were struggling with personal and legitimacy problems. They reactivated their old national organisation, *GRAS*, under the new name of *Grünes Bündnis Schweiz (GBS)*. No further attempt was made to unite the two wings of the green movement. The *GPS* felt strong enough to stand alone and desperately avoided any association with left-wing and alternative ideas.

Speculations based upon opinion polls and the electoral success for various cantonal parliaments predicted a substantial gain for the green groups. A new majority of green, green-alternative, social-democratic and other oppositional forces together with the more concerned members of the bourgeois parties seemed possible - especially with regard to environmental issues.

Confronted with such a challenge, the traditional parties turned green. Environmental problems dominated the preelectoral period and the traditional cleavages seemed to disappear. Hence the Greens once again showed quite disappointing results. With 5.1 percent of the vote, nine of the 200 seats in the National Council (*Nationalrat*) went to the *GPS* and 4.3 percent of the vote and five seats to the *GBS*. The would-be coalition partner, the Social Democrats, lost six seats and the bourgeois parties (the Free Democratic, the Christian Democratic Party and the Swiss People's Party) were able to hold their share. If there was any change, apart from the few new seats gained, it took place within the traditional parties. Environmental candidates were widely preferred. Apparently, environmental problems did not polarize the party system as much as the left-right dimension had in the past. Concerned voters could choose from a variety of candidates from right, left and green lists, all of whom were putting forward ecologist demands.

The failure of the green groups to live up to the high expectations must be scrutinized through a closer look at the electoral system. Elections for the National Council are held according to a system of proportional representation (*Proporz-System*). By the *Proporz-System* the number of the seats each party receives depends on its share of the vote. This system, in fact, is meant to give smaller parties more weight. But since voting districts are drawn along cantonal lines, the less populous cantons send only a few representatives to the *Nationalrat* and the number of votes needed to win a seat lays far beyond the means of new and smaller parties. The green parties therefore presented themselves in only 18 of the 26 cantons, and in quite a few of these they did not stand any real chance of winning a seat.

Organisational Structure

On the national level, the moderate *Grüne Partei der Schweiz* (*GPS*) is a federally grown coalition of 11 branches in 10 cantons with a weak organisational structure. Up to two branches per canton can be members of the national party as long as they do not compete with one another. A special "observer" status is reserved for groups which can not or do not wish to become full members immediately. Two bodies coordinate the national activities: the Meeting of Delegates and the Executive Board. At the Meeting of Delegates (legislative) which takes place twice a year, the branches send their representatives according to their vote in cantonal elections. Decisions require a double majority: a majority of branches as well as a majority of delegates must agree. The executive is comprised of one member from each branch. The president is elected every two years, but a reelection is possible. It was not until the end of the 1987 elections that a national secretariat was set up.

The *Grüne Bündnis Schweiz* (*GBS*) the national organisation of the green-alternative parties still exists only pro forma. They came together and agreed on a common agenda, primarily so that they might participate in the 1987 national elections, and in order to gain the necessary media support. Time will tell whether a national body will be established to coordinate the activities of the green alternative forces. Up to now, the *GBS* is not much more than a name for a group of politically diverse and very active parties in different parts of Switzerland.

For both green wings the emphasis is on the regional level. Most decisions are made at general meetings. An executive deals with everyday politics and puts forward political issues on behalf of the members. Nevertheless, since neither the decision-making process nor the selection of candidates is highly formalized, the party control is rather weak. Party leaders and representatives can acquire a far - reaching autonomy and sometimes go their own ways. A *GPS*-member of the national parliament, for example, suddenly joined another parliamentary group, very much against the will of his own party.

Members of parliament (MP´s) are of vital importance to the green parties finances. *GPS* Delegates are required to pay 10 percent of the income from their parliamentary job to the party fund. Parliamentary fractions (usually five MP´s from one party) receive a special refund which allows their parties to establish a paid secretariat. The costly elections usually cause the green parties enormous financial problems. At the time of the 1987 elections, the *GBS* was prepared to pay interest on loans.

It is not easy to establish the exact number of members of political parties. Some parties refuse to disclose these figures, while others do not know them themselves. Today the *GPS* has approximately 4,500 members. They have considerably increased their support from less than 1000 members in 1983. Compared to the four big parties (*FdP, CVP, SPS* and *SVP*), which claim to have between 60,000 and 140,000 members, this does not seem overwhelming, but more important for party activities is the number of active members. Here, the green parties have a considerable advantage over traditional parties.

Although politicans from the fringe of the traditional parties joined the moderate *GPS,* most of the members do not have a political background. *GPS* members cover a wide age range, and include a remarkable share of women. They are mainly middle class, home owners, teachers, architects, doctors and engineers. Quite a few deal with ecological problems professionally. Loose personal and ideological connections to environmental organisations such as the World Wildlife Fund (*WWF*), the Swiss Association for the Protection of the Environment (*SGU*), and an alternative automobile organisation (*VCS*) are also common.

Green alternative groups borrow their members from a broad array of social-change-oriented political movements. The *GPS* unites people from many left-wing parties and progressive unions, as well as from social movements such as the womens movement, the anti-nuclear movement, the peace movement, the Third World movement, army opponents and activists in grassroot mobilisation. Many members are previously acquainted as a result of other common political activities. Rather strong ties still exist with progressive and alternative groups or movements, on the individual as well as the collective level.

Electoral Support

As the Swiss green parties have not yet established strong party ties and a large and loyal electoral base, floating voters are of a vital importance. At the national elections in 1983 almost half of the vote for the *GPS* came from people without firm party relations. This is more than twice as many as for the traditional parties. A representative sample of voters reveals that the Green Party (*GPS*) finds its strongest support among people under forty years of age, from women and from those living in the German-speaking part of Switzerland. No significant urban-rural difference was found (Longchamp 1984).

Switzerland is a highly federalistic country comprised of 26 relativey autonomous cantons and communities. Accordingly, its political system is divided into three levels - federal, cantonal and communal (local) - each of which has its own executive and legislative bodies. Environmental groups are powerful in the large agglomerations such as Zurich, Bern, Geneva and Lausanne. New and smaller parties are usually more successful on the regional level. They do not have the recources to lead a nationwide campaign and to put forward a homogenous program. The branches are relatively independent and have the flexibility to take regional characteristics in account. And since most local and cantonal parliaments follow the principle of proportional representation, by which there is no quorum (except in the French-speaking part of Switzerland, where the quorum lies between 5 and 10 percent of the vote) the minimum percentage of the vote required to send a representative to the parliament is lower than on the national level.

Considering the usual stability of the Swiss political system, there has been an important shift toward the greens in the cantonal elections of the past five years. Since 1983 the moderate GPS has gained 44 seats and now holds 56 seats in six cantonal parliaments. This amounts to just over 6 percent of the total of 900 seats in these cantons. Environmentalists were most successful in Zurich and in Baselland, where they won more than 10 percent of the vote. A total of 21 ecologist groups, eight of which belong to the moderate greens

(*GPS*), are represented in 16 cantonal parliaments. In nine of these they reached fractional size (five or more seats).

As electoral success on the national level is more elusive, only half of the cantons in which green and green alternative parties are represented have sent an environmentalist to the national parliament. These are usually cantons in which a green parliamentary group already exists in the cantonal parliament. Since their emergence on the national scene, the green parties have continuously increased their share of vote, but at the slow pace which characterizes political change in Switzerland.

Table 13.1
Green Representation in the National Parliament in Switzerland

| | Green Party (*GPS*) | | Green Alternative Parties | | |
	% of Vote	Seats	% of Vote	Seats	
1979	0.7%	1	-	-	
1983	2.6%	4	0.8%	-	(GRASS)
1987	5.1%	9	4.3%	5	(GBS)

Source: Official Electoral Statistics

It is apparently even more difficult to bring a canditate into the executive. Here the elections are held according to the "Majorz"-system which clearly favours the large parties. A closer look at the results of green candidates at executive elections shows that the voters seem to be willing to give the executive a "green consciousness", but prefer not to give executive power to an environmentalist. Nevertheless, there are a few environmentalists in communal and cantonal executive bodies. They are most strongly represented in the canton of Bern, where the moderate *GPS* (*Freie Liste Bern*) holds two of the nine executive mandates.

Government Participation
As a whole, the Swiss electoral system is quite conducive to the participation of new and small parties. The *Konkordanzsystem* - a deliberate power-sharing effort, whereby the leaders of the largest parties have agreed to co-govern - has, however, a stabilizing effect. On the national level, for example, the Free Democratic Party (*FdP*),

the Christian Democratic Party (*CVP*), the Social Democratic Party (*SPS*) and the Swiss People´s Party (*SVP*) have formed an agreement to constitute the government. Following the so-called "magic formula" (*Zauberformel*), the federal executive (*Bundesrat*) was - for the past thirty years - composed by the following number of party representatives: *FdP* (2), *CVP* (2), *SPS* (2), *SVP* (1). From 1947 to 1963 their share of the vote at the national elections was well over 80 percent. Mainly due to the losses of the Social Democrats, this share fell to 72 percent in 1987. The three bourgeois parties (*FdP*, *CVP* and *SVP*) were able to hold their shares. As yet, the new and small parties have failed to acquire the strength to make new alliances possible. Small oppositional parties are thus forced to collaborate in parliamentary groups. This brings them more power and allows them special rights in the parliament. However, such cooperation often proves to be a rather difficult task, since all the cultural and ideological differences between the parties tend to reemerge within one parliamentary group.

For the 1987 elections the *GPS* tried to avoid connections to existing parties, as well as references to traditional right-left distinctions. They claimed a pragmatic openness to all forces seriously concerned with environmental problems. All proposals from other parties to set up a common fraction were turned down by the *GPS*. At the first meeting of the *GPS* after the 1987 elections the possibility of forming a parliamentary group with the radical *GBS* was discussed. Potential conflicts between conservative parties from the French-speaking part of Switzerland (Vaud, Neuchâchtel) and progressive organisations from the German-speaking part (Zürich and Bern) reemerged already.

Programatic Profile

In the light of different groups united in the *GPS,* the party program is - or must be - very vague, restraining from clear positions on actual political issues. The policy of the *GPS* is based on the following five principles which hold for the national party as well as for the cantonal branches: decentralisation, humanism, quality of life, anti-technology and long-term perspectives (Rebeaud 1987). At the core of their political commitment stands the protection of the environment. Although they are opposed to high technology, they do not oppose progress as long as it promotes a better quality of life. This can only be achieved through small-scale and decentralised modes of production. According to the *GPS*, natural resources should not be wasted and an intact world should be left to future generations.

Violence and the manipulation of masses is also clearly rejected. Their activities are aimed at saving the environment and the party is conceived solely as a means to "save the world"" from destruction. Should this end be achieved, the party organisation is no longer justified and should disolve.

Toward the state the *GPS* holds quite a liberal position: Not a strong state, but rather responsible citizens are needed. Because they have attempted to distance themselves from the traditional right-left controversies, they do not take a clear position regarding social issues. In order to "save the world", they demand sacrifice. In such a rich country as Switzerland, the slogan "We must get poorer!" has not been completely unsuccessful. Although they favour limiting army expenses, they do not support the successfully launched initiative to abolish the Swiss army. The *GPS´s* interpretation of the state´s role in society, their suspicion of the right-left dichotomy and their position towards the army render problematic any contacts with the radical greens which go beyond a purely pragmatic cooperation.

The different groups of the *GBS* also agreed on a minimal program, which reveals some clear points of view with regard to current political disputes: They support withdrawal from nuclear energy, equal rights for men and women and the elimination of the patriarchal role-division, social solidarity with regard to social security and human working conditions, an active peace policy, open borders to political refugees and immigrants, and support for national liberation movements in other countries (Grünes Bündnis 1987). All these positions clearly reveal the parents of the *GBS*: progressive left wing and alternative movements. Since the position of a political group vis-à-vis the highly integrated and widely accepted army is of crucial importance to its success in Switzerland, the initiative to abolish the army was considered too delicate an issue, and was not addressed.

Outlook

The resistance by the greens to establishing a single "umbrella" party - such as the Greens in West Germany - cannot be understood without taking into account the social and the political system in Switzerland. In a historically grown, multilingual, confederation of culturally diverse cantons, the subunits have a remarkable autonomy. The national organisations, even those of the traditional parties, are not "monolithic centralized edificies, but large "girders" uniting the cantonal organisations" (Gruner 1967). The parties are much more important on a cantonal level. Within the same party there are great differences between the branches. This results in different positions on specific issues and different paroles for plebiscites. Green and alternative parties also reflect regional cleavages. These cleavages, together with the moderate-radical dimension, lead to important differences and make a unification even more difficult. The Social Democrats, the largest "oppositional" party, share governmental responsibilities, but - even if they have been quite progressive on environmental issues - they have failed to integrate other oppositional forces. Since the political system to some extent allows the participation of smaller parties, there is less pressure on green forces to organize into a single party. If both green wings joined forces, the environmentalists would constitute the fifth-largest party on the national level. But such a party would be more heterogenous and prone to unresolvable conflicts. A closer look at the differences in party programs between *GPS* and *GBS* supports this argument. The division into two green parties externalizes the eternal conflict between the pragmatic and moderate greens and the progressive alternative greens, thus avoiding endless theoretical discussions which usually hinder party activities. In any case, the national organisations of both green wings, are already quite heterogenous.

Surely, one of the most important factors in the relative success of the environmentalists is the increasing concern with environmental problems. In such a densely populated country as Switzerland, where nature is considered -not at least for the sake of the tourist industry - to be an important resource, the necessity for environmental protection is becoming widely accepted. Even some nationalists from the extreme right therefore promote environmental causes. Environmental catastrophes contribute to the feeling that "something has to be done". The traditional parties have lost considerable support. Weak party ties, low voter turnout and increasing unconventional political activities (Kriesi 1985) provide evidence for a lack of responsiveness and a certain distrust of the traditional political representation system. A new party which claims to remain above the rigid political structures, which does not mind traditional social cleavages and which offers to fight pragmatically for a better environment undoubtedly has a certain attractiveness.

The Swiss political system has, on the other hand, proved to be very stable over many decades, and according to puplic opinion, this is one of the reasons for the great welfare of this country. The integration of small parties channels and eventually appeases social discontent. Despite all social changes, the four large parties have been more or less able to keep their shares over time. The green parties cannot rely on a historically grown stable constituency, and since their concern cuts across the traditional lines of conflict and social cleavages, support has to be constantly negotiated.

Ultimately, it is neither power itself, nor government participation which the moderate Green party (*GPS*) seeks. Their success can therefore not be measured solely in terms of election results. They have clearly helped to raise awareness of environmental problems and they have forced traditional parties to be more sensitive in this regard. They have even spurred a kind of new polarisation within some of the major parties: the more environmentally-concerned candidates in these traditional parties proved to be more successful in the latest elections. The success of the more ambitious *GBS* will, of course, have to be measured otherwise. Fundamental social changes are more difficult to achieve.

The future of the moderate *GPS* will depend primarily on the ability of the government to cope with environmental problems and on the responsiveness of the traditional parties and their ability to integrate ecologist demands into theit party platforms. If government and parties fail, there will be an increasing demand for a party like the *GPS*. If they succeed, the moderate greens will be bound to disappear, with some of their members joining existing parties and some of them falling back into inactivity. The future of the *GBS* is more difficult to predict. Whether they will be able to build a viable national organisation depends on their capacity to overcome ideological differences. The union of different groups from the extreme left with alternative movements into one homogenous organisation would come close to a "new historical compromise". Should this unification fail, these groups will continue their struggles independently.

14
Europe:
The "Greens" and the "Rainbow Group" in the European Parliament

Karl H. Buck

Development of the "Greens" and the "Rainbow Group"
The European Parliament (EP) is different from national parliaments in Europe. The compentences of the EP were, until recently, limited to a strictly advisory role to the legislative body, the European Community Council of Ministers, and to a certain control of about one third of the European budget. The Single European Act has widened these competences without, however, giving real legislative functions to the EP. Until 1979, the members of the EP had been chosen by and out of their national parliaments. However, since 1979, elections to the EP are held every five years independently of national elections on the basis of highly different national electoral systems.

In the first direct elections to the EP held in 1979, various ecological and small leftist movements participated with their own candidates, however, without much electoral success. The German heterogeneous alliance of green lists, minor parties, alternative groups and citizen action groups (known as *Sonstige Politische Vereinigungen* "Die Grünen") gained 900.000 votes and received 3.2 percent of the total vote; a percentage well below the 5 percent threshold required by German electoral law (see Frankland, in this volume). Prior to the second direct elections in 1984, contacts were established with some green parties from Belgium, France, and the United Kingdom and with leftist and nonconformist parties in the Netherlands and Italy. From the very beginning, a conflict existed between the "pure" ecologists and parties which adopted ecological issues in their political strategy to radically change the contemporary "capitalist societies" in Western Europe.

Because of the dissidence among the ecological groups on the European level, the German Greens - by far the largest, politically influential and financially stable party -had, until recently, limited themselves to an observer´s role in the "European Coordination" of the ecologists. The German Greens insisted that a future parliamentary group in the EP should also incorporate radical leftist parties or movements such as the Dutch *Green Progressive Accord* (a list that consisted of left wing radicals, pacifists and communists) or the anti-European Community movement in Denmark. In opposition to this larger approach, "the Green in Europe", a new alliance of "pure" ecologists was founded in early 1984, consisting of the following groups and parties: *Les Verts* (France), *Ecology Party* (United Kingdom), *Green Alliance* (Ireland), *Agalev and Ecolo* (Belgium), *De Groenen* (Netherlands), *Miljöpartiet* (Sweden), and the *Austrian Alternative List*.

Finally, the rather generous electoral funding to be expected from the EP (altogether some 200 million US dollars) and the promising forecasts of the electoral turnout paved the way for the foundation of a minimal common platform with the following programatic points: a neutral and decentralized European Community with autonomous regions; resistance against any nuclear missiles and dissolution of all military and political blocks; environmental protection without any compromises, absolute equality of women in all spheres; ecological agriculture on the basis of small farms; partnership with the Third World and close relations with its movements for freedom and independence; unlimited exercise of fundamental democratic rights.

The electoral turnout was only satisfactory for the Greens in Germany and Belgium. The Green party in Germany gained 8.2 percent of the vote and received seven seats in the EP. The Belgium Greens won two seats. Together with the Dutch *Green Progressive Accord*, which also gained two seats, they could have officially formed a parliamentary group within the EP (see Table 14.1). However, the German Greens wanted their parliamentary group to have more political clout and thus contacted some members of the "Technical Group", an affiliation of smaller groups in the EP from 1979 to 1984. After several rounds of negotiation with the green parties, together with some radical federalists, regionalists, and anti European Community groups, the "Rainbow Group" was formed as a parliamentary group in the EP. The Rainbow consists of - The *Green-Alternative European Link* (GRAEL), which include seven members of the German Green party, two members of the Dutch *Green Progressive Accord*, one member from the Italian Proletarian

Democracy Party, one from the Belgium Agalev, and one from a Basque party after Spain joined the European Community in 1986. Meanwhile GRAEL lost one Belgium member of the Ecolo party and one Italian member of the Proletarian Unity party. One German member of the Green party from West-Berlin received complete autonomy within GRAEL.

- The *European Free Alliance* (EVA), in which the regionalist groupings (i.e. the Belgian Flemish Volksunie and the Italian Sardist party) are united with the former Belgian ecologist representative for the Wallon part of Belgium and the new Basque party member.

- The *Danish movement against the European Community* which is composed of a rather heterogenous group (among others a communist, a priest, an extreme rightwinger and a very popular leftwing woman). The Danish anti-EC movement nominates candidates only for the European and not for national elections.

Table 14.1
The Rainbow Group in the European Parliament:
Electoral Results

	1979		1984	
	%	seats	%	seats
GRAEL (1)				
German Green Party	3.2	0	8.2	7
Green Progessive Accord (Netherlands)	-	-	5.6	2
Proletarian Party (Italy)	0.7	1	1.4	1
AGALEV (Belgium)	1.4	0	4.3	1
EVA (1)				
Ecologists (Belgium)	2.0	0	3.9	1
Flemish Volksunie (Belgium)	6.0	1	8.5	2
Sardist Party (Italy)	-	-	0.5	1
Anti EC Movement				
(only in Denmark)	21.0	4	20.8	4

(1) did not exist as subgroupings in 1979

Source: Official Electoral Statistics

Since the Rainbow group does not wish to have an image as a homogenous coherent group, its internal structure is consequently minimal; the three subgroups hardly ever meet together. However, the Rainbow has the status of a parliamentary fraction and as such, the group is represented in the leading bodies of the European parliament albeit through a system of rotating presidents. The only group within the Rainbow that represents green and alternative issues in the European parliament is the GRAEL. We shall therefore focus our attention on this group.

The GRAEL: Organizational Structure, Programatic Profile, and Activities

When GRAEL entered the European parliament, non-conformist political behavior of the group members was expected. In fact, the group did not disappoint these expectations: flowers on the plenary desks, vociferous exchanges with the President of the parliament or with the representatives of right wing groups, leaflets in the Plenary sessions as well as "happenings" to denounce scandals in European agricultural policy, were all characteristics of the GRAEL group at the beginning of the second legislature of the European parliament in 1984 and early 1985. In addition, the GRAEL introduced an organizational structure that was different from all other parliamentary groups in the EP. The group intended to prevent professionalisation and elite formation by using a maximum of grassroot participation and by using a rotation of representatives. GRAEL members as well as their deputies are, for instance, both entitled to vote within the group. The group meetings are generally open to the public and the newly created working groups for studying relevant political issues were designed to be the centre of activity. As such, the working groups within the GRAEL were given a certain financial autonomy. Since GRAEL members and their staff are expected to accept revenues roughly equivalent to that of skilled workers only, the group could employ a far greater number of staff members given the balance of the rather high allowences and salaries alloted to members of the European parliament. The daily decisions in the administrative area are usually taken by a General Secretary whose very activities are politically monitored by one or two GRAEL members of parliament who are rotated themselves over time. In general, the GRAEL has decided that its members of parliament are to be replaced by their deputies after half of the five-year European parliament session has elapsed.

In terms of their programatic requests, the GRAEL is still a very heterogeneous group, however, the members still have some goals in common. "Think globally, act locally" was, for instance, one of the slogans the Greens agreed upon in view of the 1984 European elections. The slogan suggested the creation of transnational webs of activity in order to fight against transnational problems such as pollution, the arms race, persecution and the violation of human rights. The slogan, however, also indicates that the institutions of the European Community are not seen by the GRAEL as very important in political terms. The GRAEL is grassroots oriented and wishes to stay in contact with its voters residing in their respective nations. In sum, the European parliament is seen as an institution through which the "green and alternative movement" can create transnational strings and influence public consciousness. Accordingly, GRAEL has used the means and the greatly valued international image of the EP to foster cooperation between social, environmental, feminist, pacifist as well as other movements. GRAEL offered rooms and translation facilities for an "Alternative Economic Summit", for a congress on "Women and Genetic Engeneering" etc. It hosted the second World Congress of prostitutes as well as meetings by Spanish agricultural workers, small peasants organizations or regionalist extremists. It contacted independence movements from Polisario to the PLO, The African National Congress, the North American Indians as well as Philippino peasant movements and the New Caledonia Liberation front. However, it is generally admitted that these contacts and activities have not created the expected "web relationship" among the movements.

Inside the European parliament, the GRAEL members clearly became more professional. From the very beginning in 1984, GRAEL members used parliamentary instruments such as questions, and interpellations to gain attention and built up contacts with interest groups and the European Commission in order to foster interests ranging from subsidies to modernizing Belgium slaughterhouses, combating environmental pollution, giving compensating payments for unfairly treated workers, to peace settlements in Central America and the protection of Human Rights. Reports prepared by GRAEL members and carried out by the European parliament include topics such as the "System of Generalized Preferences" to the Third World, agriculture and environment, babyfood, new and renewable sources of energy, biotechnology as well as aspects of pollution, nuclear energy, and contamination.

Outlook

There are several problems currently existing within the GRAEL which might affect the future of the group. Firstly, a fundamental rule of the organization has not been respected sufficiently: only two of the seven members from the German Greens gave way to their successors as member of parliament after the two and a half years of the five year European parliamentary session (rotation principle). The others either began to like the amenities of the job, perhaps felt nobody else could do the job better, or thought the successors did not have the right ideas. Secondly, GRAEL members became increasingly aware that certain concepts of the "Greens in Europe" (such as "Europe of the regions" or "creation of a web of initiatives") turned out to be empty phrases which could not possibly be realized. Thirdly, the national party organizations show only little interest in the activities of their green representatives in the European parliament for the GRAEL members seem to be too far away from their local grassroots oriented organization. Fourthly, because of their political inefficiency, the Eurogreens risk not being taken as a serious partner in the long term both from within and from outside the European parliament - verily, their voting record is patchy. Fifthly, the GRAEL tends to underestimate or to disregard potential partners such as the Commission of the European Community, where environmental concerns are also present in some directorates. Finally, the GRAEL risks overlooking that at least some of their electorate has a considerable degree of transnational and European consciousness without necessarily being against parliamentarism (e.g. parts of the environmentalists and pacifists).

In terms of their heterogeneous composition, the GRAEL within the Rainbow group is not so different from other transnational party groups within the European parliament. However, the GRAEL is well on its way toward loosing a clear identity as well as the interest of the mass media. In order to make the group more reliable and effective within the European parliament, the GRAEL has to work out clearer political positions towards various aspects of European policy. This, however, seems to be a difficult undertaking since the various national party organizations that are united in the GRAEL have no common policy stands on European issues. The future of green and alternative groups in the European parliament is, therefore, clearly dependent upon the programmatic development of national green parties.

Comparative Conclusion

15

The "New Politics Dimension" in European Green Parties

Thomas Poguntke

Introduction

After decades of `frozen´ party systems, `ecological´ parties have had remarkable electoral success in some countries, notably in Germany and Belgium, and more recently in Italy, Switzerland and Finland. The widespread attention these cases have attracted has led to a flourishing literature on this topic. Virtually all these studies, however, have used classifications of such parties which are based on a single discriminant variable like the degree of radicalism, characteristics of the electorate, or party origin (Rüdig, 1985; Kitschelt, 1988; Müller-Rommel, 1985b). Alternatively, this chapter proposes a model that facilitates their classification according to the most important aspects of a political party: program, organization and party behavior, social bases.

It has been suggested elsewhere that the emergence of these parties is in most cases related to the surge of the new politics which has left a specific imprint on their typical ´Gestalt´: The properties of the new politics are likely to mould such parties accordingly (Poguntke, 1987a: 80f.). Based on a brief review of the major characteristics of the new politics syndrome, we suggest a set of features which can be expected to be typical of parties that are primarily based on the new politics segments of society. The model is then tested empirically in order to arrive at tentative conclusions on the extent to which the emergence and success of European Green parties is related to the surge of the new politics. In addition, we shall try to shed some light on the causes and implications of the fierce conflicts inside and between these parties.

Finally, it will be demonstrated that the model is capable of discriminating in a theoretically meaningful way between genuine New Politics parties and parties that have merely attempted to attain a `green´ image. The latter hypothesis points to a terminological problem: Although they are commonly referred to in the political debate as `green´ or `ecological´ parties, the generic term `New Politics Party´ should be used for those parties that owe their particular outlook to the surge of the new politics. This has two advantages: It refers to an established body of theoretical and empirical literature and it avoids confounding what are really two analytically distinct groups, i.e. conservative ´green´ formations, and left-wing, emancipatory political parties which are concerned with a broader set of issues than merely ecology.

Any attempt to study small and newly emerging parties on a comparative basis is inevitably plagued with the lack of comprehensive information. The data that has been used for this analysis was therefore collected from the following sources: Keesing´s Contemporary Archives, election reports in periodicals, some case studies, and party publications. It covers the period from 1976 to mid-1988. Given the aim of obtaining a complete overview about European green parties, the method of relying on sources of information which often do not report in great detail appears to be adequate. Using more detailed and specific sources would necessarily confine us to the analysis of very few cases and hence render a truly comparative perspective impossible. The scope of analysis extends to those twelve West European countries which have been covered in this book. All parties or electoral formations were included which either call themselves `green´ or `ecological´. Since we are dealing with a relatively recent phenomenon, many of these parties are electorally rather weak. Hence, no specific cut-off point was applied.

Since this article is not concerned with new politics theory, we shall only give a very brief account of the major lines of argument. Subsequently, three dimensions of measurement are specified and applied in the third section. The results are given for each of them in a separate table. Finally, the findings are summarized and analyzed in the fourth part, where a quantitatively based judgement is presented as to how likely the various green parties are to conform with the suggested family of New Politics parties.

New Politics Theory

New Politics theory is concerned with the rise of a cluster of new political issues and related changes in participatory dispositions and behavior. Writers like Inglehart (1971, 1977, 1981) and Barnes, Kaase et al., (1979) - to mention only the more pioneering ones - have tried to explain these changes primarily by referring to the surge of postmaterialist value orientations:

Younger age groups, and particularly those with higher education and a new middle class background amongst them, have been socialized in a way which makes them emphasize social and self-actualization needs - like less impersonal society, participation at the workplace and in political decision-making, freedom of expression, beautiful environment and the appreciation of creativity (Inglehart, 1977, p. 42).

Other authors give more weight to changes in the social structure of modern societies and the related cognitive mobilization (Kitschelt, 1988; Dalton, 1984). However, there is no fundamental contradiction between both approaches (Chandler/Siaroff, 1986: 303). Value change cannot be explained merely by the socialization hypothesis which translates period effects into aggregate changes. There is no doubt that shifts toward new politic issue orientations and related behavioral dispositions are intimately related to changes in the social structure of advanced industrial societies.

It is this cross-nationally validated anchorage of the new politics that casts some doubt on theories that interpret new politics as a transitory phenomenon. It has been argued for the German case, that the surge of the new politics and the subsequent success of the Green party is primarily a reaction to the failure of the political and economic system to provide adequate career prospects for young university graduates (Alber, in this volume; Bürklin, 1984: 46; 1985a; 1985b: 286-90). Although it is certainly true that new politics demands represent a convenient focus for such a counter-elite strategy, the argument fails to explain the high portion of well paid party militants.

In their `pure´ form, new politics demands run counter to the dominant political paradigm of the postwar period, which centres around economic and security (old politics) issues. (Cotgrove/Duff, 1980: 339) Also, the old politics is characterized by the predominance of representative forms of decision-making and conventional political behavior. Since many new politics demands are widely perceived as challenging conventional wisdoms of economic policy, sympathy with such policies is likely to rise with growing distance from the production process. Therefore, members of the new middle classes should be disposed to be more favorable to new politics demands - regardless of their actual value orientation (Baker et al.: 152ff.).

This change of the political agenda is accompanied by shifting particpatory norms and dispositions among similar social groups. It means the increase of a qualitatively different, i.e. elite-challenging form of political participation which employs protest techniques like unofficial strikes, boycotts, blocades, or rent strikes (Barnes/Kaase, 1979). A considerable portion of individuals who are prepared to engage in protest action also participates through conventional channels and is hence available for mobilization by new politics parties.

New Politics parties should therefore display the essential elements of new politics on three dimensions: *program, political style, and electoral profile.* Their embedding in new politics should make them distinct from established parties which - though different with respect to ideology and electoral basis - belong to the old politics cluster in terms of conventional political style and a common political agenda. The radical new politics-oriented sections are therefore largely excluded from their electoral market as soon as a genuine New Politics party has emerged.

It is obviously an over-simplification to speak of only two groups of parties from the old-new politics perspective. Inherently, the three dimensions which will now be specified involve many continous variables: Few parties are either completely hierarchical or participatory, for example, and some parties may not endorse all of the new politics issues. Furthermore, most issue areas allow for positions with varying degrees of radicalism. This means that it would be more appropriate on theoretical grounds to elaborate measures which allowed us to place parties on a old-new politics continuum. Our data-base, however, is not suited for such detailed analysis. Hence, we have used relatively rigid dichotomous measures in order to clearly tap the new politics end of this underlying continuum.

Dimensions of Measurement and Analysis

On the following pages we shall now discuss the ideal-typical outlook of an ecological or green party that has been moulded by the surge of the new politics. Our model consists of three dimensions that are conventionally regarded to be central to political parties: program, organization and party behavior, social bases. The specific properties of this ideal-typical model follow from the characteristics of the new politics.

Dimension I: Programmatic Features - New Politics Orientation

Subsequently, we have identified the central programmatic elements of the new politics.

Ecology
Concern with ecological politics is one of the most prominent themes of the new politics. The link to the underlying causes of the new politics is quite evident: First, an intact environment caters to aesthetic needs. Second, persons who are less concerned about the functioning of the economy are likely to shift their attention to the protection of nature. In political terms, this implies that the imperatives of the ecological system assume priority over conventional economic rationality out of principled considerations. First and foremost, this leads to the rejection of unlimited and unregulated economic growth, which is seen to pose a fundamental threat to the ecological balance. It involves opposition to large-scale projects in general and often concentrates on resistence against nuclear power stations, which have come to symbolize all the detrimental impacts of big technology on the environment and on liberal freedoms (Nelkin/Pollack 1980: 129). Alternatively, small-scale, environmentally adapted and resource-concious production is demanded.

Mere opposition to nuclear power stations, may be combined with endorsement of conventional economic strategies which does not represent an `ecological´ political orientation. Therefore, we have used two variables: *Opposition to Nuclear Power Stations (Anti-Nuc)*, and *Ecological Orientation (Ecol)*, which describes the whole syndrome discussed in this section.

Individualism
Emphasis on individuality is a necessary element of self-actualization and as such an integral part of new politics. This dimension covers concern with individual self-determination in the widest sense: It includes all the classical Liberal freedoms, but transcends this tradition by emphasizing more strongly the individual components and aspects of these rights. Loosely formulated, it extends Liberalism towards the direction of Anarchism. To clarify: if we conceptualize a continuum `state/patrimonial´ power - `individual freedom´, Social Democracy and Conservatism would be positioned on one side, Liberalism closer to the other end with Anarchism occupying the extreme `freedom´ position.

Hence, in the context of new politics, emphasis on individual liberties is not so much about areas protected from too much state interference rather than about `state-free zones´. To give an example: Liberals would strive for exact codification of police or secret service powers, whereas the Greens in the German Land Hesse have actually demanded the complete dissolution of the *Verfassungsschutz* (domestic secret service). In order to grasp the different aspects of this issue area we have used three variables:

Classical Liberal Issues: traditional Liberal concerns, including liberalized abortion and divorce, respect for minorities, etc.; they represent a logical first step; *(Class Lib)*

Self-Determination: transcends classical Liberalism and is expressed by demands for a minimum of state interference with individual life and a maximum of tolerance for `alternative´ life styles. *(Self Deter)*

Feminism: as specific expression of individual self-actualization and self-determination, it could have been included under `Self-Determination´, but was treated as a separate variable because of its independent existence as a political force. *(Fem)*

Participatory Democracy/Direct Democracy
For many adherents of new politics, the strong emphasis on individualistic, self-determined participation describes both a normative goal and their actual mode of behavior. This is also reflected in the parties´ unconventional outlook and will be discussed below.

On the ideological level, it gives rise to the concept of `Basisdemokratie´ (grass roots democracy) as the main principle of political and societal organization. The essence of it is direct participation in decision-making on specific issues as opposed to the usual choice between political programs which are then specified and realized by professional politicians (Kaase, 1982: 185-86). It means that the lower units of any societal organization ought to have extensive decision-making powers, which implies decentralized structures. Ideally, the lowest unit has the most resources and competences, and the higher-level bodies only take over tasks which the basic unit is structurally incapable of mastering. Access to decentralized bodies facilitates direct and concrete influence on decisions that affect daily life - unlike the present organization of democracy, which functions in a much more abstract and mediated way.

Appparently, decentralization is not, unlike conservative strategies, intended to shield off `big politics´ from participatory demands of the populace. On the contrary, it is seen to be the essential precondition for meaningful participatory opportunities on all levels, because it distributes power to more units and makes politics more transparent and hence intelligible.

As already indicated, this principle of organization should extend to all spheres of society, which means in concrete terms that participatory opportunities should be vastly expanded. In order to inhibit any possible tendency towards oligarchization, a strict political control of elected office-holders is proposed together with severe limitation of re-election possibilities *(Part Democ)*.

Leftism
Empirically and logically, new politics is related to some aspects of traditional left-wing policies (Inglehart, 1977; Cotgove/Duff, 1980: 344ff.). Few remarks may suffice to indicate the principal logical links: Individualism and participatory orientation are highly likely to lead to demands for more self-control and co-determination at the workplace. Openness to change and opposition to hierarchical structures, the need to assume relatively extensive control over the economy in order to restructure it in an ecologically meaningful way - the motives differ from traditional leftism, but the political implications are similar in a considerable number of policy areas. In recent years, the links between the new politics and traditional left-wing concerns have led to a partial change in the public understanding of the substantive meaning of the left-right dimension (Dalton, 1988: 121).

Furthermore, a certain level of relative material scarcity as result of non-growth policies would necessitate egalitarian measures for legitimation: If the cake is not to be ever growing, so that everybody has the reasonable expectation of getting somewhat more every year, redistributive policies are likely to become more salient. The alternative strategy, which is to resort to more repression in order to cope with the erosion of legitimacy is impossible due to the inherent anti-authoritarianism of the new politics.

Therefore, this categorie is intended to cover all demands which resemble traditional goals of the left like workers´ control, egalitarian policies or more societal control of the economic process *(Left)*.

Third World
Persons who care less about their own material well-being are obviously more likely to be prepared to make true sacrifices in order to enhance living conditions in the Third World. Such attitudes also tap the postmaterial value of belonging in the widest, that is to say global sense (cf. Baker et al., 1981: 141; Inglehart, 1977: 384). Consequently, parties are awarded a positive score on this variable if

they are strongly concerned with Third World problems and favour redistribution from North to South *(3rd World)*.

Unilateral disarmament
Postmaterialists emphasize security less than materialists but are more concerned with values like `belonging´ and `reconciliation´. Therefore, they can be expected to be more sceptical towards the dominant logic of international relations based on security. Alternatively, they may be prepared to take decisive unilateral steps in disarmament policy in order to approach a situation based on mutual trust instead of deterrence. This issue is sub-divided into two variables: opposition to the NATO twin-track decision and the quest for unilateral disarmament.

In recent years, the so-called NATO twin-track decision on the deployment of intermediate range nuclear missiles in Western Europe has dominated the debate in many countries. We have therefore used the stance on this issue as a separate variable, although it is largely irrelevant for non-NATO countries. The prominence of the missile debate justifies the inclusion of this variable despite the resolution of this conflict through the ratification of the INF-treaty *(Anti Miss)*. All more far-reaching unilaterist arms reduction proposals up to neutralist or genuinely pacifist positions are covered by the `unilateral clisarmament´ variable. *(Unil Dis)*

The following figure (15.1) gives an overview of the programmatic orientation of green parties in Western Europe. The broadly comparative perspective inevitably means that we are confined to an incomplete data base. Many of these `blanks´ can be explained by the application of a strict procedure: Broad reference in the sources to `environmental orientation´, for example, was not considered to be sufficient evidence for a given party´s ecological orientation. Some of the variables, like `Participatory Democracy´ are `open-ended´, that is to say that a potentially unlimited number of possible policy proposals and specific strategies are covered by such a variable. Hence, a positive score was awarded, if a party endorses one or more central demands covered by a variable and no contradictory information was available.

Any negative variable score led to the negative categorization of the whole dimension. Such a strictly `exclusive´ approach, which was applied throughout the analysis, seems to be necessary in order to reduce the danger of false judgements on the basis of what is essentially an incomplete data collection: Whereas a high number of positive variable scores may merely result from a large amount of available data on a certain case, any negative score carries a definite `information value`.

Since most of the issues taken by themselves could belong to another ideological framework, a party was only considered to score positively on the programmatic dimension, if it had more than 50 % (i.e. six) positive variable scores.

Symbols for figure 15.1:
+ positive score on variable or dimension
- negative score on variable or dimension
`blank`: no information on this variable/information insufficient to award score for dimension
* last column gives result for whole dimension - a positive score for the whole dimension was awarded only for six or more positive variables. Any negative variable led to a negative score for the whole dimension.
** The French ecological movement has set up electoral organizations individually for each election, where most of the various groups joined forces. The analysis is based on joint election platforms. In November 1982 the `Movement d'Ecologique Politique` and the `Confederation Ecologique` adopted a permanent party structure, but the `Friends of the Earth` did not join.
Full party names: Alternative List Austria (ALö); United Greens Austria (VGö); Environment Party (MP); Green Party Switzerland (GPS), until 1987: Federation of Green Parties (Fed.Green); Green Alliance Switzerland (GBS), until 1987: Green Alternative Switzerland (GRAS);

Figure 15.1
Programatic Orientation of Green Parties in Western Europe

Country	Party	Ecology		Individualism						Disarmament		Total		Total Dimens. Score
		Ecol	Anti- Nuc	Class Lib	Self Deter	Fem	Part Democ	Left	3rd World	Anti Miss	Unil Dis	+	−	
Austria	ALÖ		+		+	+	+	+	+		+	7	0	+
	VGÖ	+		−			−	−				1	3	−
Belgium	AGALEV	+	+	+	+		+	+	+	+	+	9	0	+
	Ecolo	+	+	+	+		+	+	+	+	+	9	0	+
Denmark	De Gronne	+	+	+	+		+	+			+	7	0	+
Finland	Greens	+	+	+	+	+		+	+		+	8	0	+
France	Greens **	+	+	+	+	+	+	+	+		+	9	0	+
Germany	Greens	+	+	+	+	+	+	+	+	+	+	10	0	+
Ireland	Green All.	+	+	+	+	+	+	+	+			8	0	+
Italy	Verdi	+	+	+	+	+	+	+	+			8	0	+
Luxemb.	GAP	+	+	+	+	+	+	+	+	+	+	10	0	+
Sweden	MP	+	+	+	+	+	+	+	+		+	9	0	+
Switzerl.	GPS	+		+				−				2	1	−
	GBS	+	+		+	+			+		+	6	0	+
UK	Ecology P	+	+	+	+	+	+	+	+	+	+	10	0	+

Dimension II: Unconventional Political Style

This dimension follows from the normative position of new politics proponents as well as from their behavioral dispositions. Obviously, normative ends are easiest to realize within one´s own party. Hence, we can expect a New Politics party to be decidedly participatory and grass-roots oriented in its outlook. Furthermore, any tendency towards oligarchization and hierarchization within such a party would not only meet ideological resistence but also elite-challenging participatory action by the party´s rank-and-file. Such a disposition of a large part of a New Politics party´s potential supporters towards unconventional political action should also be detectable in the way the party acts as a collectivity. Unfortunately, our data does not permit a very detailed exploration of these aspects. Therefore, the analysis is limited to two variables: Participatory party structure (i.e. rules) and party action (i.e. behavior) (see Figure 15.2).

Since party statutes are to a large extent influenced by normative considerations, we can expect to find a relatively straightforward translation of participatory, anti-authoritarian aspirations into the party constitution (Poguntke 1987b).

In the following schema, a positive score was awarded if the available information permitted the conclusion that the party structure is characterized by anti-hierarchy measures like involvement of the rank-and-file in specific policy decisions, open access to party meetings on all levels, public party meetings, no office accumulation, provisions for a strong control of elected office holders, or limited permitted periods in elected offices. Obviously, such a list can never be exhaustive - the potential variations of such provisions are almost unlimited and to a certain extent country-specific. Hence, qualitative judgement of individual cases was applied, not the use of a mechanistic check list *(party struct)*.

Due to the participatory composition of such a party, a strong impetus should exist for the party as a whole to engage in extra-parliamentary, unconventional forms of political action, like demonstrations, boycotts, strikes, and the like.

However, only a small fraction of a political party´s sympathy potential actually joins the party. In the case of a New Politics party, this portion may even be smaller because of the predominance of unconventional participatory dispositions within this social group. Consequently, a considerable share of these political energies will normally be invested in the `milieu´ of such a party, i.e. in citizen initiatives and extra-parliamentary movements. Therefore, a new politics party will rarely be the most numerous force in unconventional political actions and will be often confined to a participant rather than a dominant role. Hence, a positive score was awarded for this variable whenever a party engages in protest action without assuming a clearly dominant position versus the extra-parliamentary forces *(party action).*

Figure 15.2
Behavioral Change and Political Style of Green Parties in Western Europe*

Country	Party	party struct	party action	dimension score**
Austria	ALÖ	+		+
	VGÖ	-		-
Belgium	AGALEV	+	+	+
	ECOLO	+	+	+
Denmark	De Gronne	+	+	+
Finland	Greens	+	+	+
Germany	Greens	+	+	+
France	Greens	+	+	+
Ireland	Green All.	+	+	+
Italy	Verdi	+	+	+
Luxemb.	GAP	+	+	+
Sweden	MP	+	+	+
Switzerl.	GPS	+		+
	GBS	+		+
UK	Ecology P	+	+	+

* cases without available data were omitted
** one positive available score was considered to be sufficient for a positive overall evaluation on this dimension

Dimension III: Electoral Profile
As discussed earlier, the social potential for a New Politics party consists of individuals who are concerned with New Politics issues out of their postmaterial value orientations and/or because of their specific social position, which makes such issues appear to correspond particularly to their interests. An independent or

reinforcing factor can be the appeal the unconventional political style of such a party exerts on protest-inclined persons.

These groups can be defined by the empirical categories that we shall use for measurement. However, situation-specific factors like neighbourhood opposition to environmentally detrimental projects may independently compel significant numbers of electors to vote for a New Politics party and hence dilute the picture considerably. This explains why the electoral profile of such parties is normally less distinct than one would otherwise expect.

Keeping this caveat in mind, voters for New Politics parties should tend to be: *postmaterialists, young, highly educated, new middle class*. In most countries, individuals that correspond to this social profile tend to live in urban areas. Hence, the variable `urban´ has been included as an additional indicator.

We have already discussed the links between the new politics and a general left-wing orientation. Consistently, we can expect a majority of voters of a New Politics party to have voted previously for other left-wing parties and/or to place themselves on the left of the political spectrum *(left)*.

How are the indicators for electoral profile scored? Apart from postmaterialism, which includes most other variables, each of the features taken by itself is largely meaningless: Only in sufficient combination do these variables describe a distinct social group, the potential of a New Politics party. Hence, the subsequent rules were applied:

Central to our theoretical consideration is postmaterialism, which can either be measured directly by survey methods or indirectly by the variables `young´, `educated´, `new middle class´. Since these latter three variables are correlated, two of them were considered sufficient to indicate the correspondence of a party´s electoral support with our model. The remaining variables are additional variables which can help to augment the judgement. A negative score on any variable led to a negative dimension score. However, we are aware of the danger of committing an ecological fallacy. Not every party with a young educated electorate is a New Politics party and in some cases only few of the possible variables were reported in the sources. Nevertheless, the combination of programmatic, electoral, and organizational aspects minimizes the danger of false categorization (see Figure 15.3).

Figure 15.3
Electoral Profile of Green Parties in Western Europe*

Country	Party	either post mat.	young	or educ	n.mid. class	additional indicators urban	left voter	dimension score**
Austria	ALÖ	+	+	+	+	+	+	+
	VGÖ	-	+	+	+	+	-	-
Belgium	AGALEV	+	+	+		+	+	+
	Ecolo	+	+	+	+	+	+	+
Denmark	De Gronne	+				+		
Finland	Greens		+	+		+	+	+
France	Greens	+	+	+	+	+	+	+
Germany	Greens	+	+	+	+	+	+	+
Ireland	Green All.					+		
Sweden	MP		+	+	+	+	+	+
Switzerl.	GPS		+					

* cases without available data are ommitted
** requirement for positive score: `+´ on post mat., or at least on two out of young, educ., n.mid. class.

Results

We shall now summarize and discuss the results from the preceeding description. As a first step, we need to decide whether or not the analyzed parties conform to our theoretically derived model of a new politics party. Since we have applied fairly rigid scoring rules with any negative variable leading to a negative score for the whole dimension, it seems suitable to apply the subsequent four categories:

`highly likely´ - a party is considered to be highly likely to conform to our theoretical expectations if it has two or three positive dimensions.

`likely´ - condition: a positive score for one dimension and positive variable scores on at least one other dimension. Although the lack of data does not permit a definite judgement, all available information suggests conformance with our model.

`incomplete data´ - where little more than the party´s name suggests a new politics orientation, this category applies.

`negative´ - any negative information on any variable

automatically leads to a completely negative classification of the analyzed party.

Figure 15.4
Classification of Green Parties in Western Europe

Country	Party	variables total +	-	dimensions total +	-	classification
Austria	ALÖ	13	0	3	0	highly likely
	VGÖ	4	6	0	3	negative
Belgium	AGALEV	15	0	3	0	highly likely
	Ecolo	16	0	3	0	highly likely
Denmark	De Gronne	10	0	2	0	highly likely
Finland	Greens	14	0	3	0	highly likely
France	Greens	17	0	3	0	highly likely
Germany	Greens	18	0	3	0	highly likely
Ireland	Green All.	12	0	2	0	highly likely
Italy	Verdi	9	0	2	0	highly likely
Luxemb.	GAP	12	0	2	0	highly likely
Sweden	MP	16	0	3	0	highly likely
Switzerl.	GPS	4	1	1	1	negative
	GBS	7	0	2	0	highly likely
UK	Ecology P	12	0	2	0	highly likely

We have analyzed 15 parties in 12 countries. The most significant result is that in all countries we can identify at least one Green party that is clearly rooted in the new politics segments of the populace. In two cases, Green parties do not belong to the new politics family, although their existence can be understood as a reaction to the surge of the New Politics

Evaluation
Green Conservatism
Our analysis has shown that all but two Green parties share common organizational, social, and ideological characteristics that can be explained through the emergence of the new politics in advanced industrialized societies. As such, Green parties are only a subgroup

of the wider phenomenon of a new type of New Politics parties (Poguntke, 1987a,b).

The two exceptions, however, indicate the ambiguity of the ecological theme. As already mentioned in the introduction, conservative answers to the environmental crisis are conceivable. They can vary substantially with respect to their degree of right-wing orientation.

One major current is related to the tradition of green conservatism which has always resented the destruction of nature by modern industrial society (Murphy, 1985: 145). This tendency is also identifiable as a minority many new politics-oriented green parties. The political concern of these `Conservationists´ is usually confined to environmental problems. Consequently, they tend to resist the broadening of the political scope of an emergent green party. Apart from the concern with the environment, however, they have little in common with the new politics that is concerned with a much broader set of political issues. Apparently, the Green party in Switzerland has been dominated by `Conservationists´ who have successfully preserved the party´s single-issue orientation (Ladner, in this volume).

Unlike these rather apolitical environmentalists some right-wing ecologists have presented encompassing political programs that can be understood as reaction to the challenge from the new politics. More radical right-wing versions of ecologism draw on anti-democratic concepts of `naturally ordered society´ and advocate authoritarian strategies for the solution of environmental problems. One albeit politically insignificant example is the German ÖDP of the ex-CDU and ex-green politician Herbert Gruhl (Poguntke, 1987a: 83). However, our measurements have not been designed to discriminate between these variants.

The Austrian VGÖ seems to belong to the category of conservative green parties. Recent developments in Austria suggest, however, that a process of internal clarification is under way. The VGÖ set up a joint list with the progressive ALÖ for the 1986 parliamentary election (Haerpfer, in this volume). Subsequently, a conference was held in order to create a joint party organization. This led to the secession of the extreme right wing of the VGÖ - which corroborates our negative categorization for the present time.

Green New Politics Parties: Contrast and Congruence
Although the remaining green parties share a wide range of new politics-induced characteristics, they are by no means alike. On the

contrary, there are substantial differences between green parties that have led to fierce conflicts in the parliamentary group of the European parliament and brought international green cooperation for the 1984 Euro-election campaign to the brink of collapse (Müller-Rommel, 1985c: 392f; Buck, in this volume).

In the light of these contrasts, it is a legitimate question whether it makes at all sense to speak of one `new type of party´. However, provided that typologies are a useful heuristic tool if the observed cases have more in common than seperates them, the above figures give ample support for our classification. After all, experience has shown that despite all controversies, these green parties have cooperated in many events.

No doubt, the remarkable homogeneity of European green parties, as it emerges from our analysis, is partially caused by the application of categories that have been designed to clearly identify parties that are products of the new politics. However, they are not suited to grasp differences within this group of parties - a procedure that inevitably follows from the broadly comparative approach of the kind presented here. In view of the available data, any attempt to differentiate between degrees of radicalism for single variables would have been illusive. However, such differentiation is possible if we focus not on single variables but on the character of the parties.

Within the group of new politics-oriented green or ecological parties, two subgroups are identifiable, the `Moderates´ and `Fundamentalists´. At first sight, the crucial criterion of distinction seems to be the position on the traditional left-right dimension that is obviously related to the conflict over the new politics (see above). However, although this conflict is not unrelated to the left-right continuum, it is primarily motivated by a disagreement over strategies as to how to accomplish the goals that are shared by both groups of parties. Whereas the Moderates believe in the eventual success of piecemeal reform, the Fundamentalists fear the pacifying and demobilizing effects of this strategy.

Undoubtedly, the choice of strategy is related to different concepts of the state and the role of parliamentary politics. Many green activists adhere to various shades of Marxist-inspired analyses of the state as an agent of the capitalist system which they in turn hold responsible for the outlook of environment and society. From this perspective, the real power resides with those who run the industrial system, and politics is primarily seen as a phenomenon of the super-structure.

This interpretation suggests that there is little to be gained from the attempt to attain political control over the state machinery. Alternatively, the system has to be challenged frontally, through mass movements. This concept of societal `counter power´ (Gegenmacht) rests on the conviction that it is possible to effectively limit the power of state and industry through mass mobilization. Furthermore, it implies that the parliamentary arena is not considered to be the place where decisions are made. Instead, it is primarily regarded as a useful arena for voicing political opinions and mobilizing people for extra-parliamentary action.

The Moderates, on the other hand, are influenced by the traditional liberal concept of the state, that regards it as a relatively neutral and powerful instrument of those who have gained political control over it. Unlike classical Liberals, however, green Moderates are considerably more sceptical about the real power of parliamentary politics. They do not deny the power of the industrial system, but nevertheless believe in the capacity of the state to influence the course of events.

Consistent with their preference for extra-parliamentary politics, Fundamentalists usually seek to forge broad alliances. Whereas the Moderates keep a close eye on their (parliamentary) respectability, radical greens are less willing to denounce new social movement activists who get involved in violent confrontations with the police. However, this is primarily a strategic, not a substantive disagreement. Both green tendencies are opposed to violent action, but the Fundamentalists argue that it is necessary not to isolate extremist activists who share green goals.

It needs to be emphasized, however, that the preference for one of the opposing positions is not always ideologically motivated. Just as important is the organizational history. Parties that are products of social movements have frequently struggled their way into political relevance through fierce and sometimes violent confrontations with the police. Additionally, related bureaucratic and legal action by the state apparatus has not always been successful in keeping up its image of impartiality. A deeply rooted suspicion of the state and an errosion of trust in formalized political procedures is therefore likely to be widespread among movement activists.

Obviously, both tendencies are also identifiable within most new politics-oriented green parties. Besides the reasons discussed thus far, the predominance of one of these factions can also be explained by external, i.e. party system-specific or political factors (Müller-Rommel 1982). In countries where governmental participation is out of reach, responsible opposition may not be very attractive.

Consistently, the German Fundamentalists gained influence in the party after the collapse of the first red-green coalition in Hesse.

The radicalism of a green party is also likely to be determined by the configuration of the national party system. Where an established Left Socialist - or even Euro-Communist - party occupies the political space left of Social Democracy, a newly emergent green party will find it more promising to embark on a moderate strategy.

Clearly, the distinction between moderate and fundamentalist green parties is closer to a theoretical construct than to an empirical description. However, if we conceive of these two types as representing the opposite ends of a continuum on which all genuine New Politics parties can be situated, the following pattern emerges:

The green parties of Ireland, Great Britain, Belgium (Ecolo), Sweden, Finland and parts of the fluid coalitions of the French Ecologists are closer to the moderate end, whereas the Belgium AGALEV, the Austrian ALÖ, the Swiss GBS, the other tendency of the French Greens, and the Greens in Luxemburg, Italy, and Germany lean towards the fundamentalist side.

Naturally, most of our categorizations are not entirely on safe grounds. The bulk of the green parties is of relatively recent vintage, which means that the process of internal ideological clarification - including secessions - is still going on. The state of some parties is also very fluid due to their small size which makes all kind of internal coups possible.

Conclusion

The foregoing analysis has demonstrated that our proposed model represents a suitable tool for identifying parties that owe their `Gestalt´ primarily to shifts towards the new politics. The integration of the most iimportant aspects of a political party has led to a clearer image of the qualitative effects of such changes. These parties share common ideological, organizational and sociological properties that are associated with shifts towards new politics. This makes them differ substantially from established parties which are predominantly rooted in the political traditions of the old politics. Even our `negative´ cases are only negative with respect to the whole new politics syndrome. Their concern with some of these issues, particularly with environmental pollution, can be understood as a reaction to the rise of new politics.

The emergence of New Politics parties is likely to create severe difficulties for parties of the Left in many countries. For many years, they could count on getting a good share of the young and educated vote which is now defecting to these parties, whereas the Conservative parties go largely unaffected. Hence, in countries with non-fragmented party systems, the Right is likely to enjoy a structural advantage for a considerable period of time, if the dominant party on the Left does not succeed in coming to terms with the new politics. Given the fundamental conflict involved, compromise is hard to achieve.

Presently, it is difficult to predict which green tendency will be dominant in the end. Clearly, much hinges on the format of the party system and systematic factors like the electoral system. However, as long as the spread of bureaucracy impinges on individual self-determination, as long as the menace of nuclear annihilation is not banned, and as long as one environmental catastrophe is only backstaged by yet another - frequently worse - disaster, it is highly likely that green parties of various kinds are here to stay.

16
Modernization, Cleavage Structures, and the Rise of Green Parties and Lists in Europe

Jens Alber

Freezing or Melting of the Western European Party Systems?

In their famous article on *cleavage structures, party systems and voter alignments* Lipset and Rokkan postulated a "freezing" of the Western European party systems since the 1920s. Their often cited freezing hypothesis is not only based on the empirical observation of remarkable continuity, but also rooted in the conceptual consideration that the narrowing of the support market brought about through the growth of mass parties and the high level of organizational mobilization of most sectors of the community "left very few openings for new movements" or new alternatives (Lipset/Rokkan 1967: 51).

On the other hand, Talcott Parsons - the author from whom Lipset and Rokkan derived their conceptual framework - seems to foretell profound changes in the politics of western societies. Departing from his famous A-G-I-L scheme, Parsons postulated three (and only three) revolutions in modern western history: the industrial revolution as the differentiation between the societal community and the economy, the democratic revolution signifying the differentiation between the societal community and the polity, and the educational revolution marking the differentiation between the societal community and the cultural subsystem (Parsons 1971). For Parsons this third rupture is just as deep reaching as the first two. In his opinion it will give rise to new quests for solidarity, community, participation, and decentralization, and markets and bureaucracies as dominant forms of organization will increasingly be complemented by new forms of collegial associations, rooted in the rise of the professions. At least implicitly, it seems, Parsons foresees a melting rather than a freezing of western party systems.

It seems evident that something close to an educational revolution has taken place during the last decades. Since 1950 enrollment ratios in institutions of higher learning have quadrupled in Western European countries (Schneider 1983). From various political studies we also know that the Western European party systems are no longer marked by the traditional degree of persistence. Mogens Pedersen (1983) has shown that there is a widespread trend towards increasing electoral volatility. Maria Maguire's replication of the Rose/Urwin studies showed that since the 1960s parties register significant changes in electoral support, with old and leading parties being particularly susceptible to losses (Maguire 1983). Klaus von Beyme (1982) demonstrated that in the 1970s there has also been a trend towards increasing party fragmentation, as the number of parties polling more than 2 percent of the vote has been growing. From single country studies, we also know that the political salience of the old cleavages seems to be diminishing. Thus, the major longitudinal study of German elections in the post-war period found that the combined explanatory power of the four traditional cleavages decreased by some 20 percent between 1953 and 1976 (Baker et.al 1981).

Does this mean that we have already entered a new stage of political development as suggested by Parsons? The results of the empirical studies are somewhat equivocal. They allow the reader to find the extent of persistence just as remarkable as the amount of change. Neither volatility nor the number of parties increased throughout all Western European countries. Within single countries, social class and religion seem to remain the strongest single predictors of partisanship. Clearly, there is change and persistence. The binding force of the old cleavages has diminished but not disappeared.

In this situation it is somewhat premature, if some scholars - maybe under the impression of the great success of Inglehart's book on the Silent Revolution (1977) - turn to individual life-styles and value preferences rather than structurally rooted interests in the search for social bases of political behavior. "Values" are certainly important, but as a tool for macroanalysis the concept seems useful only, if values are conceived as stable orientations which may be linked to specific milieus in the social structure. In the tradition of Lipset and Rokkan, and in the light of Parsons' arguments it appears more fruitful to inquire whether we can detect new cleavages which might become foci of group formations, how such new cleavages interact with the old cleavages, and how the existing political institutions and party organizations channel the new demands. In a second step we should then examine whether the development of green parties can meaningfully be related to new cleavage structures. As a first step, I have prepared the conceptual framework, shown below. It presents some speculation about the development of new cleavage lines together with a schematic summary of factors which seem likely to diminish the salience of the old cleavages.

Modernization and the Restructuration of Cleavages

My attempt to specify potential new cleavages departs from the Lipset/Rokkan typology, but it interprets their approach in the light of the Weberian sociology of domination. Seen from this perspective, Lipset and Rokkan discuss cleavages in four analytical dimensions: (1) the realm of sector-specific property classes (primary vs. secondary sector), (2) the dimension of acquisition classes (workers vs. employers), (3) the realm of the power struggle between the state and the power contending associations (state vs. church), and (4) the dimension of authority relations between governing elites and the subject population (dominant vs. subject culture). In this adaption, the territorial axis of the Lipset/Rokkan scheme is understood as an institutional centre-periphery axis which captures the growing importance of the state and hence of authority relations focussing on issues of political control and legitimation.

The question then is if we can observe societal trends which create potentials for new cleavages in these dimensions. My conceptual scheme is an attempt to specify hypotheses in this respect, and to suggest topics for research on new group formations that we can actually observe.

Let me first turn to a discussion of *property classes*. All western nations have witnessed the twin process of an enormous growth of the welfare state and of the service sector. The bulk of the labour force is shifting from the production of goods to the production of services. Within the service sector, public employment in the fields of health and education records particularly heavy increases. In this process new kinds of property rights differentiate. The educational revolution and the increasing dependence of economic growth upon technological innovation make academic degrees a new form of educational capital which is usable for returns.

With the growth of the public sector, the right to tenured office becomes another new form of property of some quantitative importance. The growth of the welfare state, finally, has created welfare entitlements as a third new type of property.

198

Figure 16.1
Modernization and Changing Cleavage Structures in Western Europe

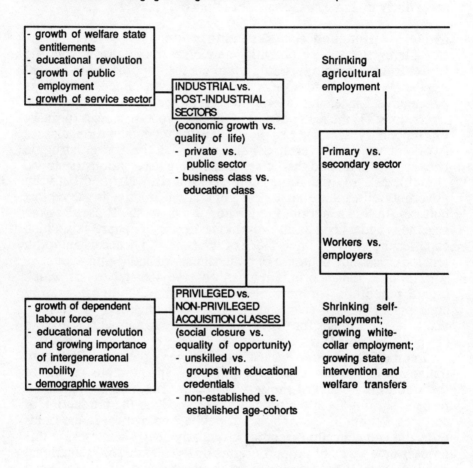

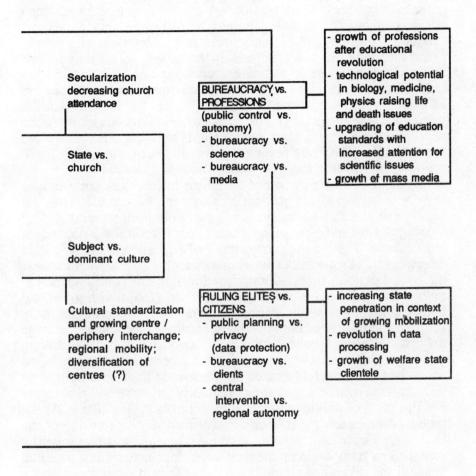

Secularization
decreasing church
attendance

State vs.
church

Subject vs.
dominant culture

Cultural standardization
and growing centre /
periphery interchange;
regional mobility;
diversification of
centres (?)

BUREAUCRACY vs.
PROFESSIONS
(public control vs.
autonomy)
- bureaucracy vs.
  science
- bureaucracy vs.
  media

RULING ELITES vs.
CITIZENS
- public planning vs.
  privacy
  (data protection)
- bureaucracy vs.
  clients
- central
  intervention vs.
  regional autonomy

- growth of professions
  after educational
  revolution
- technological potential
  in biology, medicine,
  physics raising life
  and death issues
- upgrading of education
  standards with
  increased attention for
  scientific issues
- growth of mass media

- increasing state
  penetration in context
  of growing mobilization
- revolution in data
  processing
- growth of welfare state
  clientele

This differentiation of new property classes creates novel potentials for cleavage. Since civil servants and welfare beneficiaries are paid from state coffers, conflicts over the tax ratio between groups living from the private and the public sector appear likely. Demographic changes making for a growing number of pensioners probably exacerbate these tensions. A second potential for tensions my arise from the growing employment in the service sector. Producing services rather than goods, and interacting with people rather than with machines, persons in the service sector may be less inclined towards formal rationality than persons socialized in the industry sector. As they earn their incomes outside industry, they are afflicted by the negative effects of industrial production without participating in the positive effects of growth. Tensions between the new "educated service class" and the old "business class" therefore appear likely. The issue "economic growth vs. quality of life" will probably become the focus of such tensions.

As the overwhelming part of the labour force in western countries is by now working in dependent employment, the old class conflict between workers and employers will probably be complemented by cleavages between new *acquisition classes* within the dependent labour force. The growing importance of educational credentials as determinants of mobility chances makes such a development appear likely in a double respect. First, the educational revolution tends to reverse the quantitative relationship between groups with lower and higher schooling. While in preceding decades those having only fulfilled the period of compulsory schooling represented the large majority of an age cohort, they now become a rapidly shrinking minority. This entails a potential for the emergence of an unskilled underclass with severely limited possibilities in the labour market. In this situation conflicts over the opportunity structure and the degree and direction of public labour market controls appear likely. As the mobilization in the Third World countries and the extension of the European Communities will increase the inflow of competing unskilled migrant workers, the new underclass appears as a potential base for the revival of ethnic prejudice and right wing movements. The recent developments in France may already be an expression of these tendencies.

A second aspect of the educational revolution entails a potential for the formation of acquisition classes among those who possess degrees of higher learning. If vocational careers become more closely linked to educational credentials, intergenerational mobility replaces career mobility as the dominant channel of advancement. In this situation, changes of the occupational structure will largely be effected through the succession of generations. This implies a growing potential for a differentiation of life-chances between various age-cohorts and hence intergenerational cleavage.

While the growth of this potential seems inherent in the increasing importance of educational credentials and intergenerational mobility, its actualization will largely hinge upon phase-specific constellations of factors which structure mobility chances. In a constellation where the cohorts graduating from the universities meet with structurally blocked mobility chances, they become a negatively privileged acquisition class which is likely to voice an intergenerational cleavage. During the phase of heavy enrollment expansion, the chance to define the situation in these terms is even enhanced, as many students are recruited from strata living in social distance to institutions of higher learning. These students probably enter the academic world with only diffuse expectations which seem particularly prone to generate frustration. Since the growth of mass universities concentrates the student cohorts in a common setting, the organizational chances for an effective mobilization are high.

In several European countries this constellation seems to have been present in recent years. The enrollment revolution occured among the large cohorts born during the baby-boom years, so that the absolute number of graduates mushroomed. At the same time the expansion of the service sector in general and the public sector in particular slowed down. The stock of positions in these fields is occupied by relatively young cohorts who will keep their posts for decades. In this situation the potential for a cleavage between established and non-established cohorts is high. Whereas those inside the system will defend the status quo, those not finding qualified openings in the labour market will press for more equality of opportunity, for the expansion of services, and for more participation. Being young, not integrated into a stable system of social control, and barred from the assumption of responsible positions, they may also be prone to cultivate an ethic of commitment rather than an ethic of responsibility in public affairs.

The educational revolution also affects the relationship between the *state and associations*. The growing output of academics swells the ranks of the professions. These groups are the traditional strongholds of liberal resistance against an increasing state penetration. They are highly cohesive, socially closed groups with high organizational capacity. Organized along collegial rather than hierarchic lines, they are alien to bureaucratic control and tend to resist public encroachments upon their autonomy. On the other hand, the advancements in medicine, biology, and physics confront the public much more immediately with the consequences of professional work than before, because they involve basic questions about human life and death. The array of problems ranges from genetic manipulation, extra-corporal fertilization, and the selection of patients for life-saving organ transplantations to the utilization of nuclear energy. In this situation demands for a public regulation of professional work are likely to grow, especially since the upgrading of educational standards presumably enhances the attention for scientific issues among the public. A cleavage between the professionals´ quest for autonomy and public pressures for control thus appear likely.

A second cleavage between the state and associations may centre around the role of the media. The growth of the mass media has given the journalists and owners of media strong legitimation and control functions which in some ways echo the traditional role of the hierocratic powers in western countries. This poses new problems for the relationship between the state and the press. Here, as in the case of the professions, the balance between associational autonomy and public responsibility will probably be at the heart of conflicts.

A potential for a new *centre-periphery* cleavage between governing elites and subject citizens builds up, because the past decades have been marked by an upsurge of both state penetration and social mobilization. The "citizens" are such an inclusive category, however, that it seems much easier to specify issues of conflict than to locate specific social carriers of the antagonisms. Two foci of conflicts seem to be generic. First, the revolution in data processing makes for a cleavage between the planning interests of public bureaucracies and the citizens´ interest in privacy. The question which groups articulate this conflict seems structurally underdetermined, however. A second potential for new cleavages arises from the growth of welfare state schemes. As an increasing number of persons live from politically regulated transfer payments, the contacts between state authorities and citizens multiply. Since the outlooks of bureaucracies and clients are inevitably at variance - the former deal with claims in a standardized, universalistic form as "cases", the latter see them as highly particularistic "personal requests" - a cleavage between bureaucracies and clients breaks forth. This creates a certain potential for the formation of client organizations which seek to influence the budgetary process and to defend the claimants´ interest against the bureaucracies. If internal differentiations within the group of clients are high, however, an individual settlement of grievances via the judicial process seems more likely than an effective collective mobilization, especially if we consider that there are no pre-structured channels of contact or communication among various client groups.

A certain potential for territorially based defense movements against central interventions is probably kept alive, as the increasing state penetration meets with increasing mobilization in the peripheries. The realization of this potential will probably remain sporadic, however, depending on specific issues such as the installment of nuclear power plants.

I am fully aware that all of this is speculation. The interesting part of the exercise, of course, is to see if and how movements and party organizations that we can actually observe fit into this framework. In this respect the scheme suggests topics for research, as it contains hypotheses about the likely social carriers and the issues of new movements. For illustrative purposes I want to apply the framework to an analysis of green parties in Western Europe. The question then is if the Greens can be interpreted as representatives of one of the new cleavages which the scheme specifies.

Such an analysis is not merely an exercise in classification. It immediately relates to the broader theoretical approaches I have outlined at the beginning. From the perspective of the Parsonian theory of the three basic revolutions we would interpret the Greens as harbingers of a new phase of post-industrial politics which are here to stay. If this interpretation were correct we should expect to find the party supporters predominantly among those groups whose rise is a trend pattern linked to the educational revolution: the new educational class in the service sector, and the professions. The perspective of the freezing hypothesis, on the other hand, would suggest to interpret the Greens merely as a transitory appearance on the political scene. In this case we would expect the green party support to come predominantly from groups whose rise is rooted in phase-specific conditions rather than long-term trends, such as the non-established age cohorts whose formation we related to a specific macro-constellation.

An Illustrative Application of the Conceptual Scheme: Green Parties in Western Europe

Nearly all case studies on green parties in this book explicitly define the Greens as a movement of the educated new middle class. It has been shown that many green party followers have earned an educational degree qualifying for academic studies. Furthermore, the upper educational strata are clearly overrepresented among the Greens. However, this does not yet indicate where to place the Greens in our scheme. Are they the representatives of the new educated middle class concentrated in the public sector (e.g. the teachers)? Are they the sounding board of the professions? Or are they the vanguard of a new negatively privileged acquisition class with blocked mobility chances?

Unfortunately, the available studies do not present their findings in the analytical break-downs that our conceptual framework would suggest. Thus, they usually do not differentiate between private and public employment, or between traditional and professional categories among the self-employed. They also say very little about the propensity for green voting in various social groups. However, they do allow some conclusions about the categories which are most heavily represented among the followers of the Greens.

The central result of the case studies in this book is that the bulk of green party support comes from students and other groups outside the labour force. In Germany, about two thirds of the green followers are not economically active. Roughly one third are students, almost another third are either unemployed of do not belong to the labour force. In France, green party followers have high educational qualifications. In Italy, the majority of green party followers are students, housewives, retired or unemployed persons. For Austria, it has been stated that the absolute majority of voters in both green parties are not occupationally active as full-time working employees. One quarter of the green vote consists of college and university students.

In terms of the Weberian sociology of domination, the majority of green party supporters may thus be characterized as groups living in social distance to the routine of everyday economic life. In most countries, among the three non-active categories only students and unemployed persons are overrepresented; pensioners who account for a high proportion of voters for the other parties are underrepresented. The proportion of white-collar employees and civil servants among green party voters roughly correspond to their proportion in the population: Clearly, then, the Greens can not be interpreted solely as the party of the educated new middle class of higher employees and civil servants or the professions.

But how do we account for the fact that green party voters are so frequently found to be in possession of higher educational degrees?

The answer is: because they are young. Most studies agree that the bulk of green paarty supporters is below 30 years, and that the propensity for green voting diminishes with increasing age. This suggests to see the association between educational status and green party voting largely as a spurious one, explained by the enrolment revolution among the younger age cohorts. The only study that examined the effect of education by controlling for age is on the Greens in West Germany and concurs with this view (Bürklin 1984). While academics in Germany have a much higher propensity for green voting than the population at large (35 versus 16 percent), academics over 40 report green party preferences only marginally more frequently than all respondents (20 versus 16 percent). If we compute an index of educational voting following the logic of the Alford index of class voting, the difference between the groups with the lowest and the highest educational degrees shrinks from 33 percentage points in the age cohorts below 30 years to 20 points in the age group 30 to 39, and to 12 points among respondents over 40 (calculated from Bürklin, 1984: 88).

In terms of our conceptual scheme, these findings are best compatible within an interpretation that sees the Greens as the representation of highly trained age cohorts with blocked mobility chances. A closer analysis of the political preferences of unemployed persons - again only available for the West-German case - fully sustains this view (Feist et. al. 1985). Among the unemployed, the Greens are the second strongest party, outrunning the Christian Democrats and falling short only of the Social Democrats. This implies that in the absence of mass unemployment the greens would probably not have been able to surpass the five percent threshold of German electoral law. Among unemployed academics voting for the Greens is found seven times more frequently than in the population. The typical supporter of the greens, we may conclude, is young, highly trained, and unemployed or not economically active. This makes the Greens appear as a party of frustrated academic plebeians rather than as an organization of the educated new leading strata of post-industrial societies.

This result has political and sociological implications. Politically, it makes a difference whether a party is advertised as the vanguard of future trends or as a representation of alienated academics on the dole. Sociologically, it means that we should interpret the greens not as a harbinger of Parsonian evolutionary trends, but as the out-growth of a maybe unique historical macro-constellation in which the heavy expansion of educational enrollment coincided with the demographic wave of the baby boom cohorts, and with fiscal problems of the state which curbed the expansion of the tertiary sector.

If this interpretation is correct, we would also expect that the issues the Greens advocate conform to the classification. Movements of ascendant, but socially blocked acquisition classes are traditionally found on the political left rather than on the political right. They usually stress issues of equality, of membership, participation and improved opportunities. If we follow Max Weber's analysis of the ideological orientation of groups living in distance to the routine of everyday economic life, they may also be prone to adhere to a rationality of values rather than a rationality of means and to cultivate an ethic of commitment rather than an ethic of responsibility (Weber 1956).

The empirical findings of the German, the Austrian and the Italian studies are compatible with these assumptions. On an eleven point left-right-scale, the average green party supporter in Germany ranks himself one point left to the average SPD supporter (Fogt/Uttitz 1984: 222). Nearly one third (29 percent) of the Greens rank themselves as leftist, as compared to merely 17 percent of the Social Democrats' followers (Schmidt 1984: 5). The fear nourished by opponents and critical foreign observers of the Greens that the party might be a modern equivalent of the fascist movements in the inter-war period does not seems warranted. Clearly, the Greens in Germany are a party of the new left rather than the new right. The same is true for the green activists in Italy and the Alternative List followers in Austria (Diani and Haerpfer in this volume).

The issues that the supporters and candidates of the Greens advocate, centre around two basic themes: equality of opportunity and quality of life. When asked about the most urgent problems on the political agenda, green followers in Germany name economic issues much less frequently than other respondents. For the German Greens, only job protection is an economic issue with high priority which falls short, however, of environmental protection and peace politics (Veen 1984: 11). An analysis of value priorities among voters across countries found related topics to be most characteristic of a "new politics" orientation which green supporters favour (Müller-Rommel 1985b; Poguntke in this volume).

Hence, the empirical findings seem to justify our classification of the Greens as a representation of age cohorts which form a negatively privileged acquisition class. They draw their support overproportionately from non-established groups, and they advocate better opportunities for access to social and political positions. They also stress quality of life issues, however, which according to the logic of our scheme should also be strong among established groups in the service sector. While the interests of these two categories thus clash in the labour market, they seem to coincide in the commodity market. As I suggested before, the non-established groups seem prone to pursue quality of life issues because of their general distance to the routine of economic life, the established groups in the service sector may follow this track because of their social distance to industry which produces visible negative effects without being their source of renumeration. Given these partially clashing and partially overlapping interests of established and non-established groups, an aggregation of their interests under the roof of a common political party can not be precluded.

If it is correct to assume that the potential for a cleavage between age cohorts with discrepant mobility chances hinges upon a phase-specific constellation, the crucial question with respect to the stability of party systems is under what conditions the existing parties can not aggregate the new demands. As Giovanni Sartori keeps telling us, once a party has achieved a certain organizational consolidation, it becomes a potent agent of mobilization which not only reflects social conditions, but actively shapes them (Sartori 1969). The decisive question then is, under what conditions a phase-specific cleavage becomes transformed into viable party formations.

Institutional and Organizational Contexts Shaping the Success of New Green Parties

In the tradition of the Lipset/Rokkan approach, an attempt to answer this question should follow a double strategy. First, we should try to develop a typology of the alternatives of coalition building; second, we should examine, how the institutionalization of the old cleavages creates macro-settings which either promote or impede the transformation of new cleavages into parties. The first strategy is certainly tempting, but it may be less fruitful than the second. To a large extent, the formation of coalitions is structurally underdetermined. In Imperial Germany, for instance, even the coalition between landed and industrial interests, which the Lipset/Rokkan typology seems to foreclose, materialized. Therefore, I only want to hint at this possibility, but not pursue it any further.

The second approach seems particularly helpful for an understanding of national variations in the emergence of green parties. The question, of course, is why the Greens are so strong in

Germany. One hypothesis following from Stein Rokkan´s work seems obvious, if not trivial: The lower the institutional thresholds of representation, the higher the chances that green parties will be formed. However, we can go a bit further than this. Since we understand the Greens as a variety of new left parties, the salience of the old class cleavage should be one of the crucial factors structuring their chances. The more intense this old conflict is, and the higher the degree of mobilization it generates, the less chances for a new left organizational mobilization will probably exist. The same reasoning may be applied to the political arena. Where the major left parties pursue a strategy of conflict rather than of cooperation, forcefully voicing leftist demands for equality of opportunity, participation, and control of the business sector, the electoral space remaining available for green protest parties is probably small. Finally, the chances of the old left parties to channel radical demands appear higher when they are on the opposition bench than when they are forced to compromise as governing parties.

The following "typology of settings" combines the hypotheses which condition the chances for the emergence of new left parties. The salience of the old class conflict is measured by the frequency of strikes, the degree of political conflict or compromise between "left" and "right" parties is indicated by the length of joint coalitions, the position in government refers to the second half of the 1970s when the increased output of academics combined with structurally blocked mobility chances. The potential for new green parties representing non-established age cohorts with educational degrees results as highest in Germany, Austria, and Switzerland. In fact, the green parties in Europe gained the highest electoral success in those three countries (see Müller-Rommel in this volume).

A rigid empirical test of this hypothesis is clearly beyond the scope of this article. Müller-Rommel (1981; 1982) has already made some steps into this direction. However, a sound test of the suggestions made here would imply the laborious task to develop empirical measures of cohort-specific mobility chances which the typology had to assume as constant throughout all Western European nations.

In sum, I have argued that the educational mobilization and state penetration constitute two central processes of modernization which restructure societal cleavages. I have then suggested a conceptual framework for the empirical study of new cleavages. One of the new cleavage potentials hinges upon phase-specific constellations which structure the mobility chances of age cohorts graduating from

Figure 16.2
Typology of Settings Shaping the Formation of New Left Parties

Salience of Class Conflict (Strikes)	Low				High			
Degree of Conflict or Consensus Politics Between Left and Right (Coalitions)	Consensus		Conflict		Consensus		Conflict	
	SZ, AU, GE, NE		SW, DA, NO		BE, (IR)		IL, FR, UK, FI	
Position of Left Party in Mobilization Phase	Govern.	Oppos.	Govern.	Oppos.	Govern.	Oppos.	Govern.	Oppos.
	GE, AU, SZ	NE	DA, NO	SW	(BE)	(IR)	UK, FI	FR, IL

(Top-level cells: Low → SZ, AU, GE, NE, SW, DA, NO; High → BE, IR, FI, UK, FR, IL)

Abreviation: Sz= Switzerland; AU= Austria; GE= West-Germany; NE= Netherlands; SW= Sweden; DA= Denmark; NO= Norway; BE=Belgium; IR= Ireland; FI= Finland; UK= United Kingdom; FR= France; IT= Italy.

institutions of higher learning. In a situation of structurally blocked mobility chances these age cohorts will constitute a negatively privileged acquisition class with a high potential for political mobilization. The organizational transformation of this potential is filtered by socio-political macro-settings (e.g. intensity of old conflicts; conflict or consensus politics; party in government) which may favour or impede the formation of green parties. If new cleavages are translated into new green party organizations, they may remain politically relevant, even if the constellation that made for their rise no longer prevails, because parties with a certain organizational consolidation become independent agents of mobilization.

General References

BARNES, S.H., M. KAASE et. al. (1979) Political Action. Beverly Hills, California: Sage Publications.

BAKER, K. et.al. (1981) Germany Transformed. PoliticalCulture and the New Politics. Cambridge / London: Harvard University Press.

von BEYME, K. (1982) Parteien in westlichen Demokratien. München.

BÜRKLIN, W.P. (1984) Grüne Politik. Opladen: Westdeutscher Verlag.

BÜRKLIN, W.P. (1985a) "The German Greens. The Post-Industrial Non-Established and the Party System." International Political Science Review 6: 463-481.

BÜRKLIN, W.P. (1985b) "The Split between the Established and the Non-Established Left in Germany." European Journal of Political Research 13 : 283-293.

COTGROVE, S. and A. DUFF (1980) "Environmentalism, Middle-Class Radicalism and Politics." Sociological Review 2: 333-352.

CHANDLER, W.M. and A. SIAROFF (1986) "Postindustrial Politics in Germany and the Origins of the Greens." Comparative Politics 18: 303-325.

DALTON, R.J. (1984) "Cognitive Mobilization and Partisan Dealignment in Advanced Industrial Democracies." Journal of Politics 46: 264-284.

DALTON, R.J. (1988) Citizen Politics in Western Democracies. Chatham: Chatham House.

FEIST, U., D. FRÖHLICH and H. KRIEGER (1984) "Die politische Einstellung von Arbeitslosen." Aus Politik und Zeitgeschichte B45: 3-17.

FISHER,ST (1980) "The `Decline of Parties´Thesis and the Role of Minor Parties," in P.Merkl (ed.) Western European Party Systems. New York: Free Press.

FOGT, H. and P. UTTITZ (1984) "Die Wähler der Grünen 1980-1983: Systemkritischer neuer Mittelstand." Zeitschrift für Parlamentsfragen 15: 210-226.

INGLEHART, R. (1971) "The Silent Revolution in Europe: Intergenerational Change in Post-Industrial Societies." American Political Science Review 65: 991-1017.

INGLEHART, R. (1977) The Silent Revolution. Princeton:

Princeton University Press.

INGLEHART, R. (1981) "Post-Materialism in an Environment of Insecurity." American Political Science Review 75: 880-900.

INGLEHART, R. (1984) " The Changing Structure of Political Cleavages in Western Societiy " in R. J. Dalton et.al. (eds.) Electoral Change in Advanced Industrial Democracies. Princeton: Princeton University Press.

INGLEHART, R . and H.D. KLINGEMANN (1976) "Party Identification, Ideological Preference, and the Left-Right Dimension among Western Mass Publics," in I. Budge et.al. (eds.) Party Identification and Beyond. London: Wiley Press.

KAASE, M. (1982) "Partizipatorische Revolution - Ende der Parteien?" in J. Raschke (ed.) Bürger und Parteien. Opladen: Westdeutscher Verlag.

KITSCHELT, H. (1988) "Left-Libertarian Parties: Explaining Innovation in Competitive Systems." World Politics 15: 194-234.

LIPSET, S.M. and ROKKAN, S. (1967) "Cleavage Structures, Party Systems, and Voter Alignments: An Introduction," in S.M. Lipset and S. Rokkan (eds.) Party Systems and Voter Alignments. New York: Free Press.

MAGUIRE, M. (1983) "Is there still Persistence? Electoral Change in Western Europe, 1948-1979," in H. Daalder and P. Mair (eds.) Western European Party Systems. Continunity and Change. London: Sage.

MÜLLER-ROMMEL, F. (1981) "Ecology Parties in Western Europe." West European Politics 5: 68-74.

MÜLLER-ROMMEL, F. (1982) "`Par 9 teien neuen Typs´ in Westeuropa: Eine vergleichende Analyse." Zeitschrift für Parlamentsfragen 13: 369-390.

MÜLLER-ROMMEL, F. (1985a) "New Social Movements and Smaller Parties: A Comparative Perspective." West European Politics 8: 41-54.

MÜLLER-ROMMEL, F. (1985b) "The Greens in Western Europe. Similar but Different." International Political Science Review 6: 483-499.

MÜLLER-ROMMEL, F. (1985c) "Das grün-alternative Parteibündnis im Europäischen Parlament: Perspektiven eines neuen Phänomens." Zeitschrift für Parlamentsfragen 16: 391-404.

MÜLLER-ROMMEL, F. (1990) "New Political Movements and New Politics Parties in Western Europe," in R. Dalton and M. Küchler (eds.) Challenging the Political Order. Oxford: Oxford University Press (forthcoming).

MÜLLER-ROMMEL, F. and T. POGUNTKE (1989) " The Unharmonius Family: Green Parties in Western Europe," in E. Kolinsky (ed.) The Greens in West Germany. Oxford: Berg Publisher.

MÜLLER-ROMMEL, F. and G. PRIDHAM (eds.) (1990) Small Parties in Western Europe. London: Sage Publishers.

MURPHY, D. (1985) "Von Aldermaston nach Greenham Common. Politischer Protest und neue soziale Bewegungen in Großbritannien," in K.-W. Brand (ed.) Neue Soziale Bewegungen in Westeuropa und den USA. Frankfurt: Campus Verlag.

NELKIN, D. and M. POLLAK (1980) "Political Parties and the Nuclear Debate in France and Germany." Comparative Politics 2: 127-42.

PARSONS, T. (1951) The Social Sytem. New York: Free Press.

PEDERSEN, M.N: (1983) "Changing Patterns of Electoral Volatility in European Party Systems 1948-1977: Explorations in Explanations," in H. Daalder and P. Mair (eds.) Western European Party Systems. Continuty and Change. London: Sage.

POGUNTKE, T. (1987a) "New Politics and Party Systems: The Emergence of a New Type of Party?" West European Politics 10: 76-88.

POGUNTKE, T. (1987b) "Grün-alternative Parteien: Eine neue Farbe im westlichen Parteiensystemen." Zeitschrift für Parlamentsfragen 18: 368-382.

RÜDIG, W. (1985) "The Greens in Europe: Ecological Parties and the European Elections of 1984." Parliamentary Affairs 38: 56-72-

SARTORI, G. (1969) "From the Sociology of Politics to Political Sociology," in S.M. Lipset (ed.) Politics and Social Sciences. New York: Free Press

SCHMIDT, M.G. (1984) "Demokratie, Wohlfahrtsstaat und neue soziale Bewegungen." Aus Politik und Zeitgeschichte B11: 3-14.

SCHNEIDER, R. (1982) "Die Bildungsentwicklung in den westeuropäischen Staaten 1870-1975." Zeitschrift für Soziologie 11: 207-226.

VEEN, H.-J. (1984) "Wer wählt Grün?" Aus Politik und Zeitgeschichte B35-36: 3-17.

WEBER, M. (1980) Wirtschaft und Gesellschaft. Tübingen: Mohr Verlag.

Country References

AUSTRIA

CHRISTIAN, R. (1983) "Die Grünen - Momentaufnahme einer Bewegung in Österreich. "Österreichisches Jahrbuch für Politik 1982: 55-81

DACHS, H. (1983) "Eine Renaissance des `mündigen Bürgers´? Über den Aufstieg der Salzburger Bürgerliste." Österreichische Zeitschrift für Politikwissenschaft 3: 311-330.

FRÖSCHL, E. (1982) "Salzburger Bürgerliste - pseudogrün und konservstiv." Zukunft, Nov.: 8-11.

HAERPFER, C. (1985) "Austria" in I. Crewe and D. Denver (eds.) Electoral Change in Western Democracies. Beckenham: Croom Helm.

MERLI, F. and M. HANDSTANGER (1984) "Die Alternative Liste Graz als Erweiterung des Kommunalpolitischen Systems." Österreichisches Jahrbuch für Politik 1983: 295-318.

NICK, R, (1986) "Rahmenbedingungen und Entwicklung der grün-alternativen Szene in Voralberg." Österreichische Zeitschrift für Politikwissenschaft 2: 157-169

PELINKA, A. (1983) "The Nuclear Power Referendum in Austria." Electoral Studies 2: 253-261.

PLASSER, F. (1985) "Die unsichtbare Fraktion: Struktur und Profil der Grün-Alternativen in Österreich." Österreichisches Jahrbuch für Politik 1984: 133-149.

PLASSER, F. (1987) "Vom Ende der Lagerparteien. Perspektivenwechsel in der österreichischen Parteien- und Wahlforschung." Österreichische Zeitschrift für Politikwissenschaft 3: 241-258.

PLASSER, F. and F. SOMMER, (1985) "Eine `grüne´Premiere. Analyse der Voralberger Landtagswahl 1984." Österreichisches Jahrbuch für Politik 1984: 55-65.

BELGIUM

BEAUFAYS, J., M. HERMANS, and P. VERJAUS (1983) "Les élections à Liège: cartels, polarisation, et les écologistes au pouvoir." Res Publica 25: 391-415.

DESCHOUWER, K. and P. STOUTHUYSEN (1984) L`electorat d`AGALEV. Bruxelles: Centre de Recherche et d`Information Socio-Politiques.

LAMBERT, G.,J.-M. PIERLOT, and J.L. ROLAND (1982) "Les Ecoles voient l`avenir autrement." La Revue Nouvelle 76: 543-547.

LEROY, P. (1984) "Waar staan `degroenen´voor?" Ons Erfdeel: 481-494.
PEETERS, A. and I. VERMEIEREN (1981) De Jaren Zeventig: Van Groen tot Groenen. Borgerhout.
STOUTHUYSEN, P. (1983) "De politieke identiteit van de Vlaamse Groene Partij AGALEV." Res Publica 25: 349-375.

DENMARK
ANDERSEN, J.(1982) Politiske partier og politisk magt i Danmark. Copenhagen.
ANDERSEN, J. (1981) "Partisystemet i opbrud." Politica 13: 87-102.
ANDERSEN,J. (1988) "Miljopoltiske skillelinjer i Danmark." Politica 20: 393-413.
BORRE, O. (1977) "Recent Trends in Danish Voting Behaviour" pp. 3-37 in K.H. Cerny (ed.) Scandinavia at the Polls. Washington D.C.: American Enterprise Institute.
BORRE, O. (1985) "Denmark," pp. 372-399 in I. Crewe and D. Denver (eds.) Electoral Change in Western Democracies. Beckenham: Croom Helm.
DAMGAARD, E. (ed.) (1980) Folkets veje i dansk politik. Copenhagen.
FITZMAURICE; J. (1981) Politics in Denmark. London.
KRISTENSEN, O.P. (1980) "Deltagelse i partpolitiske aktiviteter," pp. 31-61 in E. Damgaard (ed.) Folkets veje i dansk politik. Copenhagen
MÜLLER ROMMEL, F. (1985) "New Social Movements and Smaller Parties: A Comparative Perspective." West European Politics 8: 41-54.
PEDERSEN, M. (1989) "The Birth, the Life , and the Death of Small Parties in Danish Politics, " in F. Müller-Rommel and G. Pridham (eds.) Small Parties in Western Europe. London: SAGE.
POGUNTKE, T. (1987) "Grün-alternative Parteien: Eine neue Farbe in westlichen Parteiensystemen." Zeitschrift für Parlamentsfragen 18: 368-382.
RUBART, F. (1984) "Dänemark: Kleinbürgerkultur im Wandel, " in P. Reichel (ed.) Politische Kultur in Westeuropa. Frankfurt/New York: Campus Verlag.

Federal Republic of Germany
BAHRO, R. (1986) Building the Green Movement. Baltimore: New Society Publishers.

216

BERGER, M., W.G. GIBOWSKI, D. ROTH, W. SCHULTE, B. GOPPERT, E. SIEBERT, and B. WEBER (1987a) Bundestagswahl 1987: Eine Analyse der Wahl zum 11. Deutschen Bundestag am 25. Januar 1987. Mannheim: Forschungsgruppe Wahlen e.v..
BERGER, M., W.G. GIBOWSKI, M. JUNG, D. ROTH, and W. SCHULTE (1987b) "Die Konsolidierung der Wende" Zeitschrift für Parlamentsfragen 18: 253-284.
BÜRKLIN, W.P. (1981) "Die Grünen und die `Neue Politik'" Politische Vierteljahresschrift 22:359-382.
CHANDLER, W.M. and A. SIAROFF (1986) "Postindustrial Politics in Germany and the Origions of the Greens." Comparative Politics 18:303-325.
FRANKLAND, E.G. (1988) "The Role of the Greens in the West Germen Parliamentary Politics, 1980-87." The Review of Politics 50:99-123.
HALLENSLEBEN, A. (1984) "Wie alles anfing ... zur Vorgeschichte der Partei Die Grünen" in T. Kluge (ed.) Grüne Politik. Frankfurt: Fischer Taschenbuch.
HERENBERG, W. (1982) "Sicherer Platz links von der SPD?" in J.R. Mettke (ed.) Die Grünen: Regierungspartner von morgen? Hamburg: Spiegel-Verlag.
HELM, J.A. (1980) "Citizen Lobbies in West Germany" in P.H. Merkl (ed.) Western European Party Systems. New York: Free Press.
HÜLSBERG, W. (1988) The German Greens. London: Verso Press.
KALTEFLEITER, W. (1980) "A Legitimacy Crisis of the German Party System?" in P.H. Merkl (ed.) Western European Party Systems. New York: Free Press
KELLY, P.K. (1982) "Interview." Der Spiegel (June 14, 1982): 47-52
KOLINSKY, E. (1984) "The Greens in Germany: Prospects of a Small Party." Parliamentary Affairs 37: 434-447.
KOLINSKY, E. (1988) "The West-German Greens - A Women's Party?" Parliamentary Affairs 41: 129-148.
KOLINSKY, E. (ed.) (1989) The Greens in West Germany.Oxford: Berg Publisher.
KRAUSHAAR, W. (1983) Was sollen die Grünen im Parlament? Frankfurt: Verlag Neue Kritik.
KVISTAD, G. (1987) "Between State and Society: Green Political Ideology in the Mid-1980's." West European Politics 10: 211-228.
LANGGUTH, G. (1986) The Green Factor in German Politics.

Boulder: Westview.
MEWES, H. (1983) "The West German Green Party." New German Crtique 28: 51-85.
MÜLLER-ROMMEL, F. (1985) "Social Movements and the Greens: New Internal Politics in West-Germany." European Journal of Political Research 13: 53-67.
MÜLLER-ROMMEL, F. (1989) "The Consolidation of a New Party in an Old Party System." Political Studies (forthcoming).
NAGLE, J.D. (1977) System and Succession. Austin: University Texas Press.
PAPADAKIS, E. (1984) The Green Movement in West-Germany. New York: St. Martin´s Press.
PAPADAKIS, E. (1987) "The Green Alternative: Interpretations of Social Protest and Political Action in West Germany." Journal of Politics and History 32: 443-454.
POGUNTKE, T. (1987) "The Organization of a Participatory Party - the German Greens." European Journal of Political Research 15: 609-633.
POGUNTKE, T. (1989) Establishing Alternative Politics: The German Greens. Doctoral Dissertation: European University Florence.
ROTH, D. (1985) "A Red-Green Coalition? Changing Attitudes of West German Voters." Paper presented at the annual meeting of the German Studies Association, Washington D.C., Oct. 4, 1985.
ROTHACKER, A. (1984) "The Green Party in German Politics." West European Politics 7: 109-116.
SARETZKI, T. (1987) "Die Wahl zur Hamburger Bürgerschaft vom 9. November 1986." Zeitschrift für Parlamentsfragen 18:16-37.
SCHMID, C.L. (1987) "The Green Movement in West-Germany: Resource Mobilization and Institutionalization." Journal of Political and Military Sociology 15: 33-46.
SCHMID, T. and E. HOPLITSCHEK (1985) "Auf dem Weg zur Volkspartei" in W. Bickerrich (ed.) SPD und Grüne: Das neue Bündnis? Hamburg: Spiegel-Verlag.
SCHRÜFER, G. (1985) Die Grünen im Deutschen Bundestag. Nürnberg: Pauli-Balleis-Verlag.
SCHULTZE, R.-O. (1987) "Die bayrische Landtagswahl vom 12. Oktober 1986" Zeitschrift für Parlamentsfragen 18: 38-56.
STROHM, H. (1978) "Warum die Bunten bunt sind" in R. Brun (ed.) Der grüne Protest. Frankfurt: Fischer.
STÖSS, R. (1980) Vom Nationalismus zum Umweltschutz. Opladen: Westdeutscher Verlag, 1980.

TOLMEIN, O. (1986) Ökorepublik Deutschland. Hamburg: Konkret Literatur.
TROITZSCH, K.G. (1980) "Die Herausforderung der `etablierten`Parteien durch die `Grünen`'" in H.Kaack and R. Roth (eds.) Handbuch des deutschen Parteiensystems. vol. I. Opladen: Leske.

FINLAND

ARTER, D. (1978) Bumpkin Against Bigwig: The Emergence of a Green Movement in Finnish Politics. Tampere: Institute of Political Science Research.
EVA (1985) Murras vai muutos. Helsinki: elinklinoelämän valtuuskunta.
HYVÄRINEN, M. and J. PAASTELA (1985) "The Finnish Communist Party: The Failure of Attempts to Modernize a C. P." Occasional paper 35. Tampere: University of Tampere, Department of Political Science.
JÄRVIKOVSKI, T. (1981) "Alternative Movements in Finland: The Case of Koijarvi." Acta Sociologica 24: 313-320.
JÄRVIKOVSKI, T. and J. KYLÄMÄKI (1982) "Koijarvi-liikkeen synnysta ja ideologiasta." Sosiologia: 175.
JALINEN, M. (1986) "Vihreät valtuutetut. Empiirinen tutkimus kunnallisvaaleissa valittujen vihreiden valtuutettujen sociaalisen taustan ja mielipiteitten pääpiirteista." Unpublished master's thesis. Tampere: University of Tampere.
LINKOLA, P. (1986) Vihreän liikken tavoiteohjelma. Dublication.
PAASTELA, J. (1986) "TheProblem of Leadership and Organization in an Emerging Political Movement: The Case of the Finnish Greens." Paper presented in the third bilateral Polish-Finnish Colloquim in political science, Sept. 8-14. Mogilany.
PAASTELA, J. (1987) "Finland`s New Social Movements in a Frozen Political System." Paper for ECPR-workshop "New social movements and the political system". April 10-16.
SÄNKIAHO, R. (1985) "Vihreiden politiikka, kysymyksia mistä, vastauksia mihin." Politiikka 3: 219-220.
SIISIÄINEN, M.(1987) "The Finnish Greens and Hegemonic Projects of Modern Corporatism." Paper for the ECPR-workshop "New social movements and the political system", April 10-16.
SIISIÄINEN, M. (1985) "`Vihreän` politiikkan ulottuvuuksia." Politiikka 3: 209.
SOININVAARA, O. (1983) Vihreää valoa. Kirja Suomen Muuttamisesta. Vaasa `83.

SOININVAARA, O. (1986) "A lecture on the Finnish Greens."
March 14. Tampere: University of Tampere.

FRANCE
BOY, D. (1981) "Le vote écologiste en 1978." Revue francaise de
science politique 24: 394-416.
BRIDGFORD, J. (1978) "The Ecologist Movement and the French
General Election 1978." Parliamentary Affairs 31: 314-323.
CERNY, P.G. (ed.) (1982) Social Movements and Protest in
France. London: St. Martin's Press.
CHAFER; T. (1983) "The Greens and the Municipal Elections."
Newsletter for the Study of Modern and Contemporary France: 11-
16.
CHAFER, T. (1984a) "The Greens in France: An Emerging Social
Movement." Journal of Area Studies 10: 36-43.
CHAFER, T. (1984b) "Ecologists and the Bomb" in P. Chilton and
J. Howorths (eds.) Defence and Dissent in Contemporary France.
London: Croom Helm.
DUPOIRIER, E. and J. JAFFEÈ (1980) "Le vote écologiste 1974 -
1979." Association 1980.
GORZ, A. (1980) Adiuex au Prolétariat. Paris: Ed Galilée.
JOURNES, C. (1979) "Les idées politiques du mouvement
écologique." Revue francaise de science politique: 230-254.
MARMOT, G. (1987) Rapport d'Activité. Paris: AGM
MÜLLER-ROMMEL, F. and H. WILKE (1981) "Sozialstruktur und
'Postmaterialistische' Werteorientierungen von Ökologisten: Eine
empirische Analyse am Beispiel Frankreichs." Politische
Vierteljahresschrift 22: 383-397.
NULLMEIER, F. et.al. (1983) Umweltbewegungen und
Parteiensystem: Frankreich - Schweden. Berlin: Quorum.
PARODI, J.L. (1979) "Les écologistes et la tentation politique."
Revue politique et parlamentaire, January.
PRENDIVILLE, B. (1987) "The Return of the Elusive Social
Movement? Le Printemps de Décembre." Modern and Contemporary
France 29: 19-24.
PRENDIVILLE, B. (1989) The Political Ecology Movement in
France. PhD. Reading University.
VADROT, C.-M. (1978) L'écologie, histoire d'une subversion.
Paris: Syros.
VADROT, C.-M. (1980) "Historique des mouvements ecologistes."
Association 1980.

GREAT BRITAIN

BERRINGTON, H. (1985) "New Parties in Britain. Why some live and most die." International Political Science Review 6: 441-461.

BYRNE, P. (1988) The Campaign for Nuclear Disarmament. For a Discussion of CND´s Renaissance in the Eighties and its `Friendly Competition´with the Green Party and other Environmental Groups. London: Croom Helm.

BYRNE, P. and LOVENDUSKI, J. (1983) "Two New Protest Groups: The Peace and Women`s Movement" in H. Drucker et.al. (eds.) Development in British Politics. New York: St. Martin Press.

CO-CHAIRS OF THE GREEN PARTY (1987) "Report to Conference." Green Party Annual Conference. Aston University.

GREEN PARTY (1987) Manifest for a Suitable Society. "Green Votes: Springing in Britain?" (1978) The Economist, Oct. 21.

LOWE, P. and J. GOYDER (1983) Environmental Groups in Politics. London: George Allen & Unwin.

MARSH, A. (1981) "Environmental Issues in Contemporary European Politics" in G. Goodman (ed.) Europe´s Transition from Oil. London: Academic Press.

McCULLOCH, A. (1983) "The Ecology Party and Constituency Politics: The anatomy of a grassroots party." Paper presented at the Political Studies Association Conference. Newcastle upon Tyne, April.

PORITT, J. (1984) Seeing Green: The Politics of Ecology Explained: London: Basil Blackwell.

RÜDIG, W. and P.D. LOWE (1986) "The Withered `Greening´of British Politics: A Study of the Ecology Party." Political Studies 34: 262-284.

IRELAND

CHUBB, B. (1983) Source Book of Irish Government. Dublin: Institute of Public Administration.

GALLAGHER, M. (1987a) "Does Ireland need a new Electoral System?" Irish Political Studies 2: 27-48.

GALLAGHER, M. (1987b) "The Outcome" in M. Laver, P. Mair, R. Sinnoott (eds.) How Ireland Voted. Dublin: Poolbeg.

LAVER, M. et.al. (1987) "Patterns of Party Support" in M. Laver et.al. (eds.) How Ireland Voted. Dublin: Poolbeg.

MARSH, M. (1985) "Ireland" in I. Crewe and D. Denver (eds.) Electoral Change in Western Democracies. Beckenham: Croom Helm.

PENNIMAN, H. and B. FARRELL (eds.) (1988) Ireland at the Polls, 1982-1987. Washington: American Enterprise Institute / Duke University Press.
SINNOTT, R. (1986) "Party Differences and Spatial Representation: The Irish Case." British Journal of Political Science 16: 217-241.
WHYTE, J. (1974) "Ireland: Politics Without Social Bases" in R. Rose (ed.) Electoral Behaviour: A Comparative Handbook. New York: Free Press.

ITALY
AMICI DELLA TERRA (1986) Confederazione verde? Atti della tavola rotonda organizzata dagli Amici della Terra. Rome, October: unpublished paper.
BIORCIO, R. (1988a) "Gli attivisti ambientalisti tra movimento e liste verdi, " in R. Biorcio and G. Lodi (eds.) La sfida verde. Il movimento ecologista in Italia. Padova: Liviana.
BIORCIO, R. (1988b) "L`elettorato verde" in R. Biorcio and G. Lodi (eds.) La sfida verde. Il movimento ecologista in Italia. Padova: Liviana.
BIORCIO, R. (1988c) "Opinione publica, questione ambientale e movimento ecologista" in R. Biorcio and G. Lodi (eds.) La sfida verde. Il movimento ecologista in Italia. Padova: Liviana.
DEL CARRIA, R. (1986) Il potere diffuso: i Verdi in Italia. Verona: Edizioni del Movimento Nonviolento.
DE MEO, M. and F. GIOVANNINI (1985) L`onda verde. I verdi in Italia. Roma: Cooperativa Alfamedia.
DIANI, M. (1988) Isole nell`arcipelago. Il movimento ecologista in Italia. Bologna: Il Mulino.
DIANI, M. and G. LODI (1988) "Three in One: Currents in the Milan Ecology Movement " in B. Klandermans, H. Kriesi and S. Tarrow (eds.) From Structure to Action: Comparing Movement Participation Accross Cultures. Greenwich, Conn.: JAI Press.
LANGER, A. (1983) "Warum es in Italien keine Grüne, wohl aber eine Radikale Partei gibt." Freibeuter 15: 82-92.
LODI, G. (1988) "Dall`ecologia alla politica: la Lista Verde di Milano" in R. Borcio and G. Lodi (eds.) La sfida verde. Il movimento ecologista in Italia. Padova: Liviana.
MANCONI, L. (9185) "E`metropolitana L`Italia al verde." La Nuova Ecologia 15: 7.
MELUCCI, A. (ed.) (1984) Altri codici. Aree di movimento nella metropoli. Bologna: Il Mulino.
POGGIO, A. (ed.) (1983) "Arcipelago Verde," supplemento a

Panorama 899.
REICH, M. (1984) "Mobilizing for Environmental Policy in Italy and Japan." Comparative Politics 16: 379-402.

LUXEMBOURG
HIRSCH, M. (1985) "The 1984 Luxembourg Election." West European Politics 8: 116-118.

SWEDEN
ASKENSTEN, A. (1981) Mot alla odds. En berättelse om hur Stockholmspartiet mrscherade in i stadshut. Stockholm.
BERVA, J.-A. et.al. (1983) "Miljöpartiet: en studie an organisation och ledarskap." Projectwork in Administration. Stockholm School of Economics, mimeo.
FRIBERG, M. and J. Galtung (1984) Rörelserna. Stockholm: Akademilitteratur.
HOLMBERG, S. and M. GILLJAM (1987) Väljare och vali Sverige. Stockholm: Bonniers.
HOLMBERG, S. et.al. (1977) Väljarna och kärnkraften. Stockholm:Liber.
JOHANSSON, L. (1980) Kärnkraftomröstningen i kommunera. Lund: Studentlitteratur.
MEZ, L. and B. OLLROGGE (1980) "Die Ökologiebewegung in Skandinavien" in R. Roth (ed.) Parlamentarisches Ritual und politische Alternative. Frankfurt/Main: Campus.
Nu Kommer Miljöpartiet (1982). On miljöpartiet med det officiella partiprogrammet. Stockholm: Timo Förlag.
NULLMEIER, F. et.al. (1983) Umweltbewegungen und Parteiensystem: Frankreich - Schweden. Berlin: Quorum Verlag.
SÄRLVIK, B. (1974) "Sweden: The Social Bases of the Parties in a Developmental Perpective" in Richard Rose (ed.) Electoral Behaviour: A Comparative Handbook. New York: Free Press.
VEDUNG, E. (1979a) "Kärnkraften ger ny blockbildning i politiken" in: Tvärsnitt 1: 42.48.
VEDUNG, E. (1979b) Kärnkraften och regeringen Fälldins fall. Stockholm: Raben and Sjögren.
VEDUNG, E. (1980) "Kärnkraften och partisystemet i Sverige." Political 1: 108-139.
VEDUNG, E. (1981) "Tillväxt-ekologidimensionen igen" in: Sociologisk Frskning: 48-51.
VEDUNG, E. (1988) "The Environmentalist Party and the Swedish Five Party Syndrome " in K. Lawson and P. Merkl (eds.) Why

Parties Fail. Princeton: Princeton University Press.
WÖRLUND, I and S. ERSSON (1987) Miljöpartiets politiska geografi 1982-1985. Umea University: Department of Political Science, mimeo.

SWITZERLAND
BLUM, R. et.al. (1987) Hoffnungswahl. 12 Stimmen zum eidgenössischen Wahlherbst 1987. Zürich: Panda.
ENGELER, U.P. (1986) "Personalverbindungen zwischen Altparteien und neuer Politik" in: Schweizerisches Jahrbuch für Politische Wissenschaft 26. Bern: Haupt.
GRÜNES BÜNDNIS (1987) Aus-Wahlbuch 1987. Luzern: Gegendruck.
GRUNER, E. (1967) "Le fonctionnement du systeme représentatif dans la confédération suisse." Paper delivered at the 7th World Congress of the International Political Science Association, Brussel.
GRUNER, E. (1977) Parteien in der Schweiz. Bern: Francke.
GRUNER, E. and H.P. HERTIG (1983) Der Stimmbürger und die neue Politik: wie reagiert die Politik auf die Beschleunigung der Zeitgeschichte? Bern: Haupt.
GSCHWEND, H. (1986) "Die Umweltbewegungen verändern die Parteienlandschaft" in: Schweizerisches Jahrbuch für Politische Wissenschaft 26. Bern: Haupt.
KRIESI, H. (1980) Entscheidungstrukturen und Entscheidungsprozesse in der Schweizer Politik. Frankfurt: Campus.
KRIESI, H. (ed.) (1985) Bewegung in der Schweizer Politik. Fallstudien zu politischen Mobilisierungsprozessen in der Schweiz. Frankfurt: Campus.
KRIESI, H. (1986) "Perspektiven neuer Politik: Parteien und neue soziale Bewegungen" in: Schweizerisches Jahrbuch für Politische Wissenschaft 26. Bern: Haupt.
LONGCHAMP, C. (1984) Analyse der Nationalratswahlen 1983. Vox-Sondernummer 20.
LONGCHAMP, C. (1987) "Die neue Instabilität als Kennzeichen des heutigen Wahlverhaltens" in: Schweizerisches Jahrbuch für Politische Wissenschaft 27. Bern: Haupt.
REBEAUD, L. (1987) Die Grünen in der Schweiz. Bern: Zytglogge.

Europe
BUCK, K. (1986) Die Regenbogen-Fraktion im Europäischen Parlament. Saarbrücken: Europa Institut Verlag.
MÜLLER-ROMMEL, F. (1985) "Das grün-alternative

Parteienbündnis im europäischen Parlament." Zeitschrift für Parlamentsfragen 3: 391-403.
RÜDIG, W. (1985) "The Greens in Europe: Ecological Parties and the European Elections of 1984." Parliamentary Affairs 4: 56-72.

About the Editor

Ferdinand Müller-Rommel is Associate Professor of political science at the University of Lüneburg in the Federal Republic of Germany. His previous academic appointments have been the Free University of Berlin and the European University Institute in Florence. In 1981-1983 he was a policy advicer in the office of the Chancellor of the Federal Republic in Bonn.

Among his publications are *Empirische Politikwissenschaft* (1979); *Innerparteiliche Gruppierungen in der SPD* (1981); *Vergleichende Politikwissenschaft* (1987); *Cabinets in Western Europe* (1988). He is currently editing a book on small parties in Western Europe and is writing a book-length study of the changing party systems in Europe.

Notes on Contributors

Jens Alber is Associate Professor at the Max-Planck-Institute, University of Cologne (Federal Republik of Germany)
Karl H. Buck is Civil Servant in the European Commission, Brussels (Belgium)
Paul Byrne is Senior Lecturer in the Department of European Studies, Loughborough University (Great Britain)
Kris Deschouwer is Professor of Political Science at the Free University of Brussels (Belgium)
Mario Diani is Assistant Professor of Sociology at the Bocconi University of Milan and Research Assistant in the Department of Sociology at the State University of Milan (Italy)
David Farrell is Lecturer in the Department of Government at the University of Manchester (Great Britain)
E. Gene Frankland is Professor of Political Science at Ball State University, Muncie, Indiana (USA)
Christian Haerpfer is Deputy Director of the Institute for Conflict Research (Vienna) and Lecturer in Political Science at the University of Vienna and Salzburg (Austria)
Thomas Koelble is Assistant Professor of Political Science at the University of California, San Diego (USA)
Andreas Ladner is Researcher in the Department of Sociology at the University of Zurich (Switzerland)

226

Jukka Paastela is Lecturer in the Department of Political Science at the University of Tampere (Finland)

Thomas Poguntke is Research Fellow in the Research Unit for Societal Developments at the University of Mannheim (Federal Republic of Germany)

Brendan Prendiville is Researcher in the Department of Political Science at Reading University (Great Britain)

Suzanne S. Schüttemeyer is Associate Professor of Political Science at the University of Lüneburg (Federal Republic of Germany)

Evert Vedung is Associate Professor of Political Science at Uppsala University (Sweden)

Addresses of Green Party Headquarters

AUSTRIA
VEREINTE GRÜNE ÖSTERREICHS Obere Weisgerberstr. 16/16, 1030 Vienna
ALTERNATIVE LISTE ÖSTERREICHS Margaretengürtel 122-124/1, 1050 Vienna
BELGIUM
AGALEV Tweekerkenstraat 78, 1040 Brussels
ECOLO Rue de la Sabloniere 9, 1000 Brussels
DENMARK
DE GRONE Landsseketariatet c/o Elit Skovbo Jensen Rosenlundvej 12, 4863 Eskildstrup
EUROPE
GRAEL European Parliament 79-81, Rue Belliard, 1040 Brussels, Belgium
FINLAND
VIHREÄ LIITTO Eerikinkatu 7 C 10, 00100 Helsinki
FRANCE
LES VERTS 90 Rue Vergniaud, 75013 Paris
GREAT BRITAIN
THE GREEN PARTY 10 Station Parade, Balham High Road, London SW 12 9AZ
IRELAND
GREEN ALLIANCE 5 Upper Fownes Street, Dublin 2
ITALY
GRUPPO VERDE Via Uffici del Vicario 21, 00186 Rome
LUXEMBOURG
DIE GRENG ALTERNATIV Boite Postale, 2711 Luxembourg
SWEDEN
MILJÖPARTIET DE GRÖNA Rikskansliet, Urvädersgränd 11, POB 15264, 10465 Stockholm
SWITZERLAND
GRÜNE PARTEI DER SCHWEIZ Postfach 1441, 3001 Bern
GRÜNES BÜNDNIS (GBS) c/o Grünes Bündnis Luzern, Postfach, 6004 Luzern
WEST GERMANY
DIE GRÜNEN Bundesgeschäftstelle, Colmannstraße 36, 5300 Bonn 1

Index